30.10.98

# REGENTS CRITICS SERIES

General Editor: Paul A. Olson

# LITERARY CRITICISM OF
# OSCAR WILDE

C0-AYQ-762

Other volumes in the Regents Critics Series are:

# Literary Criticism of Oscar Wilde

*Edited by*

STANLEY WEINTRAUB

UNIVERSITY OF NEBRASKA PRESS · LINCOLN

# Regents Critics Series

The Regents Critics Series provides reading texts of significant literary critics in the Western tradition. The series treats criticism as a useful tool: an introduction to the critic's own poetry and prose if he is a poet or novelist, an introduction to other work in his day if he is more judge than creator. Nowhere is criticism regarded as an end in itself but as what it is—a means to the understanding of the language of art as it has existed and been understood in various periods and societies.

Each volume includes a scholarly introduction which describes how the work collected came to be written, and suggests its uses. All texts are edited in the most conservative fashion consonant with the production of a good reading text; and all translated texts observe the dictum that the letter gives life and the spirit kills when a technical or rigorous passage is being put into English. Other types of passages may be more freely treated. Footnoting and other scholarly paraphernalia are restricted to the essential minimum. Such features as a bibliographical checklist or an index are carried where they are appropriate to the work in hand. If a volume is the first collection of the author's critical writing, this is noted in the bibliographical data.

PAUL A. OLSON

*University of Nebraska*

# Contents

## II. ON SHAKESPEARE

## III. ON AESTHETICS AND THE CRITIC

## IV. ON HIMSELF

# Introduction
# The Critic in Spite of Himself

*Art is the only serious thing in the world.*—Oscar Wilde

When Wilde played Oscar in the columns of a dozen journals in the eighties and nineties, as well as in his essays and stories and poems and plays, he was also being an instinctual critic. Nevertheless, that aspect of his work is usually dismissed. "Scholars and readers are generally agreed," such derogation goes, "that Wilde's criticism merits study only as a patchwork affair or as a polished form of public entertainment."[1] To the public he seemed to be playing with paradoxes, yet the way in which Wilde stood the platitudes of his time on their heads was more than clever entertainment. Without at first knowing it, he was evolving a critical position that would remain consistent and consistently provocative, unaltered by prison and disgrace, or by the reduction of his audience to a handful of loyal friends.

Wilde, like many critics, began his career in the medium because he needed the money (journalistic criticism paid regularly if not well) and because he always had something to say. The first duty of a critic of the arts, he suggested, ignoring that duty in the process, "is to hold his tongue at all times, and upon all subjects." Long before he had begun writing literary criticism regularly, Wilde busied himself with his flamboyant and notorious lectures on the arts, all the while reserving his scorn for the journeyman critic, trapped in a morass of mediocrity. "The poor reviewers," he deplored, "are apparently reduced to being the reporters of the

1. Epifanio San Juan, Jr., *The Art of Oscar Wilde* (Princeton, N.J.: Princeton University Press, 1967), p. 74.

police-court of literature, the chroniclers of the doings of the habitual criminals of art." Later, in *The Importance of Being Earnest*, Wilde's Algernon advises John Worthing about the low state of literary criticism, "You should leave that to the people who haven't been at a University. They do it so well in the daily papers." But Wilde not only had been to one university, he had been through two, having earned a degree at Trinity College, Dublin, before he went up to Oxford; and his comparative over-education reinforced his contempt for contemporary critics as well as his condescension toward the work upon which they wasted their industry. Afterwards—while inferentially praising himself as a critic—he confessed in his *Critic as Artist* dialogue that he was "a little unfair" in describing English artistic and critical activity as "mediocrity weighing mediocrity in the balance, and incompetence applauding its brother." He, of course, wrote for the smaller-circulation and higher-priced journals, for, he wrote, "as a rule, the critics—I speak . . . of the higher class, of those in fact who write for the sixpenny papers—are far more cultured than the people whose work they are called on to review. This is, indeed, only what one would expect, for criticism demands infinitely more cultivation than creation does."

Loftily, Wilde observed that he was always amused "by the silly vanity of those writers and artists of our day who seem to imagine that the primary function of the critic is to chatter about their second-rate work." For more than five years, however, he chattered about it himself, often at length, while insisting nonetheless that criticism ultimately had to be emancipated from its police-court function. His own best criticism would bend in that direction; yet visible in it would be more than merely a seriocomic police-court magistrate dispensing fines, for Oscar could not resist—epigram-matically—putting on the black cap of the hanging judge. Even the music-hall turns, he knew, would never win him the general reader. The average Englishman, he felt, would rather be flattered by being told that his own emotions were "the ultimate test of literature."[2] "Very nice of you to like my article . . . ," he wrote

2. Citations in footnotes will be given only for quotations which do not appear in the text of this book.

one well-wisher after *The Decay of Lying* first appeared in 1889. "It is meant to bewilder the masses by its fantastic form; *au fond* it is of course serious."[3] Even in his most ambitious critical efforts he could not escape his persona: the public was always more baffled and amused by the flippant Oscarisms than it was enlightened or persuaded.

Wilde's activities as critic began, almost inadvertently, in 1884. His brother Willie, then drama critic for the London journal *Vanity Fair*, had taken a midsummer holiday, leaving Oscar to fill the unsigned column whenever necessary. A few months later Oscar was writing articles on his own, for the *Pall Mall Gazette*, then for the *Dramatic Review*, *Nineteenth Century*, and other publications. He had not really come to the profession belatedly, however, for his lecture performances emphasized the domestic arts almost as much as they did Oscar, and even at Oxford he had been writing criticism as well as much else. His earliest essay, "The Rise of Historical Criticism," was first a university exercise. Later he restated its point more cogently, more memorably, and far more briefly: "The one duty we owe to history is to rewrite it."

By what was probably no coincidence, Wilde's career in the critical columns, which flourished in the late eighties, followed closely upon his marriage in 1884 and the birth of his sons in 1885 and 1886. In mid-1887 he even accepted—and with eagerness—the editorship of the magazine *Lady's World*, changing its name to *Woman's World*.[4] During his two years with the publication he strove to emphasize "literature, art, and modern life," and sought a cachet for the magazine which only recognized contributors could give it. Cajoling and flattering "name" women to contribute, he was reduced to his own poorest criticism (on women writers, for

3. Oscar Wilde to Violet Fane, January 15, 1889, in Rupert Hart-Davis (ed.), *Letters of Oscar Wilde* (London: Hart-Davis, 1962), p. 236.

4. Another contemporary writer who would seize the early-career foothold of a women's magazine was Arnold Bennett, who became assistant editor of *Woman* in 1893, and editor in 1896. One of his duties, also, was the book criticism page, which he wrote under the name of "Barbara." For the same publishers (Cassell) he briefly produced a literary column for *Hearth and Home* signed "Sarah Volatile." By 1898 he no longer needed the editorial income and was making his living as a writer.

his magazine) both in print and in private. Seeking a piece from one minor poetess, he wrote her, praising a passage in one of her verses, "Keats even would have envied you."[5] That he was able to force his pen to fashion the words is indicative of his need to make *Woman's World* a success, and thus his own position as editor secure.

Although Wilde was beginning to become known for his stories and tales, and was regularly publishing his book criticism, he needed to sell all he could bring himself to write. He had already begun to live two expensive lives, one of them farther removed than could have been imagined by the proprietors of *Woman's World* from the connotations of either its earlier title or the new one upon which Wilde had so persuasively insisted. He had by then gone over almost entirely—although still furtively—to the sub-terranean world of men. In 1886—so Robert Ross later confided— Ross at seventeen had seduced the thirty-year-old Wilde into the "love that dares not speak its name." Maintaining the façade of marriage and family, while luxuriating in the secret new joys, required moneygrubbing by those additional legitimate means he had as a writer; and the very un-naturalness of the new existence may have reinforced and intensified critical points of view he had already begun expressing—that art (or un-nature) was superior to both utility and nature, and that art was above reason as it was above respectability.

From the half-hidden double life Wilde could rationalize his esthetic attitudes with increased effectiveness. Writing at the time of the murderer and forger Thomas Wainewright (in "Pen, Pencil, and Poison"), he suggested, as he might have of himself, "His crimes seem to have had an important effect upon his art. They gave a strong personality to his style, a quality that his early work certainly lacked." When in 1897, three years before his death, Wilde lamented at length to Lord Alfred Douglas from prison, he recognized that "everything about my tragedy has been hideous, mean, repellent, lacking in style" (*De Profundis*). To Wilde, even his fall was a failure in style.

5. Oscar Wilde to Mrs. Hamilton King, ca. September, 1887, in *Letters*, p. 205.

The crime which earned Wainewright Wilde's moral castigation was not the murder of Englishmen but the misuse of the English language. Here, as scandalously stated as was possible, was the kernel of Wilde's esthetic: "The fact of the man's being a poisoner is nothing against his prose. The domestic virtues are not the true basis of art." For Wilde, a misprint was more than a murder. Inveighing constantly against shoddy editing, inept translating and poor proofreading, he once concluded a review of some lame verses by the future (and since forgotten) poet laureate Alfred Austin with the opinion that the typographical errors were less excusable than the tepid poetry: "Even the most uninteresting poet cannot survive bad editing." The same, he thought, was true of a better American poet: "Longfellow is so essentially poor in rhymes that it is unfair to rob him even of one." Errors of fact were equally errors in taste. "Why call upon us," Wilde asked in one case, "to admire a bad misquotation . . . ?" Another writer, he observed, displayed "that intimate acquaintance with Sappho's lost poems which is the privilege only of those who are not acquainted with Greek literature."

Although Wilde was often sharp in his published criticism, he reserved some of his most caustic sarcasm for his private letters, illustrating, perhaps, Shaw's comment about the profession, "I have never been able to see how the duties of a critic, which consist largely in making painful remarks in public about the most sensitive of his fellow creatures, can be reconciled with the manners of a gentleman." Early in Wilde's career as a critic, for example, A. P. T. Elder, publisher of the new American magazine *Literary Life*, sent Oscar from Chicago the December, 1884, and the January, 1885, issues, asking for an opinion of the contents. The reply was brief but devastating:

> . . . a little more care, both as regards style and substance, should be taken. Rossetti is not living (p. 190), and *"in medias res"* (p. 192) could not pass, even at a Fancy Ball, for *"in medio tutissimus"*: that a book "will be read with interest by the *illiterate"* (p. 151) is too charming to alter, but that no man was more fortunate than Carlyle was in his marriage, is a somewhat too painful paradox (p. 134). Still, there is much that is good, and the advice to read the daily papers as a method of

acquiring judgment and good sense (p. 183) is an excellent bit of American humour, on which you must allow me to congratulate the author.[6]

Similarly, when J. S. Little asked for Wilde's views of his new novel, *Whose Wife Shall She Be?*, the critic was politely negative:

> Thank you very much for your charming book, which I have read with great pleasure. You ask me to give you a criticism of it, but Gil Blas is plucking my sleeve and reminding me of the Archbishop.[7] However, here *is* my opinion.
>
> The book is a little too crowded: the motive is hardly clear enough: if Gwendoline is the heroine we should hear more of her: if she is not, the last chapters emphasise her too much. Captain Breutnall is not a success: his death is merely the premature disappearance of a shell-jacket: I decline to mourn with Gwendoline over someone who is not properly introduced.[8]

By the time Wilde left regular reviewing in 1890 he had formed heretical opinions about the mechanics as well as the objectives of the craft. "It is sometimes said of them," he observed of reviewers, "that they do not read all through the works they are called upon to criticize. They do not. Or at least they should not. . . . Nor is it necessary. To know the vintage and quality of a wine one need not drink the whole cask. It must be perfectly easy in half an hour to say whether a book is worth anything or worth nothing. Ten minutes are really sufficient, if one has the instinct for form." He may have preached more truly than his own critical practice evidenced, for even in omnibus notices he seems to have paid closer attention to the texts than many of his contemporary journeymen. Still, form was more significant to him than content. "In matters of grave importance," Wilde had one of his impossible

6. Oscar Wilde to A. P. T. Elder, ca. January, 1885, in *Letters*, p. 170.
7. In Lesage's novel, one of the tasks of Gil Blas is to copy out the homilies of the Archbishop, who makes Gil Blas promise to tell him when the homilies appear to be declining in quality. After the Archbishop has a stroke, the homilies do deteriorate, and the Archbishop is told so by Gil Blas. He is fired for his pains, teaching him the unwisdom of being truthful.
8. Oscar Wilde to J. S. Little, January 15, 1888, in *Letters*, p. 214.

young ladies in *The Importance of Being Earnest* say, "style, not sincerity, is the important thing."

Wilde the critic was drawn to style on the printed page as much as Oscar the personality was drawn to it in life. When, as an Oxford undergraduate, he had met Walter Pater, that high priest of style had asked him, "Why do you always write poetry? Why do you not write prose? Prose is so much more difficult." At the time Wilde was hard pressed for an answer, for, he recalled, those were "days of lyrical ardour and studious sonnet-writing; days when one loved the exquisite intricacy and musical repetitions of the ballade, and the villanelle with its linked long-drawn echoes and its curious completeness; days when one solemnly sought to discover the proper temper in which a triolet should be written; delightful days, in which, I am glad to say, there was far more rhyme than reason. . . . I do not think I knew then that even prophets correct their proofs." Afterwards Wilde understood that a portion of the artistic tension which gave the creator pleasure as he shaped his lines could be reproduced in the reader—the "critical pressure . . . that we receive from tracing, through what may seem the intricacies of a sentence, the working of the constructive intelligence" (*Speaker*, March 22, 1890). Yet Wilde insisted that it was not for the reader that such sentences were shaped: "The pleasure that one has in creating a work of art is purely a personal pleasure, and it is for the sake of this pleasure that one creates. . . . Nothing else interests him. . . . He is fascinated by what he has in hand. He is indifferent to others." Wilde meant it personally as well as theoretically. "I write because it gives me the greatest possible artistic pleasure to write. If my work pleases the few I am gratified. If it does not, it causes me no pain."

What often caused Wilde anguish as a critic was the violence done to style by incorrect English and inept analogies and references. And whether or not he was sure of his facts or his quotations (his memory, however, was as encyclopedic as his reading), Wilde delivered his judgments with confidence and with an ear sensitive to the balanced phrase and the well-turned epigram. Disdaining a literary fashion, he declared, "It is only an auctioneer who should admire all schools of art"; and attacking praise of a

poet grounded upon his attractiveness to "hundreds of imitators,"
Wilde observed, "Longfellow has no imitators, for of echoes them
selves there are echoes and it is only style that makes a school."
Condemning analogy-hunting, he wrote, "There is no surer way
of destroying a similarity than to strain it." Demonstrating his
point, he went on:

> . . . when Mr. [John Addington] Symonds, after genially comparing
> Jonson's blank verse to the front of Whitehall (a comparison, by the
> way, that would have enraged the poet beyond measure) proceeds to
> play a fantastic aria on the same string, and tells us that 'Massinger re-
> minds us of the intricacies of Sansovino, Shakespeare of Gothic aisles or
> heaven's cathedral . . . Ford of glittering Corinthian colonnades, Web-
> ster of vaulted crypts, . . . Marlowe of masoned clouds, and Marston,
> in his better moments, of the fragmentary vigour of a Roman ruin,' one
> begins to regret that anyone ever thought of the unity of the arts. Similes
> such as these obscure; they do not illumine. To say that Ford is like a
> glittering Corinthian colonnade adds nothing to our knowledge of either
> Ford or Greek architecture.

Wilde's sympathy with things Greek may have had something
to do with his amatory as well as his literary education. Since for
him life and art had fused, he could say, "Whatever . . . is modern
in our life we owe to the Greeks. Whatever is an anachronism is
due to mediaevalism." And it was only partly with facetious intent
that he added that generally "the forms of art have been due to
the Greek critical spirit. To it we owe the epic, the lyric, the entire
drama . . . , including burlesque, the idyll, the romantic novel,
the novel of adventure, the essay, the dialogue, the oration, the
lecture, for which we should perhaps not forgive them, and the
epigram." In fact, Wilde concluded, at the end of an even more
lighthearted catalogue of genres, to the Greeks was owed every
form of writing but "American journalism, to which no parallel
can be found anywhere, and the ballad in sham Scotch dialect."
There was one element in the Greek critical spirit, nevertheless,
from which Wilde dissented—Plato's emphasis upon "the ethical
spirit of art."

Everything in Wilde's personality inclined toward Aristotle,
who criticized art "not from the moral, but from the purely esthetic

point of view." Here Wilde realized he was diverging (but for Pater) from nine previous decades of nineteenth-century thought, for what he labeled as the confusion of ethics with esthetics was to him as much evidence of contemporary critical sterility as was Plato's added insistence—then no longer taken seriously—that poetry, or mythopoeia, because it is a form of lying, had to be condemned on moral grounds. This attitude Wilde related to the nineteenth-century schools of romanticism and realism, each of which, in its way, sought a return of literature to nature. "All bad art," he declared in *The Decay of Lying*, "comes from returning to Life and Nature, and elevating them into ideals." What parts Wilde's own self-conscious role-playing, as well as his underground activities which (by the usual standards) "went against Nature," played in formulating his critical posture can never be known, for that posture must have been as subconsciously motivated as it was deliberate. Wilde always underestimated the shaping power of the unconscious.

"All fine imaginative work" Wilde viewed (in *The Critic as Artist*) as "self-conscious and deliberate. . . . A great poet sings because he chooses to sing." Literature which seems to be "the most natural and simple product of its time is always the result of the most self-conscious effort. . . . there is no fine art without self-consciousness, and self-consciousness and the critical spirit are one." Wilde even went a step further, arguing that the function of the artist was "to invent, not to chronicle. . . . Life by its realism is always spoiling the subject-matter of art. . . . The superior pleasure in literature is to realize the non-existent."

The realization of the nonexistent is a liberation of the personality, an enrichment of experience, and thus to Wilde it was toward that end that criticism itself had to be, at its highest, "creative" (rather than elucidating). As a result the baffled disciple of the *Critic as Artist* dialogue, summing up the arguments and deliberate over-statements of the second part, muses aloud, "You have told me that . . . all Art is immoral, and all thought dangerous; that criticism is more creative than creation, and that the highest criticism is that which reveals in the work of Art what the artist has not put there; that it is exactly because a man cannot do a thing that he is the proper judge of it; and that the true critic is unfair, insincere, and not rational." Since Wilde's life had become the chief medium for his art, his paradoxes defended his practice while formulating an esthetic.

Criticism defined as creation implied the revaluation of criticism as well as the work toward which it had been a reaction. "Who cares whether Mr. Ruskin's views on Turner are sound or not?" Wilde argued. "What does it matter? That mighty and majestic prose of his, so fervid and so fiery-coloured in its noble eloquence, so rich in its elaborate symphonic music, so sure and certain, at its best, in subtle choice of word and epithet, is at least as great a work of art as any of those wonderful [Turner] sunsets that bleach or rot on their corrupted canvases in England's Gallery." Style—imagination given form—outlasted all else in art: a concept obviously dear to an artist who thought that even his own life was stylized. "My own experience," he observed in *The Decay of Lying*, "is that the more we study Art, the less we care for Nature. What Art really reveals to us is Nature's lack of design, her curious crudities, her extraordinary monotony, her absolutely unfinished condition. Nature has good intentions, of course, but, as Aristotle once said, she cannot carry them out. When I look at a landscape I cannot help seeing all its defects. It is fortunate for us, however, that Nature is so imperfect, as otherwise we should have had no art at all. Art is our spirited protest, our gallant attempt to teach Nature her proper place." Man could accomplish what nature could not—the union of content with form.

In painting as in writing, realism to Wilde was a failure: it lacked form. The only portraits in which one could believe (he used Holbein as an example) were those in which there is "very little of the sitter and a very great deal of the artist." Holbein's success was that he "compelled life to accept his conditions"—that he imposed upon life his style: "It is style that makes us believe in a thing—nothing but style." And, developing his argument further, he suggested that life imitated art more than art imitated life, sometimes realizing afterward in fact what had first been imagined by a painter or sculptor or novelist. Again he called upon his favorite Greek to support the thesis. "Scientifically speaking," he pontificated

unscientifically, "the basis of life—the energy of life, as Aristotle
would call it—is simply the desire for expression, and Art is always
presenting various forms through which the expression can be
attained. Life seizes on them and uses them." But life (or nature),
lacking artistic intellect, and thus artistic taste, was guilty—to
Wilde—of self-defeating inertia:

> Art creates an incomparable and unique effect, and, having done so,
> passes on to other things. Nature, upon the other hand, forgetting that
> imitation can be made the sincerest form of insult, keeps on repeating
> this effect until we all become absolutely wearied of it. Nobody of any
> real culture, for instance, ever talks nowadays about the beauty of a
> sunset. Sunsets are quite old-fashioned. They belong to the time when
> Turner was the last note in art. To admire them is a distinct sign of
> provincialism of temperament. Upon the other hand they go on.
> Yesterday evening Mrs. Arundel insisted on my going to the window
> and looking at the glorious sky, as she called it. Of course I had to look
> at it. She is one of those absurdly pretty Philistines to whom one can
> deny nothing. And what was it? It was simply a very second-rate Tur-
> ner, a Turner of a bad period, with all the painter's worst faults exag-
> gerated and over-emphasised.

Wilde's argument, for all its scientific unsoundness, is nonetheless
brilliantly reasoned, suggesting how art not only interprets life
but imposes upon it in ways which seemingly shape it or improve
upon it. Nature, for example, acquires direction from the landscape
painter:

> Where, if not from the Impressionists, do we get those wonderful brown
> fogs that come creeping down our streets, blurring the gas-lamps and
> changing the houses into monstrous shadows? To whom, if not to them
> and their master, do we owe the lovely silver mists that brood over our
> river, and turn to faint forms of fading grace curved bridge and swaying
> barge? The extraordinary change that has taken place in the climate of
> London during the last ten years is entirely due to a particular school of
> Art. You smile. Consider the matter from a scientific or a metaphysical
> point of view, and you will find that I am right. For what is Nature?
> Nature is no great mother who has borne us. She is our creation. It is in
> our brain that she quickens to life. Things are because we see them, and
> what we see, and how we see it, depends on the Arts that have influenced

us. To look at a thing is very different from seeing a thing. One does
not see anything until one sees its beauty. Then, and then only, does it
come into existence. At present, people see fogs, not because there are
fogs, but because poets and painters have taught them the mysterious
loveliness of such effects. There may have been fogs for centuries in
London. I dare say there were. But no one saw them, and so we do not
know anything about them. They did not exist till Art had invented
them.

Despite the axiomatic nature of these pardoxes to Wilde, he
found disturbing evidence all around him that the more trivial
world of facts was increasingly dominating and usurping the role
imagination had to play if man were to strive toward his highest
possibilities. Facts were spreading their chilling touch over everything, vulgarizing humanity. Wryly, but not seriously, Wilde—
the veteran of a cross-country American lecture tour—blamed
the forbidding climate on the "crude commercialism," the materialism, the "indifference to the poetical side of things," the lack of
imagination as well as of "high unattainable ideals" on the part
of that most influential country which had "adopted for its national
hero a man who, according to his own confession, was incapable of
telling a lie." It was "not too much to say that the story of George
Washington and the cherry-tree has done more harm, and in a
shorter space of time, than any other moral tale in our literature."
It was not truth which enlarged consciousness, Wilde complained,
for the English, too, were always "degrading truth into facts." And
when a truth became a fact, it lost all intellectual value.[9] Sin,
unsurprisingly, was a more essential element: "Sin increases the
experience of the race," and is an "intensified assertion of individualism" and a relief from "monotony of type," which "in its rejection
of the current notions about morality" is also—paradoxically—"one
with the highest ethics."

Echoing his creator, Algernon in *The Importance of Being Earnest*
notes that the truth "is rarely pure and simple. Modern life would
be very tedious if it were either, and modern literature a complete
impossibility!" Since Wilde toyed with the idea of reality as

9. Oscar Wilde, "A Few Maxims for the Instruction of the Over-Educated," in
*Letters*, p. 869.

appcarance, "with no reality in things apart from their appearances,"[10] he considered the artist's mind and mood as capable of
shaping that reality—thus Turner's burnished sunsets and literature's
London fogs. Nineteenth-century "scientific" or artistic realism,
however, reached only for concreteness and arrived instead at
dullness, leading Wilde's spokesman in *The Decay of Lying* to
lament, "Ours is certainly the dullest and most prosaic century
possible. Why, even Sleep has played us false. . . . The dreams of
the great middle classes of this country, as recorded in Mr. [Frederic
W. H.]Myers's two bulky volumes on the subject, and in the Transactions of the Psychical Society, are the most depressing things I have
ever read. There is not even a fine nightmare among them. They
are commonplace, sordid, and tedious." It was art, "absolutely
indifferent to fact," which made reality readable and intelligible
through imagination—and that through the medium of style.

In Wilde's criticism one always returns to the touchstone of
style. Things are because we perceive them, and how we do so
"depends on the arts which have influenced us. To look at a thing
is very different from seeing a thing."[11] Style was "that masterful
but restrained individuality of manner by which one artist is
differentiated from another," and one reached toward perfection
in handling style by ascertaining and utilizing the maximum
expressive powers of the artist's medium. Lack of literary style,
Wilde confessed, was the only thing that ever prejudiced him, as a
critic, against a book. In fact, he noted in an epigram which
anticipated the twentieth century but which in his own time seemed
only another infuriating paradox, "Only the great masters of style
ever succeed in being obscure."

Before style came certain qualities upon which style could then
be imposed. Wilde pointed to these in pouncing upon a lame
English rendering of a French book, which might be "up to the
intellectual requirements of Harrow schoolboys" but would "hardly
satisfy those who consider that accuracy, lucidity and ease are
essential to a good translation." Although accuracy, lucidity, and

10. Quoted from Wilde's conversation by Laurence Housman, *Echo de Paris* (New
York: D. Appleton & Co., 1924), p. 22.
11. *Ibid.*

ease were essential to *all* good writing, the writer's good intentions were not of the smallest value. Involving one's feelings with one's material was "outside the proper sphere of art," and put the artist at a stylistic disadvantage. "All bad poetry springs from genuine feeling. To be natural is to be obvious, and to be obvious is to be inartistic." Or, as André Gide later put it, cynically, "To me the worst instinct has always seemed sincere."

Artificiality, or self-consciousness, lay at the heart of style, and was impossible to achieve if "a thing is useful or necessary to us, or affects us in any way, either for pain or for pleasure, or appeals strongly to our sympathies, or is a vital part of the environment in which we live. . . . It is exactly because Hecuba is nothing to us that her sorrows are such an admirable motive for tragedy." It was an unrealizable ideal, for not even the most self-conscious artist could work effectively for very long with materials which could not concern him. Even in his most blatantly commercial writings, Wilde, contradicting his own contention about critical distance, almost always twisted the subject at hand into a perspective which permitted him to say something he wanted to say in a manner at least close to the way he wanted to say it. If it were not for that, his critical journalism would possess neither interest nor vitality; yet it has both, often in spite of the dauntingly dismal quality of the publications he found himself forced to review.

Wilde's major critical works, *The Decay of Lying* and *The Critic as Artist*, were in part spill-overs from his book-reviewing phase, then in its waning months.[12] Their perspectives parallel the earlier reviews, while also reinforcing earlier judgments about particular authors. But their self-conscious brilliance creates the atmosphere of a performance, an effect the dialogue form sustains. As a result his views about writers and writing seem more geniune in the reviews, where he usually appeared anonymously and had no cause for calling attention to Oscar Wilde. Because he took his work as critic more seriously than his pose suggested (and very likely more seriously than he at first intended), he did have cause for some mild despair. Wilde felt, for example, that the high level of poetry

12. Wilde's first and last review columns appeared in the *Pall Mall Gazette*, on October 14, 1884, and May 24, 1890.

in his time was only relative to the extremely low quality of contemporary fiction and drama, and made the best of a depressing situation by concluding, "We have been able to have fine poetry in England because the public do not read it, and consequently do not influence it."[13] In his *Pall Mall Gazette* days he had appealed not only for *readers* for books of new poetry, but for *purchasers* of the books. He may have believed in a relationship between coterie and quality—later, in fact, he subsidized the private publication of John Gray's verses, *Silverpoints*—but Wilde realistically understood that trade publishers had to sell books in order to stay in business. "It would be sad indeed," he wrote, "if the many volumes of poems that are every year published in London found no readers but the authors themselves and the authors' relations; and the real philanthropist should recognize it as part of his duties to buy every new book of verse that appears. Sometimes, we will acknowledge, he will be disappointed, often he will be bored; still now and then he will be amply rewarded for his reckless benevolence."

Wilde's own such rewards as a critic were few, but one was the young Yeats, whose *Wanderings of Oisin* seemed to him so remarkable that he could "hardly resist the fascinating temptation of recklessly prophesying a fine future for its author. . . . Here we find nobility of treatment and nobility of subject-matter, delicacy of poetic instinct and richness of imaginative resource." He reviewed few other living poets he could admire. Swinburne, who "once set his age on fire by a volume of very perfect and very poisonous poetry," disappointed Wilde by developing crippling limitations, "the chief of which is . . . the entire lack of any sense of limit. His song is nearly always too loud for his subject." The best of the later Swinburne was to Wilde empty of everything but technical excellence: "Out of the thunder and splendour of words he himself says nothing." "Art for art's sake" may have been a splendid contemporary watchword, but Wilde expected art to provide some "revelation of human life." Now and then the mask slipped.

The criticism from which Wilde most shrank was that of religious poetry, and his reasons were much the same—"that quality of absolute unintelligibility that is the peculiar privilege of the verbally

13. *The Soul of Man Under Socialism.*

inspired." More orthodox religious verse was seldom an improvement. "There seems to be some curious connection between piety and poor rhymes," he discovered. "Ordinary theology has long since converted its gold into lead, and words and phrases that once touched the heart of the world have become wearisome and meaningless through repetition. If Theology desires to move us, she must re-write her formulas." His skepticism included a "little volume . . . of poems on the Saints. Each poem is preceded by a brief biography of the Saint it celebrates—which is a very necessary precaution, as few of them ever existed. It does not display much poetic power and such lines as these on St. Stephen . . . may be said to add another horror to martyrdom. Still it is a thoroughly well-intentioned book and eminently suitable for invalids."

Wilde often pinpointed the appropriate audience for a book, a useful way to indicate a bad book's meager appeal, and the method was a critical staple of his right up to the last line of his last review column: "On the whole *Primavera* is a pleasant little book, and we are glad to welcome it. It is charmingly 'got up,' and undergraduates might read it with advantage during lecture hours." It was an early effort by four young Oxonians, two of whom would be famous in a decade, and nearly forgotten in two—Laurence Binyon and Stephen Phillips. One earlier young poet—who died young— remained in Wilde's thinly populated literary pantheon. Thomas Chatterton, he thought, was "one of England's greatest poets." Wilde's 1886 lecture on the "marvellous boy," given at Birkbeck College, London, was promised for publication in Herbert Horne's *Century Guild Hobby Horse,* but although the extant manuscript runs to seventy pages, it was apparently never ready for the printer.[14]

In at least one case Wilde's pantheon was occupied by a poetess, and one might hope that Oscar the gentleman rather than Oscar the critic made the choice. Belying his own dicta about overpraise rendering the criticism suspect,[15] he intoned that the author of

14. *Letters,* p. 192 n. The MS is in the William Andrews Clark Memorial Library, Los Angeles.

15. "No one survives being over-estimated, nor is there any surer way of destroying an author's reputation than to glorify him without judgment and to praise him without tact."

*Sonnets from the Portuguese* was "unapproachable by any woman who has ever touched lyre or blown through reed since the days of the great Aeolian poetess. . . . Of all the women of history, Mrs. Browning is the only one that we could name in any possible or remote connection with Sappho." Another Greek analogy was more appropriate. To Wilde, England's greatest poet was Milton, and it was to his loss of sight that the language owed "the sonorous splendour of his later verse." There was a lesson to be learned. "When Milton became blind he composed, as everyone should compose, with the voice purely, and so the pipe or reed of earlier days became that mighty many-stopped organ whose rich reverberant music has all the stateliness of Homeric verse. . . . Yes: writing has done much harm to writers. We must return to the voice." Mrs. Browning's husband fared worse, for reasons consistent with Wilde's attitude toward Milton. "Meredith," he wrote in an observation on the contemporary novel, "is a prose Browning, and so is Browning. He used poetry as a medium for writing in prose."

In some cases Wilde found reason to praise a poet for largely nonpoetical values. The worth of Whitman's poetry was "in its prophecy, not in its performance." He found in Whitman (whom he had met in the old poet's home in Camden) "a largeness of vision, a healthy sanity and a fine ethical purpose"—all qualities none of Whitman's detractors noted, and all qualities which had little to do with Wilde's theories of art. Longfellow, a lesser poet, he praised as "one of the first true men of letters America has produced," for that reason alone a writer who deserved "a high place in any history of American civilization. . . . But his poems are not of the kind that call for intellectual analysis or for elaborate description or, indeed, for any serious discussion at all." It was the very problem which afflicted Wilde whenever he had a column to fill on the latest output in verse, for few writers he criticized even measured up to the modest Longfellow standard.

Wilde reviewed few contemporary plays, either in print or in performance. It was a thin period for the theater. "The only link between Literature and the Drama left to us in England at the present moment," he complained, "is the bill of the play."[16] Like

16. "A Few Maxims for the Instruction of the Over-Educated."

Shaw, he defended paradoxically the serious place in the theater of the play of wit. "I was on the point of explaining to Gerald," says his Lord Illingworth, "that the world has always laughed at its own tragedies, that being the only way in which it has been able to bear them. And that, consequently, whatever the world has treated seriously belongs to the comedy side of things" (*A Woman of No Importance*). Comedy appealed to him too because it was the self-conscious side of theater—"an audience looks at a tragedian, but a comedian looks at his audience." In comedy, he thought, "situations predominate over characters," while tragedy was the "exaggeration of the individual." But plays, in any case, were meant to be acted rather than read, for in no other way could they combine the literary and plastic arts. "On the stage," he wrote hopefully, "literature returns to life and archaeology becomes art. A fine theatre is a temple where all the muses may meet." It was foolish, he thought, to complain "of the passion of a play being hidden by paint, and of sentiment being killed by scenery. . . . A noble play, nobly mounted, gives us double artistic pleasure. The eye as well as the ear is gratified, and the whole nature is made exquisitely receptive of the influence of imaginative work."

Shakespeare helped sustain a number of contentions basic to Wilde's criticism. He was, for example, "indifferent to historical accuracy." Of course, Wilde added, "the aesthetic value of Shakespeare's plays does not, in the slightest degree, depend upon their facts, but on their Truth, and Truth is independent of facts always, inventing or selecting them at pleasure." Truth in stage performance could take many forms, one aspect being the truth suggested by paradox, as Wilde observed about a famous scene in *Hamlet*:

> The whole point of Hamlet's advice to the players seems to me to be lost unless the Player himself has been guilty of the fault which Hamlet reprehends, unless he has sawn the air with his hand, mouthed his lines, torn his passion to tatters, and out-Heroded Herod. The very sensibility which Hamlet notices in the actor, such as his real tears and the like, is not the quality of a good artist. The part should be played after the manner of a provincial tragedian. It is meant to be a satire, and to play it well is to play it badly.

*Hamlet* was Wilde's favorite play, and the curious pair of Rosencrantz and Guildenstern were among his favorite characters, perhaps because he could read so much into their shadowy existences. As late as his 1897 letter-essay *De Profundis* he was discovering new depths in the pair; but reviewing an 1885 performance, he pretended not to be able to tell them apart. "Mr. Norman Forbes . . . he wrote, "played either Guildenstern or Rosencrantz very gracefully. I believe one of our budding Hazlitts is preparing a volume to be entitled 'Great Guildensterns and Remarkable Rosencrantzes,' but I have never been able to discern any difference between these two characters. They are, I think, the only characters Shakespeare has not cared to individualise."

Rosencrantz and Guildenstern were useful to Wilde in other ways as well, as he drew upon them to develop what has since become a cliché of biographical criticism. "Formerly we used to canonise our great men; nowadays we vulgarise them," he wrote, with Joseph Knight's life of Dante Gabriel Rossetti in mind. It was "just the sort of biography Guildenstern might have written of Hamlet. Nor does its unsatisfactory character come merely from the ludicrous inadequacy of the materials at Mr. Knight's disposal. . . . Rossetti's was a great personality, and great personalities do not easily survive shilling primers. Sooner or later they have inevitably to come down to the level of their biographers." Wilde could pillory the biographer as deftly as the biography, observing about a mild and reticent life of George Sand that it was "the biography of a very great man from the pen of a very ladylike writer."

After reading Hall Caine's *Coleridge* he was reminded of what Wordsworth had once said on viewing a bust of himself: "It is not a bad Wordsworth, but it is not the real Wordsworth; it is not Wordsworth the poet, it is the sort of Wordsworth who might be Chancellor of the Exchequer." It was what Wilde later called in *The Decay of Lying* and *The Critic as Artist* the failure of realism. "The incidents of the life are duly recounted . . . , as no doubt they should be in every popular biography; but of the spiritual progress of the man's soul we hear absolutely nothing. Never . . . are we brought near to Coleridge; the magic of that wonderful personality is hidden from us by a cloud of mean details." For Wilde "the goings-out and comings-in of a man, his places of sojourn and his roads of travel are but idle things to chronicle, if that which is the man be left unrecorded." There was much that was mysterious in an artist's "thoughts, dreams and passions, his moments of creative impulse, their source and secret, his moods of imaginative joy, their marvel and their meaning, and not his moods merely but the music and the melancholy that they brought him; . . . and though we may not be able to pluck out the heart of his mystery, still let us recognise that mystery is there."

In the later major essays Wilde not only borrowed ideas from the reviews, but epigrams as well, including the lines about vulgarization replacing canonization in biography, and about cheap editions of great books being replaced by cheap editions of great men. "Every great man nowadays has his disciples, and it is always Judas who writes the biography." Not always, he should have noted in the interests of consistency: sometimes the biographer was Guildenstern.

Wilde found contemporary fiction no better than writing in other forms. The *Peerage*, Lord Illingworth observes in *A Woman of No Importance*, "is the best thing in fiction the English have ever done." In conversation Wilde added, "No *modern* literary work of any worth has been produced in the English language—except of course *Bradshaw*."[17] His Gwendolen Fairfax, in *The Importance of Being Earnest*, resorts to even more offbeat literature in order to find something satisfactory: "I never travel without my diary. One should always have something sensational to read in the train." She might have found history more exciting. Miss Prism, in fact, warns Cecily to omit from her schoolwork the chapter "on the Fall of the Rupee . . . . It is somewhat too sensational."

Because Wilde always insisted that facts did not add up to truth, it was characteristic of him to blur the line between fiction and history. "The only form of fiction in which real characters do not seem out of place," he wrote, "is history." In fact, he added afterwards, "The ancient historians gave us delightful fiction in the form of fact; the modern novelist presents us with dull facts

17. *Bradshaw* was an English railway timetable named for a nineteenth-century printer.

under the guise of fiction." The historical writings of Carlyle, he
thought, proved his paradox, for in Carlyle's *French Revolution*, "one
of the most fascinating historical novels ever written, facts are
either kept in their subordinate position, or else entirely excluded
on the general ground of dullness." He was convinced that the
"one duty we owe to history is to re-write it. That is not the least
of the tasks in store for the critical spirit. When we have fully
discovered the scientific laws that govern life, we shall realise that
the one person who has more illusions than the dreamer is the man
of action."

Fiction, Wilde's observation about Carlyle suggested, was guilty
of literature's worst crime—dullness; and the reasons only proved
in his manner the validity of his critical theses. "What are American
dry goods?" Lady Hunstanton asks. "American novels," says Lord
Illingworth.[18] Traditionally swollen Victorian fiction fared no
better. "Anybody can write a three-volumed novel," Wilde declared
in *The Critic as Artist*. "It merely requires a complete ignorance of
both life and literature." In *The Importance of Being Earnest* the
worldly Lady Bracknell describes Miss Prism's mislaid early manuscript as being that "of a novel of more than usually revolting
sentimentality." No change is discernible in Miss Prism's later
critical position. When Cecily Cardew—that paradoxically modern
spirit—complains that she dislikes novels which end happily because
they depress her so much, Miss Prism restates the case for the
traditional novel: "The good ended happily, and the bad un-
happily. That is what Fiction means." Such fiction was not only
unlike life, but was not art, any more than was the new documentary
novel to Wilde a work of literary art. The Zolaesque novelists of
East End slum life "find life crude, and leave it raw." (That this
could have social utility did not impress Wilde, for social utility
itself was outside art.) Zola himself, with all his narrative power
and exactitude of description, left Wilde unmoved, although he
defended Zola against the moral indignation he correctly analyzed

18. *A Woman of No Importance*. Wilde had used the quip earlier in *Dorian Gray*:
   "Dry goods! What are American dry-goods?" asked the Duchess, raising
her large hands in wonder, and accentuating the verb.
   "American novels," answered Lord Henry, helping himself to some quail.

as "simply the indignation of Tartuffe on being exposed." The
problem of the naturalist novel was that it dealt with the "dreary
vices" and "drearier virtues" of people whose lives were "absolutely
without interest." Whatever their interest to the newly literate
classes emancipated by board-school English, the characters brought
to life by this new breed of novel were not for Wilde. "Who cares
what happens to them?" The justification of a character in a novel
for him was not that character's realistic basis, "but that the author
is what he is. Otherwise the novel is not a work of art."

Wilde bore the cross of novel-reviewing with wit and patience.
He observed (an idea he borrowed for his best play) that some of
the most inept fiction-writing was "done with the best intentions,
and that people are never so trivial as when they take themselves
seriously." Yet he did not feel that he had to be very severe with the
contemporary English novels he reviewed, for they were "the only
relaxation of the intellectually unemployed." Bad writing, however,
irritated him: "The nineteenth century may be a prosaic age, but
we fear that, if we are to judge by the general run of novels, it is not
an age of prose." The explanation, he quipped, might have been
that the novelists of his day were caught in a dilemma—"if they do
not go into society, their books are unreadable; and if they do go
into society, they have no time left for writing." One group of
inexpensively priced novels he found so unworthy of publication
that he concluded, "We sincerely hope that a few more novels like
these will be published, as the public will then find out that a bad
book is very dear at a shilling."

There were consolations, too, for the critic of fiction. An English
edition of Balzac prompted his declaration that the *Comédie humaine*
was "the greatest moment that literature has produced in this
century. . . . Balzac's aim . . . was to do for humanity what Buffon
had done for animal creation. As the naturalist studied lions and
tigers, so the novelist studied men and women. . . . A steady course
of Balzac reduces our living friends to shadows, and our acquaintances to the shadows of shades." Frugally, he reused some of the
lines from the review in *The Decay of Lying*, adding to them a
sentence linking his observations to a theme of the essay: "Balzac
is no more of a realist than Holbein was." But Wilde had no patience

with Englishmen who claimed Dickens as the domestic Balzac.
"One must have a heart of stone," he joked, "to read the death of
Little Nell without laughing." More seriously, he wrote that "in
some respects Dickens might be likened to those old sculptors of
our Gothic cathedrals, who could give form to the most fantastic
fancy, and crowd with grotesque monsters a curious world of
dreams, but saw little of the grace and dignity of the men and
women among whom they lived, and whose art, lacking sanity,
was therefore incomplete. Yet at least they knew the limitations
of their art, while Dickens never knew the limitations of his."

Few contemporary writers earned Wilde's encomiums. His old
mentor Walter Pater (whom Wilde often paraphrased) wrote sentences which had "the charm of an elaborate piece of music" as
well as "the unity of such music." George Meredith, however,
"as a writer . . . [had] mastered everything except language," while
as a novelist (Wilde admired his characterization) Meredith could
do "everything, except tell a story." Henry James wrote fiction "as
if it were a painful duty, and wastes upon mean motives and
imperceptible 'points of view' his neat literary style, his felicitous
phrases, his swift and caustic satire." Hall Caine, aiming rather at the
grandiose, wrote "at the top of his voice. He is so loud that one
cannot hear what he says." Carlyle was once dismissed with the
remark that "the whole of the Philosophy of Clothes is to be found
in Lear's scene with Edgar—a passage which has the advantage of
brevity and style over the grotesque wisdom and somewhat mouthing metaphysics of *Sartor Resartus*." Earnestness as well as bad
writing condemned Mrs. Ward's much esteemed *Robert Elsmere*, "a
masterpiece of the *genre ennuyeux*, the one form of literature that the
English people seems thoroughly to enjoy." F. Marion Crawford's
popular American expatriate novels were also moral and dull:
"He is always telling us that to be good is to be good, and that to
be bad is to be wicked." Charles Reade's novels of moral indignation
drew Wilde's saddest reproaches, for he felt that after one of the
most distinguished and beautiful books of the age, *The Cloister and
the Hearth*, Reade, "an artist, a scholar, a man with a true sense of
beauty," wasted the rest of his career "raging and roaring over
the abuses of contemporary life like a common pamphleteer." By

placing himself too close to his material, by substituting subjectivity for self-consciousness, Reade—by Wilde's standards—forsook the necessary critical perspectives. Wilde never altered this view, even from the sobering vantage of prison. From Reading Gaol he wrote Robert Ross about a posthumous collection of Robert Louis Stevenson's letters that they were "most disappointing. . . . I see that romantic surroundings are the worst surroundings possible for a romantic writer. In Gower Street Stevenson could have written a new *Trois Mousquetaires*. In Samoa he wrote letters to *The Times* about Germans."[19]

Wilde seemed almost to anticipate prison, if not actually to aspire toward it, for reasons related to his subterranean life yet capable of rationalization from a critical point of view. While he lived as if he could evade the morals laws forever, he knew better and prepared his case for himself by equating courageous wrongdoing with the artist's search for enrichment of experience. What one shouldn't do *had* to be done, in order to explore new possibilities in self-consciousness—a concept Algernon applies to literature in *The Importance of Being Earnest*: "Oh! it is absurd to have a hard-and-fast rule about what one should read and what one shouldn't. More than half of modern culture depends on what one shouldn't read." What one shouldn't *do* might be enforced by prison regulations, Wilde wrote more than six years before his own days in the dock, but prison nonetheless could have an "admirable effect," while in no way limiting or constraining "the freedom of a man's soul." Approvingly, he quoted Wilfrid Blunt as reporting after his own experience that prison, "like a sickness or a spiritual retreat . . . purifies and ennobles; and the soul emerges from it stronger and more self-contained." *The Importance of Being Earnest* was only in its second month at the St. James's Theatre when its author had the opportunity of prison forced upon him, and in *De Profundis*, written in his last months of incarceration, he applied his experience to his theories.

"Everything that is realised is right," Wilde insisted in *De Profundis*, thus continuing to equate sin—artistically mastered—with truth. "The books that the world calls immoral books," he had written in *The Picture of Dorian Gray*, "are books that show the

19. Oscar Wilde to Robert Ross, April 6 [1897], in *Letters*, p. 520.

world its own shame." In *The Soul of Man Under Socialism* he explained, "When the public say a work of art is grossly unintelligible, they mean that the artist has said or made a beautiful thing that is true." It was a paradox he had to believe in: it explained himself. It also explained his art. "Romantic art," he wrote in defending *Dorian Gray*, "deals with the exception and the individual. Good people, belonging as they do to the normal, and so, commonplace, type, are artistically uninteresting. Bad people are, from the point of view of art, fascinating studies. They represent colour, variety and strangeness. Good people exasperate one's reason; bad people stir one's imagination." The sinister double life of Dorian Gray was more relevant to the author's own condition than the reading public then knew. On the surface Wilde was in the novel no more than creatively consistent with his own esthetic theories. Yet it was through more than critical uniformity that Wilde's essays, stories, and plays talked of masks and of lying, and pivoted cleverly upon deception and double lives.[20] "It is proper," Wilde wrote, intending perhaps only a half-truth, "that limitation should be placed on action. It is not proper that limitation should be placed on art. To art belong all things that are and all things that are not."

The Wildean ideal was an artist who "has no ethical sympathies at all. Virtue and wickedness are to him simply what the colours on his palette are to the painter." The proposed public for that ideal was less realizable—one which would understand that the "sphere of art and the sphere of ethics" were "absolutely distinct and separate." It was to the confusion between ethics and art, he explained, "that we owe the appearance of Mrs. Grundy, that amusing old lady who represents the only original form of humour that the middle classes of this country have been able to produce."

Grundyism, Wilde understood, was not entirely a laughing matter, for it implied some *de facto* censorship over imaginative literature. Literature possessed certain rights and freedoms inherent in art, he insisted. "A Government might just as well try to teach painters how to paint, or sculptors how to model, as attempt to interfere

20. *Lord Arthur Savile's Crime*, "Pen, Pencil and Poison," "The Portrait of Mr. W. H.," and all the plays are additional cases in point.

with the style, treatment and subject-matter of the literary artist."
Censorship "would degrade literature far more than any didactic
or so-called immoral book could possibly do." The problem was
that although Wilde was right, he was evading the equally crucial
question as to whether the immoral literary artist (in his capacity not
as artist, but as human being) degraded literature. And it remains
to the confusion between the two inescapable questions that we
owe some skepticism about Wilde the literary critic. In Oscar's
heyday, the young Max Beerbohm, in his first published essay (he
was still at Merton College, Oxford), pointed out the problem.
"Apart from the truth that the excellence of a work lies not in the
possession of any ulterior motive or original conviction of its
author, but in the aspect of the work itself," Max wrote, "to say
that Mr. Wilde is not in earnest is manifestly false. No writer has
pleaded with greater zeal and consistency for the preference
of Aesthetics to Ethics . . . [yet] it is not by his works alone that
we must judge him, but by the personality of which his works
are a part."[21] Wilde could have agreed with the dangerously
accurate and prophetic judgment. "I treated art as the supreme
reality and life as a mere mode of fiction," he afterwards wrote
(from prison) to Douglas in *De Profundis*. But he might have added,
as was his method, a diversionary paradox. "Not that I agree with
everything that I have said in this essay," he had already explained
in *The Truth of Masks*. "There is much with which I entirely disagree.
. . . For in Art there is no such thing as a universal truth. A truth in
art is that whose contradiction is also true."

A critic in spite of himself, then a critic to explain himself,
Wilde sought to bring art into harmony with his life, and his life
into harmony with art. It is a paradox entirely consistent with his
life that such criticism has proved to be as enduring as it is entertaining. But like his John Worthing (who was Ernest in the country),
Wilde might have confessed his surprise "to find out suddenly that
all his life he has been speaking nothing but the truth."

21. Max Beerbohm (as "An American"), "Oscar Wilde," *Anglo-American Times*,
March 25, 1893, identified and reprinted in Rupert Hart-Davis (ed.), *Max
Beerbohm's Letters to Reggie Turner* (Philadelphia and New York, Lippincott, 1965),
pp. 290–291.

*A Note on the Texts*

The texts, with one exception, follow their reproduction in the first (1908) authorized edition of Wilde, which reprinted most of Wilde's publications from their first printed versions. Wilde began writing for *Dramatic Review* on March 14, 1885; *Nineteenth Century* in May, 1885; *Society* on July 4, 1885; *Saturday Review* on May 7, 1887; *Woman's World* in June, 1887; *The Lady's Pictorial* in December, 1887; *Queen* on December 8, 1888; *The Speaker* in February, 1890. "The Rise of Historical Criticism" appeared in Wilde's lifetime only in a truncated version at the end of *Lord Arthur Savile's Crime and Other Prose Pieces*. A revised edition of his collected major critical essays appeared as *Intentions* in 1891. Earlier, "The Decay of Lying" appeared in *Nineteenth Century* (January, 1889); "Pen, Pencil and Poison" in *The Fortnightly Review* (January, 1889); "The Artist as Critic" (as "The True Function and Value of Criticism") in *Nineteenth Century* (Part I in July, 1890, and Part II in September, 1890); "The Portrait of Mr. W. H." in *Blackwood's Magazine* (July, 1889); and "The Truth of Masks" (as "Shakespeare and Stage Costume") in *Nineteenth Century* (May, 1885). The brief extract from *De Profundis*, the letter-autobiographical essay first published incompletely in 1906, follows that text as corrected in the 1962 printing in *The Letters of Oscar Wilde*.

*The Soul of Man [Under Socialism]*, first published in 1891, has been excluded as not being primarily literary criticism. *Pen, Pencil and Poison* (1889, revised 1891) is excluded as being primarily a tongue-in-cheek biographical essay, while the *Portrait of Mr. W. H.* (1889), often considered to be a criticism of Shakespeare's *Sonnets*, is more a facetious exercise in pseudobiography. All three are examined in the editor's Introduction.

The texts are reprinted here as they appeared in the sources, with no substantive alterations or changes in spelling. Only the printing style of quotation marks has been regularized to follow the American style (double quotation marks on the first quotation, with single quote marks for a quote within a quote). Generally, foreign words and phrases are translated either in a footnote or, if very brief, in brackets in the text following the original; an exception has been made, however, for less well known languages, which are given in translation in the text, with the original in footnotes. Editorial deletions are indicated by three asterisks (* * *); ellipses are the author's own.

STANLEY WEINTRAUB

*Pennsylvania State University*

# I. ON BOOKS AND AUTHORS

# To Read or Not to Read

*The* Pall Mall Gazette *had been running a series on "The Best Hundred Books" by "The Best Hundred Judges." Wilde's rejoinder appeared under the editorial note "As we have published so many letters advising what to read, the following advice 'what not to read' from so good an authority as Mr. Oscar Wilde may be of service."*

Books, I fancy, may be conveniently divided into three classes:

1. Books to read, such as Cicero's *Letters*, Suetonius, Vasari's *Lives of the Painters*, the *Autobiography of Benvenuto Cellini*, Sir John Mandeville, Marco Polo, St. Simon's *Memoirs*, Mommsen, and (till we get a better one) Grote's *History of Greece*.

2. Books to re-read, such as Plato and Keats: in the sphere of poetry, the masters not the minstrels; in the sphere of philosophy, the seers not the *savants*.

3. Books not to read at all, such as Thomson's *Seasons*, Rogers's *Italy*, Paley's *Evidences*, all the Fathers except St. Augustine, all John Stuart Mill except the essay on *Liberty*, all Voltaire's plays without any exception, Butler's *Analogy*, Grant's *Aristotle*, Hume's *England*, Lewes's *History of Philosophy*, all argumentative books and all books that try to prove anything.

The third class is by far the most important. To tell people what to read is, as a rule, either useless or harmful; for, the appreciation of literature is a question of temperament not of teaching; to Parnassus there is no primer and nothing that one can learn is ever worth learning. But to tell people what not to read is a very different matter, and I venture to recommend it as a mission to the University Extension Scheme.

Indeed, it is one that is eminently needed in this age of ours, an age that reads so much, that it has no time to admire, and writes so much, that it has no time to think. Whoever will select out of the chaos of our modern curricula "The Worst Hundred Books," and publish a list of them, will confer on the rising generation a real and lasting benefit.

After expressing these views I suppose I should not offer any suggestions at all with regard to "The Best Hundred Books," but I hope you will allow me the pleasure of being inconsistent, as I am anxious to put in a claim for a book that has been strangely omitted by most of the excellent judges who have contributed to your columns. I mean the *Greek Anthology*.[1] The beautiful poems contained in this collection seem to me to hold the same position with regard to Greek dramatic literature as do the delicate little figurines of Tanagra to the Phidian marbles, and to be quite as necessary for the complete understanding of the Greek spirit.

I am also amazed to find that Edgar Allan Poe has been passed over. Surely this marvellous lord of rhythmic expression deserves a place? If, in order to make room for him, it be necessary to elbow out someone else, I should elbow out Southey, and I think that Baudelaire might be most advantageously substituted for Keble.

No doubt, both in the *Curse of Kehama* and in the *Christian Year*[2] there are poetic qualities of a certain kind, but absolute catholicity of taste is not without its dangers. It is only an auctioneer who should admire all schools of art.

*Pall Mall Gazette*, February 8, 1886.

1. A collection of some 4,500 short Greek poems dating from about the time of Alexander the Great to early medieval times.
2. *The Curse of Kehama*, a poem by Robert Southey based on Hindu mythology and folklore, was first published in 1810. *The Christian Year*, published anonymously in 1823, was a volume of sacred poems by John Keble, professor of poetry at Oxford for many years. It was immensely popular in its time.

# A New Calendar [Alfred Austin]

*Review of* Days of the Year: A Poetic Calendar from the Works of Alfred Austin, *selected and edited by A. S., with introduction by William Sharp. At this time Austin (1835–1913) was editor of the* National Review, *a post he held until his appointment as poet laureate in 1896. The Scottish poet and man of letters William Sharp (1856–1905) is best known today for the stories and sketches he wrote under the name of "Fiona Macleod," but the secret of his authorship was not revealed until after his death.*

Most modern calendars mar the sweet simplicity of our lives by reminding us that each day that passes is the anniversary of some perfectly uninteresting event. Their compilers display a degraded passion for chronicling small beer, and rake out the dust-heap of history in an ardent search after rubbish. Mr. Walter Scott, however, has made a new departure and has published a calendar in which every day of the year is made beautiful for us by means of an elegant extract from the poems of Mr. Alfred Austin. This, undoubtedly, is a step in the right direction. It is true that such aphorisms as

> Graves are a *mother's dimples*
> When we complain,

or

> The primrose wears a constant smile,
> And captive takes the heart,

can hardly be said to belong to the very highest order of poetry, still, they are preferable, on the whole, to the date of Hannah More's birth, or of the burning down of Exeter Change, or of the opening of the Great Exhibition; and though it would be dangerous

5

to make calendars the basis of Culture, we should all be much improved if we began each day with a fine passage of English poetry. How far this desirable result can be attained by a use of the volume now before us is, perhaps, open to question, but it must be admitted that its anonymous compiler has done his work very conscientiously, nor will we quarrel with him for the fact that he constantly repeats the same quotation twice over. No doubt it was difficult to find in Mr. Austin's work three hundred and sixty-five different passages really worthy of insertion in an almanac, and, besides, our climate has so degenerated of late that there is no reason at all why a motto perfectly suitable for February should not be equally appropriate when August has set in with its usual severity. For the misprints there is less excuse. Even the most uninteresting poet cannot survive bad editing.

Prefixed to the Calendar is an introductory note from the pen of Mr. William Sharp, written in that involved and affected style which is Mr. Sharp's distinguishing characteristic, and displaying that intimate acquaintance with Sappho's lost poems which is the privilege only of those who are not acquainted with Greek literature. As a criticism it is not of much value, but as an advertisement it is quite excellent. Indeed, Mr. Sharp hints mysteriously at secret political influence, and tells us that though Mr. Austin "sings with Tityrus" yet he "has conversed with Aeneas," which, we suppose, is a euphemistic method of alluding to the fact that Mr. Austin once lunched with Lord Beaconsfield. It is for the poet, however, not for the politician, that Mr. Sharp reserves his loftiest panegyric and, in his anxiety to smuggle the author of *Leszko the Bastard* and *Grandmother's Teaching* into the charmed circle of the Immortals, he leaves no adjective unturned, quoting and misquoting Mr. Austin with a recklessness that is absolutely fatal to the cause he pleads. For mediocre critics are usually safe in their generalities; it is in their reasons and examples that they come so lamentably to grief. When, for instance, Mr. Sharp tells us that lines with the "natural magic" of Shakespeare, Keats and Coleridge are "far from infrequent" in Mr. Austin's poems, all that we can say is that we have never come across any lines of the kind in Mr. Austin's published works, but it is difficult to help smiling when Mr. Sharp gravely calls upon us to note "the illuminative significance" of such a commonplace verse as

> My manhood keeps the dew of morn,
>     And what have I to give;
> Being right glad that I was born,
>     And thankful that I live.

Nor do Mr. Sharp's constant misquotations really help him out of his difficulties. Such a line as

> A meadow ribbed with *drying* swathes of hay,

has at least the merit of being a simple, straightforward description of an ordinary scene in an English landscape, but not much can be said in favour of

> A meadow ribbed with *dying* swathes of hay,

which is Mr. Sharp's own version, and one that he finds "delightfully suggestive." It is indeed suggestive, but only of that want of care that comes from want of taste.

On the whole, Mr. Sharp has attempted an impossible task. Mr. Austin is neither an Olympian nor a Titan, and all the puffing in Paternoster Row cannot set him on Parnassus.

His verse is devoid of all real rhythmical life; it may have the metre of poetry, but it has not often got its music, nor can there be any true delicacy in the ear that tolerates such rhymes as "chord" and "abroad." Even the claim that Mr. Sharp puts forward for him, that his muse takes her impressions directly from nature and owes nothing to books, cannot be sustained for a moment. Wordsworth is a great poet, but bad echoes of Wordsworth are extremely depressing, and when Mr. Austin calls the cuckoo a

> Voyaging voice [1]

---

1.                     O Cuckoo! shall I call thee Bird,
                       Or but a wandering voice?

                              (Wordsworth, "To the Cuckoo")

and tells us that

> The stockdove *broods*
> Low to itself,[2]

we must really enter a protest against such silly plagiarisms.

Perhaps, however, we are treating Mr. Sharp too seriously. He admits himself that it was at the special request of the compiler of the Calendar that he wrote the preface at all, and though he courteously adds that the task is agreeable to him, still he shows only too clearly that he considers it a task and, like a clever lawyer or a popular clergyman, tries to atone for his lack of sincerity by a pleasing over-emphasis. Nor is there any reason why this Calendar should not be a great success. If published as a broad-sheet, with a picture of Mr. Austin "conversing with Aeneas," it might gladden many a simple cottage home and prove a source of innocent amusement to the Conservative working-man.

*Pall Mall Gazette*, February 17, 1887.

2.          Over his own sweet voice the stock-dove broods. . . .

(Wordsworth, "Resolution and Independence")

# Balzac in English

*Review of Balzac's* The Duchesse de Langeais and Other Stories *and* César Birotteau, *translated by Poulet-Malassis, in the series "Balzac's Novels in English" published by Routledge and Company.*

Many years ago, in a number of *All the Year Round*, Charles Dickens complained that Balzac was very little read in England, and although since then the public has become more familiar with the great masterpieces of French fiction, still it may be doubted whether the *Comédie Humaine* is at all appreciated or understood by the general run of novel readers. It is really the greatest monument that literature has produced in our century, and M. Taine hardly exaggerates when he says that, after Shakespeare, Balzac is our most important magazine of documents on human nature. Balzac's aim, in fact, was to do for humanity what Buffon had done for the animal creation. As the naturalist studied lions and tigers, so the novelist studied men and women. Yet he was no mere reporter. Photography and *procès-verbal* were not the essentials of his method. Observation gave him the facts of life, but his genius converted facts into truths, and truths into truth. He was, in a word, a marvellous combination of the artistic temperament with the scientific spirit. The latter he bequeathed to his disciples; the former was entirely his own. The distinction between such a book as M. Zola's *L'Assommoir* and such a book as Balzac's *Illusions Perdues* is the distinction between unimaginative realism and imaginative reality. "All Balzac's characters," said Baudelaire, "are gifted with the same ardour of life that animated himself. All his fictions are as deeply coloured as dreams. Every mind is a weapon loaded to the muzzle with will. The very scullions have genius." He was, of course, accused of being immoral. Few writers who deal directly with life

9

escape that charge. His answer to the accusation was characteristic and conclusive. "Whoever contributes his stone to the edifice of ideas," he wrote, "whoever proclaims an abuse, whoever sets his mark upon an evil to be abolished, always passes for immoral. If you are true in your portraits, if, by dint of daily and nightly toil, you succeed in writing the most difficult language in the world, the word immoral is thrown in your face." The morals of the personages of the *Comédie Humaine* are simply the morals of the world around us. They are part of the artist's subject-matter; they are not part of his method. If there be any need of censure it is to life, not to literature, that it should be given. Balzac, besides, is essentially universal. He sees life from every point of view. He has no preferences and no prejudices. He does not try to prove anything. He feels that the spectacle of life contains its own secret. "Il crée un monde et se tait."[1]

And what a world it is! What a panorama of passions! What a pell-mell of men and women! It was said of Trollope that he increased the number of our acquaintances without adding to our visiting list; but after the *Comédie Humaine* one begins to believe that the only real people are the people who have never existed. Lucien de Rubempré, le Père Goriot, Ursule Mirouët, Marguerite Claës, the Baron Hulot, Madame Marneffe, le Cousin Pons, De Marsay— all bring with them a kind of contagious illusion of life. They have a fierce vitality about them: their existence is fervent and fiery-coloured; we not merely feel for them but we see them—they dominate our fancy and defy scepticism. A steady course of Balzac reduces our living friends to shadows, and our acquaintances to the shadows of shades. Who would care to go out to an evening party to meet Tomkins, the friend of one's boyhood, when one can sit at home with Lucien de Rubempré? It is pleasanter to have the entrée to Balzac's society than to receive cards from all the duchesses in Mayfair.

In spite of this, there are many people who have declared the *Comédie Humaine* to be indigestible. Perhaps it is: but then what about truffles? Balzac's publisher refused to be disturbed by any such criticism as that. "Indigestible, is it?" he exclaimed with

1. "He creates a world and is silent."

what, for a publisher, was rare good sense. "Well, I should hope so; who ever thinks of a dinner that isn't?" And our English publisher, Mr. Routledge, clearly agrees with M. Poulet-Malassis, as he is occupied in producing a complete translation of the *Comédie Humaine*. The two volumes that at present lie before us contain *César Birotteau*, that terrible tragedy of finance, and *L'Illustre Gaudissart*, the apotheosis of the commercial traveller, the *Duchesse de Langeais*, most marvellous of modern love stories, *Le Chef d'Oeuvre Inconnu*, from which Mr. Henry James took his *Madonna of the Future*, and that extraordinary romance *Une Passion dans le Désert*. The choice of stories is quite excellent, but the translations are very unequal, and some of them are positively bad. *L'Illustre Gaudissart*, for instance, is full of the most grotesque mistakes, mistakes that would disgrace a schoolboy. "Bon conseil vaut un oeil dans la main" is translated "Good advice is an egg in the hand"! "Ecus rebelles" is rendered "rebellious lucre," and such common expressions as "faire la barbe," "attendre la vente," "n'entendre rien," "pâlir sur une affaire," are all mistranslated. "Des bois de quoi se faire un cure-dent" is not "a few trees to slice into toothpicks," but "as much timber as would make a toothpick"; "son horloge enfermée dans une grande armoire oblongue" is not "a clock which he kept shut up in a large oblong closet" but simply a clock in a tall clock-case; "journal viager" is not "an annuity," "garce" is not the same as "farce," and "dessins des Indes" are not "drawings of the Indies." On the whole, nothing can be worse than this translation, and if Mr. Routledge wishes the public to read his version of the *Comédie Humaine*, he should engage translators who have some slight knowledge of French.

*César Birotteau* is better, though it is not by any means free from mistakes. "To suffer under the Maximum" is an absurd rendering of "subir le maximum"; "perse" is "chintz," not "Persian chintz"; "rendre le pain bénit" is not "to take the wafer"; "rivière" is hardly a "*fillet* of diamonds"; and to translate "son coeur avait un calus à l'endroit du loyer" by "his heart was a callus in the direction of a lease" is an insult to two languages. On the whole, the best version is that of the *Duchesse de Langeais*, though even this leaves much to be desired. Such a sentence as "to imitate the rough logician who marched before the Pyrrhonians *while denying his own movement*" entirely misses the point of Balzac's "imiter le rude logicien qui marchait devant les pyrrhoniens, qui niaient le mouvement."

We fear Mr. Routledge's edition will not do. It is well printed and nicely bound; but his translators do not understand French. It is a great pity, for *La Comédie Humaine* is one of the masterpieces of the age.

*Pall Mall Gazette*, September 13, 1886.

# Poetry and Prison [Wilfrid Blunt]

*Review of* In Vinculis *by Wilfrid Scawen Blunt (1840–1922). Blunt, a poet, orientalist, traveler, anti-imperialist, sportsman, and breeder of Arabian horses, had been imprisoned for political agitation in Ireland. Arthur James Balfour (1848–1930), who was Chief Secretary for Ireland at the time of Blunt's imprisonment, later became Prime Minister (1902– 1905). His* Defence of Philosophic Doubt *(1879), to which Wilde alludes, was Balfour's first book.*

Prison has had an admirable effect on Mr. Wilfrid Blunt as a poet. The *Love Sonnets of Proteus*, in spite of their clever Musset-like modernities and their swift brilliant wit, were but affected or fantastic at best. They were simply the records of passing moods and moments, of which some were sad and others sweet, and not a few shameful. Their subject was not of high or serious import. They contained much that was wilful and weak. *In Vinculis*, upon the other hand, is a book that stirs one by its fine sincerity of purpose, its lofty and impassioned thought, its depth and ardour of intense feeling. "Imprisonment," says Mr. Blunt in his preface, "is a reality of discipline most useful to the modern soul, lapped as it is in physical sloth and self-indulgence. Like a sickness or a spiritual retreat it purifies and ennobles; and the soul emerges from it stronger and more self-contained." To him, certainly, it has been a mode of purification. The opening sonnets, composed in the bleak cell of Galway Gaol, and written down on the fly-leaves of the prisoner's prayer-book, are full of things nobly conceived and nobly uttered, and show that though Mr. Balfour may enforce "plain living" by his prison regulations, he cannot prevent "high thinking" or in any way limit or constrain the freedom of a man's soul. They are, of course, intensely personal in expression. They

13

could not fail to be so. But the personality that they reveal has nothing petty or ignoble about it. The petulant cry of the shallow egoist which was the chief characteristic of the *Love Sonnets of Proteus* is not to be found here. In its place we have wild grief and terrible scorn, fierce rage and flame-like passion. Such a sonnet as the following comes out of the very fire of heart and brain:

> God knows, 'twas not with a fore-reasoned plan
> I left the easeful dwellings of my peace,
> And sought this combat with ungodly Man,
> And ceaseless still through years that do not cease
> Have warred with Powers and Principalities.
> My natural soul, ere yet these strifes began,
> Was as a sister diligent to please
> And loving all, and most the human clan.
>
> God knows it. And He knows how the world's tears
> Touched me. And He is witness of my wrath,
> How it was kindled against murderers
> Who slew for gold, and how upon their path
> I met them. Since which day the World in arms
> Strikes at my life with angers and alarms.

And this sonnet has all the strange strength of that despair which is but the prelude to a larger hope:

> I thought to do a deed of chivalry,
> An act of worth, which haply in her sight
> Who was my mistress should recorded be
> And of the nations. And, when thus the fight
> Faltered and men once bold with faces white
> Turned this and that way in excuse to flee,
> I only stood, and by the foeman's might
> Was overborne and mangled cruelly.
>
> Then crawled I to her feet, in whose dear cause
> I made this venture, and "Behold," I said,
> "How I am wounded for thee in these wars."
> But she, "Poor cripple, would'st thou I should wed
> A limbless trunk?" and laughing turned from me.
> Yet she was fair, and her name "Liberty."

The sonnet beginning

> A prison is a convent without God—
> Poverty, Chastity, Obedience
> Its precepts are:

is very fine; and this, written just after entering the gaol, is powerful:

> Naked I came into the world of pleasure,
>   And naked come I to this house of pain.
> Here at the gate I lay down my life's treasure,
>   My pride, my garments and my name with men.
>   The world and I henceforth shall be as twain,
> No sound of me shall pierce for good or ill
>   These walls of grief. Nor shall I hear the vain
> Laughter and tears of those who love me still.
>
> Within, what new life waits me! Little ease,
>   Cold lying, hunger, nights of wakefulness,
> Harsh orders given, no voice to soothe or please,
>   Poor thieves for friends, for books rules meaningless
> This is the grave—nay, hell. Yet, Lord of Might,
> Still in Thy light my spirit shall see light.

But, indeed, all the sonnets are worth reading, and *The Canon of Aughrim*, the longest poem in the book, is a most masterly and dramatic description of the tragic life of the Irish peasant. Literature is not much indebted to Mr. Balfour for his sophistical *Defence of Philosophic Doubt* which is one of the dullest books we know, but it must be admitted that by sending Mr. Blunt to gaol he has converted a clever rhymer into an earnest and deep-thinking poet. The narrow confines of the prison cell seem to suit the "sonnet's scanty plot of ground," and an unjust imprisonment for a noble cause strengthens as well as deepens the nature.

*Pall Mall Gazette*, January 3, 1889.

# A New Book on Dickens

*Review of* Life of Charles Dickens *by Frank T. Marzials, in the "Great Writers" Series, published by Walter Scott.*

Mr. Marzials' *Dickens* is a great improvement on the *Longfellow* and *Coleridge* of his predecessors. It is certainly a little sad to find our old friend the manager of the Theatre Royal, Portsmouth, appearing as "Mr. Vincent Crumules" (*sic*), but such misprints are not by any means uncommon in Mr. Walter Scott's publications, and, on the whole, this is a very pleasant book indeed. It is brightly and cleverly written, admirably constructed, and gives a most vivid and graphic picture of that strange modern drama, the drama of Dickens's life. The earlier chapters are quite excellent, and, though the story of the famous novelist's boyhood has been often told before, Mr. Marzials shows that it can be told again without losing any of the charm of its interest, while the account of Dickens in the plenitude of his glory is most appreciative and genial. We are really brought close to the man with his indomitable energy, his extraordinary capacity for work, his high spirits, his fascinating, tyrannous personality. The description of his method of reading is admirable, and the amazing stump-campaign in America attains, in Mr. Marzials' hands, to the dignity of a mock-heroic poem. One side of Dickens's character, however, is left almost entirely untouched, and yet it is one in every way deserving of close study. That Dickens should have felt bitterly towards his father and mother is quite explicable, but that, while feeling so bitterly, he should have caricatured them for the amusement of the public, with an evident delight in his own humour, has always seemed to us a most curious psychological problem. We are far from complaining that he did so. Good novelists are much rarer

16

than good sons, and none of us would part readily with Micawber and Mrs. Nickleby. Still, the fact remains that a man who was affectionate and loving to his children, generous and warm-hearted to his friends, and whose books are the very bacchanalia of benevolence, pilloried his parents to make the groundlings laugh, and this fact every biographer of Dickens should face and, if possible, explain.

As for Mr. Marzials' critical estimate of Dickens as a writer, he tells us quite frankly that he believes that Dickens at his best was "one of the greatest masters of pathos who ever lived," a remark that seems to us an excellent example of what novelists call "the fine courage of despair." Of course, no biographer of Dickens could say anything else, just at present. A popular series is bound to express popular views, and cheap criticisms may be excused in cheap books. Besides, it is always open to every one to accept G. H. Lewes's unfortunate maxim that any author who makes one cry possesses the gift of pathos and, indeed, there is something very flattering in being told that one's own emotions are the ultimate test of literature. When Mr. Marzials discusses Dickens's power of drawing human nature we are upon somewhat safer ground, and we cannot but admire the cleverness with which he passes over his hero's innumerable failures. For, in some respects, Dickens might be likened to those old sculptors of our Gothic cathedrals who could give form to the most fantastic fancy, and crowd with grotesque monsters a curious world of dreams, but saw little of the grace and dignity of the men and women among whom they lived, and whose art, lacking sanity, was therefore incomplete. Yet they at least knew the limitations of their art, while Dickens never knew the limitations of his. When he tries to be serious he succeeds only in being dull, when he aims at truth he reaches merely platitude. Shakespeare could place Ferdinand and Miranda by the side of Caliban, and Life recognises them all as her own, but Dickens's Mirandas are the young ladies out of a fashion-book, and his Ferdinands the walking gentlemen of an unsuccessful company of third-rate players. So little sanity, indeed, had Dickens's art that he was never able even to satirise: he could only caricature; and so little does Mr. Marzials realise where Dickens's true strength and weakness lie, that he actually complains that Cruikshank's illustrations are too much exaggerated and that he could never draw either a lady or a gentleman.

The latter was hardly a disqualification for illustrating Dickens as few such characters occur in his books, unless we are to regard Lord Frederick Verisopht and Sir Mulberry Hawk as valuable studies of high life; and, for our own part, we have always considered that the greatest injustice ever done to Dickens has been done by those who have tried to illustrate him seriously.

In conclusion, Mr. Marzials expresses his belief that a century hence Dickens will be read as much as we now read Scott, and says rather prettily that as long as he is read "there will be one gentle and humanising influence the more at work among men," which is always a useful tag to append to the life of any popular author. Remembering that of all forms of error prophecy is the most gratuitous, we will not take upon ourselves to decide the question of Dickens's immortality. If our descendants do not read him they will miss a great source of amusement, and if they do, we hope they will not model their style upon his. Of this, however, there is but little danger, for no age ever borrows the slang of its predecessor. As for "the gentle and humanising influence," this is taking Dickens just a little too seriously.

*Pall Mall Gazette*, March 31, 1887.

# A Batch of Novels
# [Dostoevsky, Turgenev, Tolstoy]

*Review of* Injury and Insult! (The Insulted and the Injured, *according to modern translations*) *by Fedor Dostoieffski, translated from the Russian by Frederick Whishaw. This early work (1862) of Dostoevsky was one in which the influence of the more sentimental aspects of Dickens were clearly visible. The last portion of the review, not reprinted here, concerned several minor novelists now utterly forgotten.*

Of the three great Russian novelists of our time Tourgenieff is by far the finest artist. He has that spirit of exquisite selection, that delicate choice of detail, which is the essence of style; his work is entirely free from any personal intention; and by taking existence at its most fiery-coloured moments he can distil into a few pages of perfect prose the moods and passions of many lives.

Count Tolstoi's method is much larger, and his field of vision more extended. He reminds us sometimes of Paul Veronese, and like that great painter, can crowd, without over-crowding, the giant canvas on which he works. We may not at first gain from his works that artistic unity of impression which is Tourgenieff's chief charm, but once that we have mastered the details the whole seems to have the grandeur and the simplicity of an epic. Dostoieffski differs widely from both his rivals. He is not so fine an artist as Tourgenieff, for he deals more with the facts than with the effects of life; nor has he Tolstoi's largeness of vision and epic dignity; but he has qualities that are distinctively and absolutely his own, such as a fierce intensity of passion and concentration of impulse, a power of dealing with the deepest mysteries of psychology and the most hidden springs of life, and a realism that is pitiless in its

19

fidelity, and terrible because it is true. Some time ago we had occasion to draw attention to his marvellous novel *Crime and Punishment*, where in the haunt of impurity and vice a harlot and an assassin meet together to read the story of Dives and Lazarus, and the outcast girl leads the sinner to make atonement for his sin; nor is the book entitled *Injury and Insult* at all inferior to that great masterpiece. Mean and ordinary though the surroundings of the story may seem, the heroine Natasha is like one of the noble victims of Greek tragedy; she is Antigone with the passion of Phaedra, and it is impossible to approach her without a feeling of awe. Greek also is the gloom of Nemesis that hangs over each character, only it is a Nemesis that does not stand outside of life, but is part of our own nature and of the same material as life itself. Aleósha, the beautiful young lad whom Natasha follows to her doom, is a second Tito Melema, and has all Tito's charm and grace and fascination. Yet he is different. He would never have denied Baldassare in the Square at Florence, nor lied to Romola about Tessa.[1] He has a magnificent, momentary sincerity, a boyish unconsciousness of all that life signifies, an ardent enthusiasm for all that life cannot give. There is nothing calculating about him. He never thinks evil, he only does it. From a psychological point of view he is one of the most interesting characters of modern fiction, as from an artistic he is one of the most attractive. As we grow to know him he stirs strange questions for us, and makes us feel that it is not the wicked only who do wrong, nor the bad alone who work evil.

And by what a subtle objective method does Dostoieffski show us his characters! He never tickets them with a list nor labels them with a description. We grow to know them very gradually, as we know people whom we meet in society, at first by little tricks of manner, personal appearance, fancies in dress, and the like; and afterwards by their deeds and words; and even then they constantly elude us, for though Dostoieffski may lay bare for us the secrets of their nature, yet he never explains his personages away; they are always surprising us by something that they say or do, and keep to the end the eternal mystery of life.

1. Tito Melema, Baldassare, Romola, and Tessa are all characters in George Eliot's novel *Romola* (1862–1863).

Irrespective of its value as a work of art, this novel possesses a deep autobiographical interest also, as the character of Vania, the poor student who loves Natasha through all her sin and shame, is Dostoieffski's study of himself. Goethe once had to delay the completion of one of his novels till experience had furnished him with new situations, but almost before he had arrived at manhood Dostoieffski knew life in its most real forms; poverty and suffering, pain and misery, prison, exile, and love, were soon familiar to him, and by the lips of Vania he has told his own story. This note of personal feeling, this harsh reality of actual experience, undoubtedly gives the book something of its strange fervour and terrible passion, yet it has not made it egotistic; we see things from every point of view, and we feel, not that fiction has been trammelled by fact, but that fact itself has become ideal and imaginative. Pitiless, too, though Dostoieffski is in his method as an artist, as a man he is full of human pity for all, for those who do evil as well as for those who suffer it, for the selfish no less than for those whose lives are wrecked for others and whose sacrifice is in vain. Since *Adam Bede* and *Le Père Goriot* no more powerful novel has been written than *Insult and Injury.* * * *

*Pall Mall Gazette*, May 2, 1887.

# A Note on Some Modern Poets
## [W. E. Henley]

*Book of Verses by W. E. Henley (1849–1903), which included the poems of an earlier volume,* In Hospital: Rhymes and Rhythms, *appeared in 1888. In that year Henley became literary editor of the* Scots Observer *(later the* National Observer*), assuming the editorship in 1889. Henley—particularly after this salvo—had no affection for Wilde, and maligned him at every opportunity, both public and private. When Wilde's* Dorian Gray *was attacked in the press, Henley's* Scots Observer *was one of the leaders of the mob (see "Mr. Wilde's Rejoinder," pp. 241–243).*

*This review continued for a half-dozen pages, surveying poets now less known than Henley.*

"If I were king," says Mr. Henley, in one of his most modest rondeaus,

> "Art should aspire, yet ugliness be dear;
> Beauty, the shaft, should speed with wit for feather;
> And love, sweet love, should never fall to sere,
>     If I were king."

And these lines contain, if not the best criticism of his own work, certainly a very complete statement of his aim and motive as a poet. His little *Book of Verses* reveals to us an artist who is seeking to find new methods of expression and has not merely a delicate sense of beauty and a brilliant, fantastic wit, but a real passion also for what is horrible, ugly, or grotesque. No doubt, everything that is worthy of existence is worthy also of art—at least, one would like to think so—but while echo or mirror can repeat for us a beautiful thing, to render artistically a thing that is ugly requires the

22

most exquisite alchemy of form, the most subtle magic of transformation. To me there is more of the cry of Marsyas than of the singing of Apollo in the earlier poems of Mr. Henley's volume, *In Hospital: Rhymes and Rhythms*, as he calls them. But it is impossible to deny their power. Some of them are like bright, vivid pastels; others like charcoal drawings, with dull blacks and murky whites; others like etchings with deeply-bitten lines, and abrupt contrasts, and clever colour-suggestions. In fact, they are like anything and everything, except perfected poems—that they certainly are not. They are still in the twilight. They are preludes, experiments, inspired jottings in a note-book, and should be heralded by a design of "Genius Making Sketches." Rhyme gives architecture as well as melody to verse; it gives that delightful sense of limitation which in all the arts is so pleasurable, and is, indeed, one of the secrets of perfection; it will whisper, as a French critic has said, "things unexpected and charming, things with strange and remote relations to each other," and bind them together in indissoluble bonds of beauty; and in his constant rejection of rhyme, Mr. Henley seems to me to have abdicated half his power. He is a *roi en exil* who has thrown away some of the strings of his lute; a poet who has forgotten the fairest part of his kingdom.

However, all work criticises itself. Here is one of Mr. Henley's inspired jottings. According to the temperament of the reader, it will serve either as a model or as the reverse:

> As with varnish red and glistening
>   Dripped his hair; his feet were rigid;
>   Raised, he settled stiffly sideways:
>   You could see the hurts were spinal.
>
> He had fallen from an engine,
>   And been dragged along the metals.
>   It was hopeless, and they knew it;
>   So they covered him, and left him.
>
> As he lay, by fits half sentient,
>   Inarticulately moaning,
>   With his stockinged feet protruded
>   Sharp and awkward from the blankets,

> To his bed there came a woman,
>> Stood and looked and sighed a little,
>> And departed without speaking,
>> As himself a few hours after.
>
> I was told she was his sweetheart.
>> They were on the eve of marriage.
>> She was quiet as a statue,
>> But her lip was gray and writhen.

In this poem, the rhythm and the music, such as it is, are obvious —perhaps a little too obvious. In the following I see nothing but ingeniously printed prose. It is a description—and a very accurate one—of a scene in a hospital ward. The medical students are supposed to be crowding round the doctor. What I quote is only a fragment, but the poem itself is a fragment:

> So shows the ring
> Seen, from behind, round a conjuror
> Doing his pitch in the street.
> High shoulders, low shoulders, broad shoulders, narrow ones,
> Round, square, and angular, serry and shove;
> While from within a voice,
> Gravely and weightily fluent,
> Sounds; and then ceases; and suddenly
> (Look at the stress of the shoulders!)
> Out of a quiver of silence,
> Over the hiss of the spray,
> Comes a low cry, and the sound
> Of breath quick intaken through teeth
> Clenched in resolve. And the master
> Breaks from the crowd, and goes,
> Wiping his hands,
> To the next bed, with his pupils
> Flocking and whispering behind him.
>
> Now one can see.
> Case Number One
> Sits (rather pale) with his bedclothes
> Stripped up, and showing his foot
> (Alas, for God's image!)
> Swaddled in wet white lint
> Brilliantly hideous with red.

Théophile Gautier[1] once said that Flaubert's style was meant to be read, and his own style to be looked at. Mr. Henley's unrhymed rhythms form very dainty designs, from a typographical point of view. From the point of view of literature, they are a series of vivid, concentrated impressions, with a keen grip of fact, a terrible actuality, and an almost masterly power of picturesque presentation. But the poetic form—what of that?

Well, let us pass to the later poems, to the rondels and rondeaus, the sonnets and quatorzains, the echoes and the ballades. How brilliant and fanciful this is! The Toyokuni colour-print that suggested it could not be more delightful. It seems to have kept all the wilful fantastic charm of the original:

> Was I a Samurai renowned,
> Two-sworded, fierce, immense of bow?
> A histrion angular and profound?
> A priest? a porter?— Child, although
> I have forgotten clean, I know
> That in the shade of Fujisan,
> What time the cherry-orchards blow,
> I loved you once in old Japan.
>
> As here you loiter, flowing-gowned
> And hugely sashed, with pins a-row
> Your quaint head as with flamelets crowned,
> Demure, inviting—even so,
> When merry maids in Miyako
> To feel the sweet o' the year began,
> And green gardens to overflow,
> I loved you once in old Japan.
>
> Clear shine the hills; the rice-fields round
> Two cranes are circling; sleepy and slow,
> A blue canal the lake's blue bound
> Breaks at the bamboo bridge; and lo!
> Touched with the sundown's spirit and glow,
> I see you turn, with flirted fan,

1. Théophile Gautier (1811–1872), French critic, poet, and novelist. His theory of "art for art's sake," which influenced Pater and the English aesthetic movement, was best expressed in the preface to *Mademoiselle de Maupin* (1835), his most famous novel.

> Against the plum-tree's bloomy snow . . .
> I loved you once in old Japan!
>
> ENVOY.
>
> Dear, 'twas a dozen lives ago;
> But that I was a lucky man
> The Toyokuni here will show:
> I loved you—once—in old Japan!

This rondel, too—how light it is, and graceful!—

> We'll to the woods and gather may
> Fresh from the footprints of the rain.
> We'll to the woods, at every vein
> To drink the spirit of the day.
>
> The winds of spring are out at play,
> The needs of spring in heart and brain.
> We'll to the woods and gather may
> Fresh from the footprints of the rain.
>
> The world's too near her end, you say?
> Hark to the blackbird's mad refrain!
> It waits for her, the vast Inane?
> Then, girls, to help her on the way
> We'll to the woods and gather may.

There are fine verses, also, scattered through this little book; some of them very strong, as—

> Out of the night that covers me,
>   Black as the pit from pole to pole,
> I thank whatever gods may be
>   For my unconquerable soul.
>
> It matters not how strait the gate,
>   How charged with punishments the scroll,
> I am the master of my fate:
>   I am the captain of my soul.

Others with a true touch of romance, as—

> Or ever the knightly years were gone
>   With the old world to the grave,
> I was a king in Babylon,
>   And you were a Christian slave.

And here and there we come across such felicitous phrases as—

> In the sand
> The gold prow-griffin claws a hold,

or—

> The spires
> Shine and are changed,

and many other graceful or fanciful lines, even "the green sky's minor thirds" being perfectly right in its place, and a very refreshing bit of affectation in a volume where there is so much that is natural.

However, Mr. Henley is not to be judged by samples. Indeed, the most attractive thing in the book is no single poem that is in it, but the strong humane personality that stands behind both flawless and faulty work alike, and looks out through many masks, some of them beautiful, and some grotesque, and not a few misshapen. In the case with most of our modern poets, when we have analysed them down to an adjective, we can go no further, or we care to go no further; but with this book it is different. Through these reeds and pipes blows the very breath of life. It seems as if one could put one's hand upon the singer's heart and count its pulsations. There is something wholesome, virile and sane about the man's soul. Anybody can be reasonable, but to be sane is not common; and sane poets are as rare as blue lilies, though they may not be quite so delightful.

> Let the great winds their worst and wildest blow,
> Or the gold weather round us mellow slow;
> We have fulfilled ourselves, and we can dare,
> And we can conquer, though we may not share
> In the rich quiet of the afterglow,
> What is to come,

is the concluding stanza of the last rondeau—indeed, of the last poem in the collection, and the high, serene temper displayed in these lines serves at once as keynote and keystone to the book. The very lightness and slightness of so much of the work, its careless moods and casual fancies, seem to suggest a nature that is not primarily interested in art—a nature, like Sordello's, passionately enamoured of life, one to which lyre and lute are things of less importance. From this mere joy of living, this frank delight in experience for its own sake, this lofty indifference, and momentary unregretted ardours, come all the faults and all the beauties of the volume. But there is this difference between them—the faults are deliberate, and the result of much study; the beauties have the air of fascinating impromptus. Mr. Henley's healthy, if sometimes misapplied, confidence in the myriad suggestions of life gives him his charm. He is made to sing along the highways, not to sit down and write. If he took himself more seriously, his work would become trivial. * * *

*Woman's World*, December, 1888.

# Ben Jonson

*Review of* Ben Jonson *by John Addington Symonds in the series "English Worthies," edited by Andrew Lang and published by Longmans, Green and Company. In 1886, the year of this review, Symonds (1840–1893) completed his seven-volume classic,* The Renaissance in Italy. *Andrew Lang (1844–1912), Scottish scholar and man of letters known for his translations and his studies of folklore and myth, has been called "the greatest bookman of his age."*

In selecting Mr. John Addington Symonds to write the life of Ben Jonson for his series of "English Worthies," Mr. Lang, no doubt, exercised a wise judgment. Mr. Symonds, like the author of *Volpone*, is a scholar and a man of letters; his book on *Shakespeare's Predecessors* showed a marvellous knowledge of the Elizabethan period, and he is a recognised authority on the Italian Renaissance. The last is not the least of his qualifications. Without a full appreciation of the meaning of the Humanistic movement it is impossible to understand the great struggle between the Classical form and the Romantic spirit which is the chief critical characteristic of the golden age of the English drama, an age when Shakespeare found his chief adversary, not among his contemporaries, but in Seneca, and when Jonson armed himself with Aristotle to win the suffrages of a London audience. Mr. Symonds' book, consequently, will be opened with interest. It does not, of course, contain much that is new about Jonson's life. But the facts of Jonson's life are already well known, and in books of this kind what is true is of more importance than what is new, appreciation more valuable than discovery. Scotchmen, however, will, no doubt, be interested to find that Mr. Symonds has succeeded in identifying Jonson's crest with that of the Johnstones of Annandale, and the story of the way the literary Titan escaped from hanging, by proving that he could read, is graphically told.

On the whole, we have a vivid picture of the man as he lived. Where picturesqueness is required, Mr. Symonds is always good. The usual comparison with Dr. Johnson is, of course, brought out. Few of "Rare Ben's" biographers spare us that, and the point is possibly a natural one to make. But when Mr. Symonds calls upon us to notice that both men made a journey to Scotland, and that "each found in a Scotchman his biographer," the parallel loses all value. There is an M in Monmouth and an M in Macedon, and Drummond of Hawthornden and Boswell of Auchinleck were both born the other side of the Tweed; but from such analogies nothing is to be learned. There is no surer way of destroying a similarity than to strain it.

As for Mr. Symonds' estimate of Jonson's genius, it is in many points quite excellent. He ranks him with the giants rather than with the gods, with those who compel our admiration by their untiring energy and huge strength of intellectual muscle, not with those "who share the divine gifts of creative imagination and inevitable instinct." Here he is right. Pelion more than Parnassus was Jonson's home. His art has too much effort about it, too much definite intention. His style lacks the charm of chance. Mr. Symonds is right also in the stress he lays on the extraordinary combination in Jonson's work of the most concentrated realism with encyclopedic erudition. In Jonson's comedies London slang and learned scholarship go hand in hand. Literature was as living a thing to him as life itself. He used his classical lore not merely to give form to his verse, but to give flesh and blood to the persons of his plays. He could build up a breathing creature out of quotations. He made the poets of Greece and Rome terribly modern, and introduced them to the oddest company. His very culture is an element in his coarseness. There are moments when one is tempted to liken him to a beast that has fed off books.

We cannot, however, agree with Mr. Symonds when he says that Jonson "rarely touched more than the outside of character," that his men and women are "the incarnations of abstract properties rather than living human beings," that they are in fact mere "masqueraders and mechanical puppets." Eloquence is a beautiful thing but rhetoric ruins many a critic, and Mr. Symonds is essentially rhetorical. When, for instance, he tells us that "Jonson made masks," while "Dekker and Heywood created souls," we feel that he is asking us to accept a crude judgment for the sake of a smart antithesis. It is, of course, true that we do not find in Jonson the same growth of character that we find in Shakespeare, and we may admit that most of the characters in Jonson's plays are, so to speak, ready-made. But a ready-made character is not necessarily either mechanical or wooden, two epithets Mr. Symonds uses constantly in his criticism.

We cannot tell, and Shakespeare himself does not tell us, why Iago is evil, why Regan and Goneril have hard hearts, or why Sir Andrew Aguecheek is a fool. It is sufficient that they are what they are, and that nature gives warrant for their existence. If a character in a play is lifelike, if we recognise it as true to nature, we have no right to insist on the author explaining its genesis to us. We must accept it as it is: and in the hands of a good dramatist mere presentation can take the place of analysis, and indeed is often a more dramatic method, because a more direct one. And Jonson's characters are true to nature. They are in no sense abstractions; they are types. Captain Bobadil and Captain Tucca, Sir John Daw and Sir Amorous La Foole, Volpone and Mosca, Subtle and Sir Epicure Mammon, Mrs. Purecraft and the Rabbi Busy are all creatures of flesh and blood, none the less lifelike because they are labelled. In this point Mr. Symonds seems to us unjust towards Jonson.

We think, also, that a special chapter might have been devoted to Jonson as a literary critic. The creative activity of the English Renaissance is so great that its achievements in the sphere of criticism are often overlooked by the student. Then, for the first time, was language treated as an art. The laws of expression and composition were investigated and formularised. The importance of words was recognised. Romanticism, Realism and Classicism fought their first battles. The dramatists are full of literary and art criticisms, and amused the public with slashing articles on one another in the form of plays.

Mr. Symonds, of course, deals with Jonson in his capacity as a critic, and always with just appreciation, but the whole subject is one that deserves fuller and more special treatment.

Some small inaccuracies, too, should be corrected in the second edition. Dryden, for instance, was not "Jonson's successor on the laureate's throne," as Mr. Symonds eloquently puts it, for Sir William Davenant came between them, and when one remembers the predominance of rhyme in Shakespeare's early plays, it is too much to say that "after the production of the first part of *Tamburlaine* blank verse became the regular dramatic metre of the public stage." Shakespeare did not accept blank verse at once as a gift from Marlowe's hand, but himself arrived at it after a long course of experiments in rhyme. Indeed, some of Mr. Symonds' remarks on Marlowe are very curious. To say of his *Edward II*, for instance, that it "is not at all inferior to the work of Shakespeare's younger age," is very niggardly and inadequate praise, and comes strangely from one who has elsewhere written with such appreciation of Marlowe's great genius; while to call Marlowe Jonson's "master" is to make for him an impossible claim. In comedy Marlowe has nothing whatever to teach Jonson; in tragedy Jonson sought for the classical not the romantic form.

As for Mr. Symonds' style, it is, as usual, very fluent, very picturesque and very full of colour. Here and there, however, it is really irritating. Such a sentence as "the tavern had the defects of its quality" is an awkward Gallicism; and when Mr. Symonds, after genially comparing Jonson's blank verse to the front of Whitehall (a comparison, by the way, that would have enraged the poet beyond measure) proceeds to play a fantastic aria on the same string, and tells us that "Massinger reminds us of the intricacies of Sansovino, Shakespeare of Gothic aisles or heaven's cathedral . . . Ford of glittering Corinthian colonnades, Webster of vaulted crypts, . . . Marlowe of masoned clouds, and Marston, in his better moments, of the fragmentary vigour of a Roman ruin," one begins to regret that any one ever thought of the unity of the arts. Similes such as these obscure; they do not illumine. To say that Ford is like a glittering Corinthian colonnade adds nothing to our knowledge of either Ford or Greek architecture. Mr. Symonds has written some charming poetry, but his prose, unfortunately, is always poetical prose, never the prose of a poet. Still, the volume is worth reading, though decidedly Mr. Symonds, to use one of his own phrases, has "the defects of his quality."

*Pall Mall Gazette*, September 20, 1886.

# On the Sale by Auction of Keats's Love Letters

*The manuscript of this poem is dated March 1, 1885, the day before Keats's letters to Fanny Brawne were sold at auction at Sotheby's.*

These are the letters which Endymion wrote
  To one he loved in secret, and apart.
  And now the brawlers of the auction mart
Bargain and bid for each poor blotted note.
Ay! for each separate pulse of passion quote
  The merchant's price: I think they love not art,
  Who break the crystal of a poet's heart
That small and sickly eyes may glare and gloat!
Is it not said that many years ago,
  In a far Eastern town, some soldiers ran
  With torches through the midnight, and began
To wrangle for mean raiment, and to throw
  Dice for the garments of a wretched man,
Not knowing the God's wonder, or his woe?

*Dramatic Review*, January 23, 1886; collected in the posthumous *Poems* (1908).

# Two Biographies of Keats

*Review of* Keats *by Sidney Colvin in the "English Men of Letters" Series published by Macmillan and Company, and of* Life of John Keats *by William Michael Rossetti in the "Great Writers" Series published by Walter Scott. Sidney Colvin (1845–1926), now best remembered for his friendship with Robert Louis Stevenson and his editorship of Stevenson's writings, was at this time Keeper of the Prints and Drawings in the British Museum. William Michael Rossetti (1829–1919) had previously published a useful edition of Shelley's poems and a memoir of the poet's life (1869), an edition of Blake (1874), and the first volume of the* Collected Works *of his elder brother, Dante Gabriel Rossetti.*

A poet, said Keats once, "is the most unpoetical of all God's creatures," and whether the aphorism be universally true or not, this is certainly the impression produced by the two last biographies that have appeared of Keats himself. It cannot be said that either Mr. Colvin or Mr. William Rossetti makes us love Keats more or understand him better. In both these books there is much that is like "chaff in the mouth," and in Mr. Rossetti's there is not a little that is like "brass on the palate." To a certain degree this is, no doubt, inevitable nowadays. Everybody pays a penalty for peeping through keyholes, and the keyhole and the backstairs are essential parts of the method of the modern biographers. It is only fair, however, to state at the outset that Mr. Colvin has done his work much better than Mr. Rossetti. The account Mr. Colvin gives of Keats's boyhood, for instance, is very pleasing, and so is the sketch of Keats's circle of friends, both Leigh Hunt and Haydon being admirably drawn. Here and there, trivial family details are introduced without much regard to proportion, and the posthumous panegyrics of devoted friends are not really of so much value, in helping us to form any true estimate of Keats's actual character, as Mr. Colvin seems to imagine. We have no doubt that when Bailey wrote to Lord Houghton that common-sense and gentleness were Keats's two special characteristics the worthy Archdeacon meant extremely well, but we prefer the real Keats, with his passionate wilfulness, his fantastic moods and his fine inconsistence. Part of Keats's charm as a man is his fascinating incompleteness. We do not want him reduced to a sand-paper smoothness or made perfect by the addition of popular virtues. Still, if Mr. Colvin has not given us a very true picture of Keats's character, he has certainly told the story of his life in a pleasant and readable manner. He may not write with the ease and grace of a man of letters, but he is never pretentious and not often pedantic.

Mr. Rossetti's book is a great failure. To begin with, Mr. Rossetti commits the great mistake of separating the man from the artist. The facts of Keats's life are interesting only when they are shown in their relation to his creative activity. The moment they are isolated they are either uninteresting or painful. Mr. Rossetti complains that the early part of Keats's life is uneventful and the latter part depressing, but the fault lies with the biographer, not with the subject.

The book opens with a detailed account of Keats's life, in which he spares us nothing, from what he calls the "sexual misadventure at Oxford" down to the six weeks' dissipation after the appearance of the *Blackwood* article and the hysterical and morbid ravings of the dying man. No doubt, most if not all of the things Mr. Rossetti tells us are facts; but there is neither tact shown in the selection that is made of the facts nor sympathy in the use to which they are put. When Mr. Rossetti writes of the man he forgets the poet, and when he criticises the poet he shows that he does not understand the man. His first error, as we have said, is isolating the life from the work; his second error is his treatment of the work itself. Take, for instance, his criticism of that wonderful *Ode to a Nightingale*, with all its marvellous magic of music, colour and form. He begins by saying that "the first point of weakness" in the poem is the "surfeit of mythological allusions," a statement which is absolutely untrue, as out of the eight stanzas of the poem only three contain any mythological allusions at all, and of these not one is either forced or remote. Then coming to the second verse,

> Oh for a draught of vintage, that hath been
> Cool'd a long age in the deep-delvèd earth,
> Tasting of Flora and the country-green,
> Dance, and Provençal song, and sunburnt mirth!

Mr. Rossetti exclaims in a fine fit of "Blue Ribbon" enthusiasm: "Surely nobody wants wine as a preparation for enjoying a nightingale's music, whether in a literal or in a fanciful relation!" "To call wine 'the true, the blushful Hippocrene' . . . seems" to him "both stilted and repulsive"; "the phrase 'with beaded bubbles winking at the brim' is (though picturesque) trivial"; "the succeeding image, 'Not charioted by Bacchus and his pards' " is "far worse"; while such an expression as "light-winged Dryad of the trees" is an obvious pleonasm, for Dryad really means *Oak*-nymph! As for that superb burst of passion,

> Thou wast not born for death, immortal Bird!
> No hungry generations tread thee down;
> The voice I hear this passing night was heard
> In ancient days by emperor and clown:

Mr. Rossetti tells us that it is a palpable, or rather "palpaple (*sic*) fact that this address . . . is a logical solecism," as men live longer than nightingales. As Mr. Colvin makes very much the same criticism, talking of "a breach of logic which is also . . . a flaw in the poetry," it may be worth while to point out to these two last critics of Keats's work that what Keats meant to convey was the contrast between the permanence of beauty and the change and decay of human life, an idea which receives its fullest expression in the *Ode on a Grecian Urn*. Nor do the other poems fare much better at Mr. Rossetti's hands. The fine invocation in *Isabella*—

> Moan hither, all ye syllables of woe,
> From the deep throat of sad Melpomene!
> Through bronzèd lyre in tragic order go,
> And touch the strings into a mystery,

seems to him "a *fadeur* [an insipid thing]"; the Indian Bacchante of the fourth book of *Endymion* he calls a "sentimental and beguiling wine-bibber," and, as for Endymion himself, he declares that he cannot understand "how his human organism, *with respirative and digestive processes*, continues to exist," and gives us his own idea of how Keats should have treated the subject. An eminent French critic once exclaimed in despair, "*Je trouve des physiologistes partout!* [I find physiologists everywhere]", but it has been reserved for Mr. Rossetti to speculate on Endymion's digestion, and we readily accord to him all the distinction of the position. Even where Mr. Rossetti seeks to praise, he spoils what he praises. To speak of *Hyperion* as "a monument of Cyclopean architecture in verse" is bad enough, but to call it "a Stonehenge of reverberance" is absolutely detestable; nor do we learn much about *The Eve of St. Mark* by being told that its "simplicity is full-blooded as well as quaint." What is the meaning, also, of stating that Keats's *Notes on Shakespeare* are "somewhat strained and *bloated*"? and is there nothing better to be said of Madeline in *The Eve of St. Agnes* than that "she is made a very charming and loveable figure, *although she does nothing very particular except to undress without looking behind her, and to elope*"? There is no necessity to follow Mr. Rossetti any further as he flounders about through the quagmire that he has made for his own feet. A critic who can say that "not many of Keats's poems are highly admirable" need not be too seriously treated. Mr. Rossetti is an industrious man and a painstaking writer, but he entirely lacks the temper necessary for the interpretation of such poetry as was written by John Keats.

It is pleasant to turn again to Mr. Colvin, who criticises always with modesty and often with acumen. We do not agree with him when he accepts Mrs. Owens's theory of a symbolic and allegoric meaning underlying *Endymion*, his final judgment on Keats as "the most Shaksperean spirit that has lived since Shakspere" is not very fortunate, and we are surprised to find him suggesting, on the evidence of a rather silly story of Severn's, that Sir Walter Scott was privy to the *Blackwood* article. There is nothing, however, about his estimate of the poet's work that is harsh, irritating or uncouth. The true Marcellus of English song has not yet found his Virgil, but Mr. Colvin makes a tolerable Statius.[1]

*Pall Mall Gazette*, September 27, 1887.

1. The death of Marcus Claudius Marcellus (43–23 B.C.), a nephew and adopted son of Augustus, whose daughter he married, was mentioned by Virgil in the *Aeneid* (vi.860). Statius (ca. 45–ca. 96 A.D.), a Roman court poet to Domitian, wrote epics, *Thebis* and *Achilleis* (unfinished), and a collection, *Silvae*.

# Great Writers by Little Men
# [Longfellow and Coleridge]

*Review of* Life of Henry Wadsworth Longfellow *by Eric S. Robertson,* *and of* Life of Samuel Taylor Coleridge *by Hall Caine. Caine (1853–* *1931), who became an enormously successful popular novelist, had published* Recollections of Rossetti *in 1882.*

In an introductory note prefixed to the initial volume of "Great Writers," a series of literary monographs now being issued by Mr. Walter Scott, the publisher himself comes forward in the kindest manner possible to give his authors the requisite "puff preliminary," and ventures to express the modest opinion that such original and valuable works "have never before been produced in any part of the world at a price so low as a shilling a volume." Far be it from us to make any heartless allusion to the fact that Shakespeare's *Sonnets* were brought out at fivepence, or that for fourpence-half-penny one could have bought a Martial in ancient Rome. Every man, a cynical American tells us, has the right to beat a drum before his booth. Still, we must acknowledge that Mr. Walter Scott would have been much better employed in correcting some of the more obvious errors that appear in his series. When, for instance, we come across such a phrase as "the brotherly liberality of the brothers *Wedgewood*," the awkwardness of the expression is hardly atoned for by the fact that the name of the great potter is misspelt; Longfellow is so essentially poor in rhymes that it is unfair to rob him even of one, and the misquotation on page 77 is absolutely unkind; the joke Coleridge himself made upon the subject should have been sufficient to remind any one that "Comberbach" (*sic*) was not the name under which he enlisted, and no real beauty is added to the first line of his pathetic *Work Without Hope* by printing "lare" (*sic*) instead of "lair." The truth is that all premature panegyrics bring their own punishment upon themselves and, in the present case, though the series has only just entered upon existence, already a great deal of the work done is careless, disappointing, unequal and tedious.

Mr. Eric Robertson's *Longfellow* is a most depressing book. No one survives being over-estimated, nor is there any surer way of destroying an author's reputation than to glorify him without judgment and to praise him without tact. Henry Wadsworth Longfellow was one of the first true men of letters America produced, and as such deserves a high place in any history of American civilisation. To a land out of breath in its greed for gain he showed the example of a life devoted entirely to the study of literature; his lectures, though not by any means brilliant, were still productive of much good; he had a most charming and gracious personality, and he wrote some pretty poems. But his poems are not of the kind that call for intellectual analysis or for elaborate description or, indeed, for any serious discussion at all. They are as unsuited for panegyric as they are unworthy of censure, and it is difficult to help smiling when Mr. Robertson gravely tells us that few modern poets have given utterance to a faith so comprehensive as that expressed in the *Psalm of Life*, or that *Evangeline* should confer on Longfellow the title of "Golden-mouthed," and that the style of metre adopted "carries the ear back to times in the world's history when grand simplicities were sung." Surely Mr. Robertson does not believe that there is any connection at all between Longfellow's unrhymed dactylics and the hexameter of Greece and Rome, or that any one reading *Evangeline* would be reminded of Homer's or Virgil's line? Where also lies the advantage of confusing popularity with poetic power? Though the *Psalm of Life* be shouted from Maine to California, that would not make it true poetry. Why call upon us to admire a bad misquotation from the *Midnight Mass for the Dying Year*, and why talk of Longfellow's "hundreds of imitators"? Longfellow has no imitators, for of echoes themselves there are no echoes and it is only style that makes a school.

Now and then, however, Mr. Robertson considers it necessary

to assume a critical attitude. He tells us, for instance, that whether or not Longfellow was a genius of the first order, it must be admitted that he loved social pleasures and was a good eater and judge of wines, admiring "Bass's ale" more than anything else he had seen in England! The remarks on *Excelsior* are even still more amazing. *Excelsior*, says Mr. Robertson, is not a ballad because a ballad deals either with real or with supernatural people, and the hero of the poem cannot be brought under either category. For, "were he of human flesh, his madcap notion of scaling a mountain with the purpose of getting to the sky would be simply drivelling lunacy," to say nothing of the fact that the peak in question is much frequented by tourists, while, on the other hand, "it would be absurd to suppose him a spirit . . . for no spirit would be so silly as climb a snowy mountain for nothing"! It is really painful to have to read such preposterous nonsense, and if Mr. Walter Scott imagines that work of this kind is "original and valuable" he has much to learn. Nor are Mr. Robertson's criticisms upon other poets at all more felicitous. The casual allusion to Herrick's "confectioneries of verse" is, of course, quite explicable, coming as it does from an editor who excluded Herrick from an anthology of the child-poems of our literature in favour of Mr. Ashby-Sterry[1] and Mr. William Sharp, but when Mr. Robertson tells us that Poe's "loftiest flights of imagination in verse . . . rise into no more empyreal realm than the *fantastic*," we can only recommend him to read as soon as possible the marvellous lines *To Helen*, a poem as beautiful as a Greek gem and as musical as Apollo's lute. The remarks, too, on Poe's critical estimate of his own work show that Mr. Robertson has never really studied the poet on whom he pronounces such glib and shallow judgments, and exemplify very clearly the fact that even dogmatism is no excuse for ignorance.

After reading Mr. Hall Caine's *Coleridge* we are irresistibly reminded of what Wordsworth once said about a bust that had been done of himself. After contemplating it for some time, he remarked, "It is not a bad Wordsworth, but it is not the real Wordsworth; it is not Wordsworth the poet, it is the sort of Wordsworth who might

1. Joseph Ashby-Sterry (d. 1917), journalist, author, and art critic.

be Chancellor of the Exchequer." Mr. Caine's Coleridge is certainly not the sort of Coleridge who might have been Chancellor of the Exchequer, for the author of *Christabel* was not by any means remarkable as a financier; but, for all that, it is not the real Coleridge, it is not Coleridge the poet. The incidents of the life are duly recounted; the gunpowder plot at Cambridge, the egg-hot and oronokoo at the little tavern in Newgate Street, the blue coat and white waistcoat that so amazed the worthy Unitarians, and the terrible smoking experiment at Birmingham are all carefully chronicled, as no doubt they should be in every popular biography; but of the spiritual progress of the man's soul we hear absolutely nothing. Never for one single instant are we brought near to Coleridge; the magic of that wonderful personality is hidden from us by a cloud of mean details, an unholy jungle of facts, and the "critical history" promised to us by Mr. Walter Scott in his unfortunate preface is conspicuous only by its absence.

Carlyle once proposed in jest to write a life of Michael Angelo without making any reference to his art, and Mr. Caine has shown that such a project is perfectly feasible. He has written the life of a great peripatetic philosopher and chronicled only the peripatetics. He has tried to tell us about a poet, and his book might be the biography of the famous tallow-chandler who would not appreciate the *Watchman*.[2] The real events of Coleridge's life are not his gig excursions and his walking tours; they are his thoughts, dreams and passions, his moments of creative impulse, their source and secret, his moods of imaginative joy, their marvel and their meaning, and not his moods merely but the music and the melancholy that they brought him; the lyric loveliness of his voice when he sang, the sterile sorrow of the years when he was silent. It is said that every man's life is a Soul's Tragedy. Coleridge's certainly was so, and though we may not be able to pluck out the heart of his mystery, still let us recognise that mystery is there; and that the goings-out and comings-in of a man, his places of sojourn and his roads of travel are but idle things to chronicle, if that which is the man be

2. *The Watchman* was a periodical issued by Coleridge from March 1 to May 13, 1796. In the *Biographia Literaria* (Article X) Coleridge humorously describes his unsuccessful attempt to sell his *Watchman* to a dour, Calvinist tallow-chandler.

left unrecorded. So mediocre is Mr. Caine's book that even accuracy could not make it better.

On the whole, then, Mr. Walter Scott cannot be congratulated on the success of his venture so far. The one really admirable feature of the series is the bibliography that is appended to each volume. These bibliographies are compiled by Mr. Anderson, of the British Museum, and are so valuable to the student, as well as interesting in themselves, that it is much to be regretted that they should be accompanied by such tedious letterpress.

*Pall Mall Gazette*, March 28, 1887.

# Mr. Morris's *Odyssey*

*Review of* The Odyssey of Homer, *translated into English by William Morris. This edition appeared in two volumes. The first volume is reviewed below, and the second volume in the selection immediately following. Morris (1834–1896) was Victorian England's answer to the Renaissance Man. From the Morris chair and his intimate association with the Pre-Raphaelites to architecture, translation, fiction, and epic poetry, from typography and textile design to socialism and stained glass, he left his influence on everything he touched.*

Of all our modern poets, Mr. William Morris is the one best qualified by nature and by art to translate for us the marvellous epic of the wanderings of Odysseus. For he is our only true story-singer since Chaucer; if he is a Socialist, he is also a Saga-man; and there was a time when he was never wearied of telling us strange legends of gods and men, wonderful tales of chivalry and romance. Master as he is of decorative and descriptive verse, he has all the Greek's joy in the visible aspect of things, all the Greek's sense of delicate and delightful detail, all the Greek's pleasure in beautiful textures and exquisite materials and imaginative designs; nor can any one have a keener sympathy with the Homeric admiration for the workers and the craftsmen in the various arts, from the stainers in white ivory and the embroiderers in purple and gold, to the weaver sitting by the loom and the dyer dipping in the vat, the chaser of shield and helmet, the carver of wood or stone. And to all this is added the true temper of high romance, the power to make the past as real to us as the present, the subtle instinct to discern passion, the swift impulse to portray life.

It is no wonder the lovers of Greek literature have so eagerly looked forward to Mr. Morris's version of the Odyssean epic, and

45

now that the first volume has appeared, it is not extravagant to say that of all our English translations this is the most perfect and the most satisfying. In spite of Coleridge's well-known views on the subject, we have always held that Chapman's *Odyssey* is immeasurably inferior to his *Iliad*, the mere difference of metre alone being sufficient to set the former in a secondary place; Pope's *Odyssey*, with its glittering rhetoric and smart antithesis, has nothing of the grand manner of the original; Cowper is dull, and Bryant dreadful, and Worsley too full of Spenserian prettinesses; while excellent though Messrs. Butcher and Lang's version undoubtedly is in many respects, still, on the whole, it gives us merely the facts of the *Odyssey* without providing anything of its artistic effect. Avia's translation even, though better than almost all its predecessors in the same field, is not worthy of taking rank beside Mr. Morris's, for here we have a true work of art, a rendering not merely of language into language, but of poetry into poetry, and though the new spirit added in the transfusion may seem to many rather Norse than Greek, and, perhaps at times, more boisterous than beautiful, there is yet a vigour of life in every line, a splendid ardour through each canto, that stirs the blood while one reads like the sound of a trumpet, and that, producing a physical as well as a spiritual delight, exults the senses no less than it exalts the soul. It may be admitted at once that, here and there, Mr. Morris has missed something of the marvellous dignity of the Homeric verse, and that, in his desire for rushing and ringing metre, he has occasionally sacrificed majesty to movement, and made stateliness give place to speed; but it is really only in such blank verse as Milton's that this effect of calm and lofty music can be attained, and in all other respects blank verse is the most inadequate medium for reproducing the full flow and fervour of the Greek hexameter. One merit, at any rate, Mr. Morris's version entirely and absolutely possesses. It is, in no sense of the word, literary; it seems to deal immediately with life itself, and to take from the reality of things its own form and colour; it is always direct and simple, and at its best has something of the "large utterance of the early gods."

As for individual passages of beauty, nothing could be better than the wonderful description of the house of the Phoeacian king, or the whole telling of the lovely legend of Circe, or the manner in which the pageant of the pale phantoms in Hades is brought before our eyes. Perhaps the huge epic humour of the escape from the Cyclops is hardly realised, but there is always a linguistic difficulty about rendering this fascinating story into English, and where we are given so much poetry we should not complain about losing a pun; and the exquisite idyll of the meeting and parting with the daughter of Alcinous is really delightfully told. How good, for instance, is this passage taken at random from the Sixth Book:

But therewith unto the handmaids goodly Odysseus spake:
"Stand off I bid you, damsels, while the work in hand I take,
And wash the brine from my shoulders, and sleek them all around.
Since verily now this long while sweet oil they have not found.
But before you nought will I wash me, for shame I have indeed,
Amidst of fair-tressed damsels to be all bare of weed."
So he spake and aloof they gat them, and thereof they told the may,
But Odysseus with the river from his body washed away
The brine from his back and his shoulders wrought broad and mightily,
And from his head was he wiping the foam of the untilled sea;
But when he had throughly washed him, and the oil about him had shed
He did upon the raiment the gift of the maid unwed.
But Athene, Zeus-begotten, dealt with him in such wise
That bigger yet was his seeming, and mightier to all eyes,
With the hair on his head crisp curling as the bloom of the daffodil.
And as when the silver with gold is o'erlaid by a man of skill,
Yea, a craftsman whom Hephaestus and Pallas Athene have taught
To be master over masters, and lovely work he hath wrought;
So she round his head and his shoulders shed grace abundantly.

It may be objected by some that the line

With the hair on his head crisp curling as the bloom of the daffodil,

is a rather fanciful version of

οὖλας ἧκε κόμας, ὑακινθίνῳ ἄνθει ὁμοίας,

and it certainly seems probable that the allusion is to the dark colour of the hero's hair; still, the point is not one of much importance, though it may be worth noting that a similar expression occurs in Ogilby's superbly illustrated translation of the *Odyssey*, published in 1665, where Charles II's Master of the Revels in Ireland gives the passage thus:

> Minerva renders him more tall and fair,
> Curling in rings like daffodils his hair.[1]

No anthology, however, can show the true merit of Mr. Morris's translation, whose real merit does not depend on stray beauties, nor is revealed by chance selections, but lies in the absolute rightness and coherence of the whole, in its purity and justice of touch, its freedom from affectation and commonplace, its harmony of form and matter. It is sufficient to say that this is a poet's version of a poet, and for such surely we should be thankful. In these latter days of coarse and vulgar literature, it is something to have made the great sea-epic of the South native and natural to our northern isle, something to have shown that our English speech may be a pipe through which Greek lips can blow, something to have taught Nausicaa to speak the same language as Perdita.

*Pall Mall Gazette*, April 26, 1887.

1. Wilde's objection dramatizes (perhaps deliberately) the range and depth of his reading. Not only does he point to the 1665 precedent for Morris's translation, he observes as well that the older version and Morris's parallel rendering offer a possibly misleading suggestion. The line (vi.231; Athena transforming Odysseus before his encounter with Nausicaa) means, literally, "She sent woolly locks [upon him], like a hyacinth flower." Much learned controversy exists regarding whether the poet's simile refers to color, or shape, or both. Wilde's opinion is that while the crisply curling locks Morris suggests by "daffodil" are fitting, that flower's hue may be inappropriate.

# Mr. Morris's Completion of
# the *Odyssey*

Mr. Morris's second volume brings the great romantic epic of
Greek literature to its perfect conclusion, and although there can
never be an ultimate translation of either *Iliad* or *Odyssey*, as each
successive age is sure to find pleasure in rendering the two poems
in its own manner and according to its own canons of taste, still
it is not too much to say that Mr. Morris's version will always be
a true classic amongst our classical translations. It is not, of course,
flawless. In our notice of the first volume we ventured to say that
Mr. Morris was sometimes far more Norse than Greek, nor
does the volume that now lies before us make us alter that opinion.
The particular metre, also, selected by Mr. Morris, although
admirably adapted to express "the strong-winged music of Homer,"
as far as its flow and freedom are concerned, misses something of
its dignity and calm. Here, it must be admitted, we feel a distinct
loss, for there is in Homer not a little of Milton's lofty manner,
and if swiftness be an essential of the Greek hexameter, stateliness
is one of its distinguishing qualities in Homer's hands. This defect,
however, if we must call it a defect, seems almost unavoidable, as
for certain metrical reasons a majestic movement in English verse
is necessarily a slow movement; and, after all that can be said is
said, how really admirable is this whole translation! If we set aside
its noble qualities as a poem and look on it purely from the scholar's
point of view, how straightforward it is, how honest and direct!
Its fidelity to the original is far beyond that of any other verse-
translation in our literature, and yet it is not the fidelity of a pedant
to his text but rather the fine loyalty of poet to poet.

When Mr. Morris's first volume appeared many of the critics
complained that his occasional use of archaic words and unusual

expressions robbed his version of the true Homeric simplicity. This, however, is not a very felicitous criticism, for while Homer is undoubtedly simple in his clearness and largeness of vision, his wonderful power of direct narration, his wholesome sanity, and the purity and precision of his method, simple in language he undoubtedly is not. What he was to his contemporaries we have, of course, no means of judging, but we know that the Athenian of the fifth century B.C. found him in many places difficult to understand, and when the creative age was succeeded by the age of criticism and Alexandria began to take the place of Athens as the centre of culture for the Hellenistic world, Homeric dictionaries and glossaries seem to have been constantly published. Indeed, Athenaeus tells us of a wonderful Byzantine blue-stocking, a *précieuse* from the Propontis, who wrote a long hexameter poem, called *Mnemosyne*, full of ingenious commentaries on difficulties in Homer, and in fact, it is evident that, as far as the language is concerned, such a phrase as "Homeric simplicity" would have rather amazed an ancient Greek. As for Mr. Morris's tendency to emphasize the etymological meaning of words, a point commented on with somewhat flippant severity in a recent number of *Macmillan's Magazine*, here Mr. Morris seems to us to be in complete accord, not merely with the spirit of Homer, but with the spirit of all early poetry. It is quite true that language is apt to degenerate into a system of almost algebraic symbols, and the modern city-man who takes a ticket for Blackfriars Bridge, naturally never thinks of the Dominican monks who once had their monastery by Thames-side, and after whom the spot is named. But in earlier times it was not so. Men were then keenly conscious of the real meaning of words, and early poetry, especially, is full of this feeling, and, indeed, may be said to owe to it no small portion of its poetic power and charm. These old words, then, and this old use of words which we find in Mr. Morris's *Odyssey* can be amply justified upon historical grounds, and as for their artistic effect, it is quite excellent. Pope tried to put Homer into the ordinary language of his day, with what result we know only too well; but Mr. Morris, who uses his archaisms with the tact of a true artist, and to whom indeed they seem to come absolutely naturally, has succeeded in giving to his version by their aid that touch, not of "quaintness," for Homer is never quaint, but of old-world romance and old-world beauty, which we moderns find so pleasurable, and to which the Greeks themselves were so keenly sensitive.

As for individual passages of special merit, Mr. Morris's translation is no robe of rags sewn with purple patches for critics to sample. Its real value lies in the absolute rightness and coherence of the whole, in the grand architecture of the swift, strong verse, and in the fact that the standard is not merely high but everywhere sustained. It is impossible, however, to resist the temptation of quoting Mr. Morris's rendering of that famous passage in the twenty-third book of the epic, in which Odysseus eludes the trap laid for him by Penelope, whose very faith in the certainty of her husband's return makes her sceptical of his identity when he stands before her; an instance, by the way, of Homer's wonderful psychological knowledge of human nature, as it is always the dreamer himself who is most surprised when his dream comes true.

Thus she spake to prove her husband; but Odysseus, grieved at heart,
Spake thus unto his bed-mate well-skilled in gainful art:
"O woman, thou sayest a word exceeding grievous to me!
Who hath otherwhere shifted my bedstead? full hard for him should
   it be,
For as deft as he were, unless soothly a very God come here,
Who easily, if he willed it, might shift it otherwhere.
But no mortal man is living, how strong soe'er in his youth,
Who shall lightly hale it elsewhere, since a mighty wonder forsooth
Is wrought in that fashioned bedstead, and I wrought it, and I alone.
In the close grew a thicket of olive, a long-leaved tree full-grown,
That flourished and grew goodly as big as a pillar about,
So round it I built my bride-room, till I did the work right out
With ashlar stone close-fitting; and I roofed it overhead,
And thereto joined doors I made me, well-fitting in their stead.
Then I lopped away the boughs of the long-leafed olive-tree,
And, shearing the bole from the root up full well and cunningly,
I planed it about with the brass, and set the rule thereto,
And shaping thereof a bed-post, with the wimble I bored it through.
So beginning, I wrought out the bedstead, and finished it utterly,
And with gold enwrought it about, and with silver and ivory,

And stretched on it a thong of oxhide with the purple dye made
   bright.
Thus then the sign I have shown thee; nor, woman, know I aright
If my bed yet bideth steadfast, or if to another place
Some man hath moved it, and smitten the olive-bole from its base."

These last twelve books of the *Odyssey* have not the same marvel
of romance, adventure and colour that we find in the earlier part
of the epic. There is nothing in them that we can compare to the
exquisite idyll of Nausicaa or to the Titanic humour of the episode
in the Cyclops' cave. Penelope has not the glamour of Circe, and
the song of the Sirens may sound sweeter than the whizz of the arrows
of Odysseus as he stands on the threshold of his hall. Yet, for sheer
intensity of passionate power, for concentration of intellectual
interest and for masterly dramatic construction, these latter books
are quite unequalled. Indeed, they show very clearly how it was
that, as Greek art developed, the epos passed into the drama. The
whole scheme of the argument, the return of the hero in disguise,
his disclosure of himself to his son, his terrible vengeance on his
enemies and his final recognition by his wife, reminds us of the
plot of more than one Greek play, and shows us what the great
Athenian poet meant when he said that his own dramas were
merely scraps from Homer's table. In rendering this splendid
poem into English verse, Mr. Morris has done our literature a
service that can hardly be over-estimated, and it is pleasant to
think that, even should the classics be entirely excluded from our
educational systems, the English boy will still be able to know
something of Homer's delightful tales, to catch an echo of his grand
music and to wander with the wise Odysseus round "the shores of
old romance."

*Pall Mall Gazette*, November 24, 1887.

# Ouida's New Novel

*Review of* Guilderoy *by Ouida. Marie Louise de la Ramée (1839–1908), who used the pen name "Ouida," was one of the best-selling novelists of the day.*

Ouida is the last of the romantics. She belongs to the school of Bulwer Lytton and George Sand, though she may lack the learning of the one and the sincerity of the other. She tries to make passion, imagination, and poetry part of fiction. She still believes in heroes and in heroines. She is florid and fervent and fanciful. Yet even she, the high priestess of the impossible, is affected by her age. Her last book, *Guilderoy* as she calls it, is an elaborate psychological study of modern temperaments. For her, it is realistic, and she has certainly caught much of the tone and temper of the society of our day. Her people move with ease and grace and indolence. The book may be described as a study of the peerage from a poetical point of view. Those who are tired of mediocre young curates who have doubts, of serious young ladies who have missions, and of the ordinary figureheads of most of the English fiction of our time, might turn with pleasure, if not with profit, to this amazing romance. It is a resplendent picture of our aristocracy. No expense has been spared in gilding. For the comparatively small sum of £1, 11s. 6d. one is introduced to the best society. The central figures are exaggerated, but the background is admirable. In spite of everything, it gives one a sense of something like life.

What is the story? Well, we must admit that we have a faint suspicion that Ouida has told it to us before. Lord Guilderoy, "whose name was as old as the days of Knut," falls madly in love, or fancies that he falls madly in love, with a rustic Perdita, a provincial Artemis who has "a Gainsborough face, with wide-opened questioning eyes and tumbled auburn hair." She is poor but well-born, being the only child of Mr. Vernon of Llanarth, a curious recluse, who is half a pedant and half Don Quixote. Guilderoy marries her and, tiring of her shyness, her lack of power to express herself, her want of knowledge of fashionable life, returns to an old passion for a wonderful creature called the Duchess of Soriá. Lady Guilderoy becomes ice; the Duchess becomes fire; at the end of the book Guilderoy is a pitiable object. He has to submit to be forgiven by one woman, and to endure to be forgotten by the other. He is thoroughly weak, thoroughly worthless, and the most fascinating person in the whole story. Then there is his sister Lady Sunbury, who is very anxious for Guilderoy to marry, and is quite determined to hate his wife. She is really a capital sketch. Ouida describes her as "one of those admirably virtuous women who are more likely to turn men away from the paths of virtue than the wickedest of sirens." She irritates herself, alienates her children, and infuriates her husband:

> "You are perfectly right; I know you are always right; I admit you
> are; but it is just that which makes you so damnably odious!" said
> Lord Sunbury once, in a burst of rage, in his town house, speaking in
> such stentorian tones that the people passing up Grosvenor Street
> looked up at his open windows, and a crossing-sweeper said to a match-
> seller, "My eye! ain't he giving it to the old gal like blazes."

The noblest character in the book is Lord Aubrey. As he is not a genius he, naturally, behaves admirably on every occasion. He begins by pitying the neglected Lady Guilderoy, and ends by loving her, but he makes the great renunciation with considerable effect, and, having induced Lady Guilderoy to receive back her husband, he accepts "a distant and arduous Viceroyalty." He is Ouida's ideal of the true politician, for Ouida has apparently taken to the study of English politics. A great deal of her book is devoted to political disquisitions. She believes that the proper rulers of a country like ours are the aristocrats. Oligarchy has great fascinations for her. She thinks meanly of the people and adores the House of Lords and Lord Salisbury. Here are some of her views. We will not call them ideas:

The House of Lords wants nothing of the nation, and therefore it is the only candid and disinterested guardian of the people's needs and re-sources. It has never withstood the real desire of the country: it has only stood between the country and its impetuous and evanescent follies.

A democracy cannot understand honour; how should it? The Caucus is chiefly made up of men who sand their sugar, put alum in their bread, forge bayonets and girders which bend like willow-wands, send bad calico to India, and insure vessels at Lloyd's which they know will go to the bottom before they have been ten days at sea.

Lord Salisbury has often been accused of arrogance; people have never seen that what they mistook for arrogance was the natural, can-did consciousness of a great noble that he is more capable of leading the country than most men composing it would be.

Democracy, after having made everything supremely hideous and uncomfortable for everybody, always ends by clinging to the coat tails of some successful general.

The prosperous politician may be honest, but his honesty is at best a questionable quality. The moment that a thing is a *métier*, it is wholly absurd to talk about any disinterestedness in the pursuit of it. To the professional politician national affairs are a manufacture into which he puts his audacity and his time, and out of which he expects to make so much percentage for his lifetime.

There is too great a tendency to govern the world by noise.

Ouida's aphorisms on women, love and, modern society are somewhat more characteristic:

Women speak as though the heart were to be treated at will like a stone, or a bath.

Half the passions of men die early, because they are expected to be eternal.

It is the folly of life that lends charm to it.

What is the cause of half the misery of women? That their love is so much more tenacious than the man's: it grows stronger as his grows weaker.

To endure the country in England for long, one must have the rusticity of Wordsworth's mind, and boots and stockings as homely.

It is because men feel the necessity to explain that they drop into the habit of saying what is not true. Wise is the woman who never insists on an explanation.

Love can make its own world in a solitude *à deux*, but marriage cannot.

Nominally monogamous, all cultured society is polygamous; often even polyandrous.

Moralists say that a soul should resist passion. They might as well say that a house should resist an earthquake.

The whole world is just now on its knees before the poorer classes: all the cardinal virtues are taken for granted in them, and it is only property of any kind which is the sinner.

Men are not merciful to women's tears as a rule; and when it is a woman belonging to them who weeps, they only go out, and slam the door behind them.

Men always consider women unjust to them, when they fail to deify their weaknesses.

No passion, once broken, will ever bear renewal.

Feeling loses its force and its delicacy if we put it under the microscope too often.

Anything which is not flattery seems injustice to a woman.

When society is aware that you think it a flock of geese, it revenges itself by hissing loudly behind your back.

Of descriptions of scenery and art we have, of course, a large number, and it is impossible not to recognise the touch of the real Ouida manner in the following:

It was an old palace: lofty, spacious, magnificent, and dull. Busts of dusky yellow marble, weird bronzes stretching out gaunt arms into the darkness, ivories brown with age, worn brocades with gold threads gleaming in them, and tapestries with strange and pallid figures of dead gods, were all half revealed and half obscured in the twilight. As he moved through them, a figure which looked almost as pale as the Adonis of the tapestry and was erect and motionless like the statue of the wounded Love, came before his sight out of the darkness. It was that of Gladys.

It is a manner full of exaggeration and over-emphasis, but with some remarkable rhetorical qualities and a good deal of colour. Ouida is fond of airing a smattering of culture, but she has a certain intrinsic insight into things and, though she is rarely true, she is never dull. *Guilderoy*, with all its faults, which are great, and its absurdities, which are greater, is a book to be read.

*Pall Mall Gazette*, May 17, 1889.

# Mr. Pater's *Imaginary Portraits*

*Walter Pater (1839–1894) first used the term "aesthetic poetry" to refer to Pre-Raphaelitism (the school of poetry centered about the work of Dante Gabriel Rossetti) in 1868. By describing the parallel between medieval asceticism and sensualism which results in the imaginative and psychological paradox by which the artist can employ the symbols and sentiments of Christianity while simultaneously rebelling against them to produce an essentially pagan effect, Pater explained the new poetry and art of Rossetti, Morris, Swinburne, and others in psychological terms. Wilde borrowed heavily from Pater's criticism, which was at its peak of influence from 1873, when his* Studies in the History of the Renaissance *was published, to 1885, the date of his* Marius the Epicurean.

To convey ideas through the medium of images has always been the aim of those who are artists as well as thinkers in literature, and it is to a desire to give a sensuous environment to intellectual concepts that we owe Mr. Pater's last volume. For these Imaginary or, as we should prefer to call them, Imaginative Portraits of his, form a series of philosophic studies in which the philosophy is tempered by personality, and the thought shown under varying conditions of mood and manner, the very permanence of each principle gaining something through the change and colour of the life through which it finds expression. The most fascinating of all these pictures is undoubtedly that of Sebastian Van Storck. The account of Watteau is perhaps a little too fanciful, and the description of him as one who was "always a seeker after something in the world, that is there in no satisfying measure, or not at all," seems to us more applicable to him who saw Mona Lisa sitting among the rocks than to the gay and debonair *peintre des fêtes galantes* [society painter]. But Sebastian, the grave young Dutch philosopher, is

57

charmingly drawn. From the first glimpse we get of him, skating over the water-meadows with his plume of squirrel's tail and his fur muff, in all the modest pleasantness of boyhood, down to his strange death in the desolate house amid the sands of the Helder, we seem to see him, to know him, almost to hear the low music of his voice. He is a dreamer, as the common phrase goes, and yet he is poetical in this sense, that his theorems shape life for him, directly. Early in youth he is stirred by a fine saying of Spinoza, and sets himself to realise the ideal of an intellectual disinterestedness, separating himself more and more from the transient world of sensation, accident and even affection, till what is finite and relative becomes of no interest to him, and he feels that as nature is but a thought of his, so he himself is but a passing thought of God. This conception, of the power of a mere metaphysical abstraction over the mind of one so fortunately endowed for the reception of the sensible world, is exceedingly delightful, and Mr. Pater has never written a more subtle psychological study, the fact that Sebastian dies in an attempt to save the life of a little child giving to the whole story a touch of poignant pathos and sad irony.

*Denys l'Auxerrois* is suggested by a figure found, or said to be found, on some old tapestries in Auxerre, the figure of a "flaxen and flowery creature, sometimes wellnigh naked among the vine-leaves, sometimes muffled in skins against the cold, sometimes in the dress of a monk, but always with a strong impress of real character and incident from the veritable streets" of the town itself. From this strange design Mr. Pater has fashioned a curious mediaeval myth of the return of Dionysus among men, a myth steeped in colour and passion and old romance, full of wonder and full of worship, Denys himself being half animal and half god, making the world mad with a new ecstasy of living, stirring the artists simply by his visible presence, drawing the marvel of music from reed and pipe, and slain at last in a stage-play by those who had loved him. In its rich affluence of imagery this story is like a picture by Mantegna, and indeed Mantegna might have suggested the description of the pageant in which Denys rides upon a gaily-painted chariot, in soft silken raiment and, for head-dress, a strange elephant scalp with gilded tusks.

If *Denys l'Auxerrois* symbolises the passion of the senses and *Sebastian Van Storck* the philosophic passion as they certainly seem to do, though no mere formula or definition can adequately express the freedom and variety of the life that they portray, the passion for the imaginative world of art is the basis of the story of *Duke Carl of Rosenmold*. Duke Carl is not unlike the late King of Bavaria,[1] in his love of France, his admiration for the *Grand Monarque* and his fantastic desire to amaze and to bewilder, but the resemblance is possibly only a chance one. In fact Mr. Pater's young hero is the precursor of the *Aufklärung* [Enlightenment] of the last century, the German precursor of Herder and Lessing and Goethe himself, and finds the forms of art ready to his hand without any national spirit to fill them or make them vital and responsive. He too dies, trampled to death by the soldiers of the country he so much admired, on the night of his marriage with a peasant girl, the very failure of his life lending him a certain melancholy grace and dramatic interest.

On the whole, then, this is a singularly attractive book. Mr. Pater is an intellectual impressionist. He does not weary us with any definite doctrine or seek to suit life to any formal creed. He is always looking for exquisite moments and, when he has found them, he analyses them with delicate and delightful art and then passes on, often to the opposite pole of thought or feeling, knowing that every mood has its own quality and charm and is justified by its mere existence. He has taken the sensationalism of Greek philosophy and made it a new method of art criticism. As for his style, it is curiously ascetic. Now and then, we come across phrases with a strange sensuousness of expression, as when he tells us how Denys l'Auxerrois, on his return from a long journey, "ate flesh for the first time, tearing the hot, red morsels with his delicate fingers in a kind of wild greed," but such passages are rare. Asceticism is the keynote of Mr. Pater's prose; at times it is almost too severe in its self-control and makes us long for a little more freedom. For indeed, the danger of such prose as his is that it is apt to become somewhat laborious. Here and there, one is tempted to say of Mr.

1. Louis II (1845–1886), Wagner's patron and builder of many magnificent castles. Declared insane and deposed, he committed suicide shortly thereafter.

Pater that he is "a seeker after something in language, that is there in no satisfying measure, or not at all." The continual preoccupation with phrase and epithet has its drawbacks as well as its virtues. And yet, when all is said, what wonderful prose it is, with its subtle preferences, its fastidious purity, its rejection of what is common or ordinary! Mr. Pater has the true spirit of selection, the true tact of omission. If he be not among the greatest prose writers of our literature he is, at least, our greatest artist in prose; and though it may be admitted that the best style is that which seems an unconscious result rather than a conscious aim, still in these latter days when violent rhetoric does duty for eloquence and vulgarity usurps the name of nature, we should be grateful for a style that deliberately aims at perfection of form, that seeks to produce its effect by artistic means and sets before itself an ideal of grave and chastened beauty.

*Pall Mall Gazette*, June 11, 1887.

# Mr. Pater's Last Volume

*Review of Pater's* Appreciations, with an Essay on Style.

When I first had the privilege—and I count it a very high one—
of meeting Mr. Walter Pater, he said to me, smiling, "Why do you
always write poetry? Why do you not write prose? Prose is so much
more difficult."

It was during my undergraduate days at Oxford; days of lyrical
ardour and of studious sonnet-writing; days when one loved the
exquisite intricacy and musical repetitions of the ballade, and the
villanelle with its linked long-drawn echoes and its curious completeness; days when one solemnly sought to discover the proper
temper in which a triolet should be written; delightful days, in
which, I am glad to say, there was far more rhyme than reason.

I may frankly confess now that at the time I did not quite
comprehend what Mr. Pater really meant; and it was not till I
had carefully studied his beautiful and suggestive essays on the
Renaissance that I fully realised what a wonderful self-conscious
art the art of English prose-writing really is, or may be made to be.
Carlyle's stormy rhetoric, Ruskin's winged and passionate eloquence, had seemed to me to spring from enthusiasm rather than
from art. I do not think I knew then that even prophets correct
their proofs. As for Jacobean prose, I thought it too exuberant;
and Queen Anne prose appeared to me terribly bald, and irritatingly
rational. But Mr. Pater's essays became to me "the golden book of
spirit and sense, the holy writ of beauty." They are still this to me.
It is possible, of course, that I may exaggerate about them. I
certainly hope that I do; for where there is no exaggeration there
is no love, and where there is no love there is no understanding.
It is only about things that do not interest one, that one can give a

really unbiassed opinion; and this is no doubt the reason why an unbiassed opinion is always valueless.

But I must not allow this brief notice of Mr. Pater's new volume to degenerate into an autobiography. I remember being told in America that whenever Margaret Fuller[1] wrote an essay upon Emerson the printers had always to send out to borrow some additional capital "I's," and I feel it right to accept this transatlantic warning.

*Appreciations*, in the fine Latin sense of the word, is the title given by Mr. Pater to his book, which is an exquisite collection of exquisite essays, of delicately wrought works of art—some of them being almost Greek in their purity of outline and perfection of form, others mediaeval in their strangeness of colour and passionate suggestion, and all of them absolutely modern, in the true meaning of the term modernity. For he to whom the present is the only thing that is present, knows nothing of the age in which he lives. To realise the nineteenth century one must realise every century that has preceded it, and that has contributed to its making. To know anything about oneself, one must know all about others. There must be no mood with which one cannot sympathise, no dead mode of life that one cannot make alive. The legacies of heredity may make us alter our views of moral responsibility, but they cannot but intensify our sense of the value of Criticism; for the true critic is he who bears within himself the dreams and ideas and feelings of myriad generations, and to whom no form of thought is alien, no emotional impulse obscure.

Perhaps the most interesting, and certainly the least successful, of the essays contained in the present volume is that on *Style*. It is the most interesting because it is the work of one who speaks with the high authority that comes from the noble realisation of things nobly conceived. It is the least successful, because the subject is too abstract. A true artist like Mr. Pater is most felicitous when he deals with the concrete, whose very limitations give him finer freedom, while they necessitate more intense vision. And yet what a high ideal is contained in these few pages! How good it is for us, in these days of popular education and facile journalism, to be reminded of the real scholarship that is essential to the perfect

1. Margaret Fuller (1810–1850), transcendentalist critic and social reformer.

writer, who, "being a true lover of words for their own sake, a
minute and constant observer of their physiognomy," will avoid
what is mere rhetoric, or ostentatious ornament, or negligent
misuse of terms, or ineffective surplusage, and will be known by
his tact of omission, by his skilful economy of means, by his selection
and self-restraint, and perhaps above all by that conscious artistic
structure which is the expression of mind in style. I think I have been
wrong in saying that the subject is too abstract. In Mr. Pater's hands
it becomes very real to us indeed, and he shows us how, behind the
perfection of a man's style, must lie the passion of a man's soul.

As one passes to the rest of the volume, one finds essays on
Wordsworth and on Coleridge, on Charles Lamb and on Sir
Thomas Browne, on some of Shakespeare's plays and on the English
kings that Shakespeare fashioned, on Dante Rossetti, and on William
Morris. As that on Wordsworth seems to be Mr. Pater's last work,
so that on the singer of the *Defence of Guenevere* is certainly his earliest,
or almost his earliest, and it is interesting to mark the change that has
taken place in his style. This change is, perhaps, at first sight not very
apparent. In 1868 we find Mr. Pater writing with the same exquisite
care for words, with the same studied music, with the same temper,
and something of the same mode of treatment. But, as he goes on,
the architecture of the style becomes richer and more complex,
the epithet more precise and intellectual. Occasionally one may be
inclined to think that there is, here and there, a sentence which is
somewhat long, and possibly, if one may venture to say so, a little
heavy and cumbersome in movement. But if this be so, it comes
from those side-issues suddenly suggested by the idea in its progress,
and really revealing the idea more perfectly; or from those felicitous
after-thoughts that give a fuller completeness to the central scheme,
and yet convey something of the charm of chance; or from a desire
to suggest the secondary shades of meaning with all their accumula-
ting effect, and to avoid, it may be, the violence and harshness of
too definite and exclusive an opinion. For in matters of art, at any
rate, thought is inevitably coloured by emotion, and so is fluid
rather than fixed, and, recognising its dependence upon moods
and upon the passion of fine moments, will not accept the rigidity
of a scientific formula or a theological dogma. The critical pleasure,
too, that we receive from tracing, through what may seem the

intricacies of a sentence, the working of the constructive intelligence, must not be overlooked. As soon as we have realised the design, everything appears clear and simple. After a time, these long sentences of Mr. Pater's come to have the charm of an elaborate piece of music, and the unity of such music also.

I have suggested that the essay on Wordsworth is probably the most recent bit of work contained in this volume. If one might choose between so much that is good, I should be inclined to say it is the finest also. The essay on Lamb is curiously suggestive; suggestive, indeed, of a somewhat more tragic, more sombre figure, than men have been wont to think of in connection with the author of the *Essays of Elia*. It is an interesting aspect under which to regard Lamb, but perhaps he himself would have had some difficulty in recognising the portrait given of him. He had, undoubtedly, great sorrows, or motives for sorrow, but he could console himself at a moment's notice for the real tragedies of life by reading any one of the Elizabethan tragedies, provided it was in a folio edition. The essay on Sir Thomas Browne is delightful, and has the strange, personal, fanciful charm of the author of the *Religio Medici*, Mr. Pater often catching the colour and accent and tone of whatever artist, or work of art, he deals with. That on Coleridge, with its insistence on the necessity of the cultivation of the relative, as opposed to the absolute spirit in philosophy and in ethics, and its high appreciation of the poet's true position in our literature, is in style and substance a very blameless work. Grace of expression and delicate subtlety of thought and phrase, characterise the essays on Shakespeare. But the essay on Wordsworth has a spiritual beauty of its own. It appeals, not to the ordinary Wordsworthian with his uncritical temper, and his gross confusion of ethical and aesthetical problems, but rather to those who desire to separate the gold from the dross, and to reach at the true Wordsworth through the mass of tedious and prosaic work that bears his name, and that serves often to conceal him from us. The presence of an alien element in Wordsworth's art is, of course, recognised by Mr. Pater, but he touches on it merely from the psychological point of view, pointing out how this quality of higher and lower moods gives the effect in his poetry "of a power not

altogether his own, or under his control"; a power which comes
and goes when it wills, "so that the old fancy which made the poet's
art an enthusiasm, a form of divine possession, seems almost true
of him." Mr. Pater's earlier essays had their *purpurei panni* [purple
passages], so eminently suitable for quotation, such as the famous
passage on *Mona Lisa*, and that other in which Botticelli's strange
conception of the Virgin is so strangely set forth. From the present
volume it is difficult to select any one passage in preference to another
as specially characteristic of Mr. Pater's treatment. This, however,
is worth quoting at length. It contains a truth eminently suitable
for our age:

> That the end of life is not action but contemplation—*being* as dis-
> tinct from *doing*—a certain disposition of the mind: is, in some shape or
> other, the principle of all the higher morality. In poetry, in art, if you
> enter into their true spirit at all, you touch this principle in a measure;
> these, by their sterility, are a type of beholding for the mere joy of be-
> holding. To treat life in the spirit of art is to make life a thing in which
> means and ends are identified: to encourage such treatment, the true
> moral significance of art and poetry. Wordsworth, and other poets who
> have been like him in ancient or more recent times, are the masters,
> the experts, in this art of-impassioned contemplation. Their work is not
> to teach lessons, or enforce rules, or even to stimulate us to noble ends,
> but to withdraw the thoughts for a while from the mere machinery of
> life, to fix them, with appropriate emotions, on the spectacle of those
> great facts in man's existence which no machinery affects, "on the
> great and universal passions of men, the most general and interesting
> of their occupations, and the entire world of nature"—on "the opera-
> tions of the elements and the appearances of the visible universe, on
> storm and sunshine, on the revolutions of the seasons, on cold and heat,
> on loss of friends and kindred, on injuries and resentments, on gratitude
> and hope, on fear and sorrow." To witness this spectacle with appro-
> priate emotions is the aim of all culture; and of these emotions poetry
> like Wordsworth's is a great nourisher and stimulant. He sees nature
> full of sentiment and excitement; he sees men and women as parts of
> nature, passionate, excited, in strange grouping and connection with the
> grandeur and beauty of the natural world:—images, in his own words,
> "of men suffering, amid awful forms and powers."

Certainly the real secret of Wordsworth has never been better expressed. After having read and re-read Mr. Pater's essay—for it requires re-reading—one returns to the poet's work with a new sense of joy and wonder, and with something of eager and impassioned expectation. And perhaps this might be roughly taken as the test or touchstone of the finest criticism.

Finally, one cannot help noticing the delicate instinct that has gone to fashion the brief epilogue that ends this delightful volume. The difference between the classical and romantic spirits in art has often, and with much over-emphasis, been discussed. But with what a light sure touch does Mr. Pater write of it! How subtle and certain are his distinctions! If imaginative prose be really the special art of this century, Mr. Pater must rank amongst our century's most characteristic artists. In certain things he stands almost alone. The age has produced wonderful prose styles, turbid with individualism, and violent with excess of rhetoric. But in Mr. Pater, as in Cardinal Newman, we find the union of personality with perfection. He has no rival in his own sphere, and he has escaped disciples. And this, not because he has not been imitated, but because in art so fine as his there is something that, in its essence, is inimitable.

*Speaker*, March 22, 1890.

# A Cheap Edition of a Great Man
# [Rossetti]

*Review of* Life of Dante Gabriel Rossetti *by Joseph Knight in the* "*Great Writers*" *Series published by Walter Scott.*

Formerly we used to canonise our great men; nowadays we vulgarise them. The vulgarisation of Rossetti has been going on for some time past with really remarkable success, and there seems no probability at present of the process being discontinued. The grass was hardly green upon the quiet grave in Birchington church-yard when Mr. Hall Caine and Mr. William Sharp rushed into print with their Memoirs and Recollections. Then came the usual mob of magazine-hacks with their various views and attitudes, and now Mr. Joseph Knight has produced for the edification of the British public a popular biography of the poet of the Blessed Damozel, the painter of Dante's Dream.

It is only fair to state that Mr. Knight's work is much better than that of his predecessors in the same field. His book is, on the whole, modestly and simply written; whatever its other faults may be, it is at least free from affectation of any kind; and it makes no serious pretence at being either exhaustive or definitive. Yet the best we can say of it is that it is just the sort of biography Guilden-stern might have written of Hamlet. Nor does its unsatisfactory character come merely from the ludicrous inadequacy of the materials at Mr. Knight's disposal; it is the whole scheme and method of the book that is radically wrong. Rossetti's was a great personality, and personalities such as his do not easily 'survive shilling primers. Sooner or later they have inevitably to come down to the level of their biographers, and in the present instance nothing could be more absolutely commonplace than the picture Mr. Knight gives us of the wonderful seer and singer whose life he has so recklessly essayed to write.

No doubt there are many people who will be deeply interested to know that Rossetti was once chased round his garden by an infuriated zebu he was trying to exhibit to Mr. Whistler, or that he had a great affection for a dog called "Dizzy," or that "sloshy" was one of his favourite words of contempt, or that Mr. Gosse[1] thought him very like Chaucer in appearance, or that he had "an absolute disqualification" for whist-playing, or that he was very fond of quoting the *Bab Ballads*,[2] or that he once said that if he could live by writing poetry he would see painting d——d! For our part, however, we cannot help expressing our regret that such a shallow and superficial biography as this should ever have been published. It is but a sorry task to rip the twisted ravel from the worn garment of life and to turn the grout in a drained cup. Better, after all, that we knew a painter only through his vision and a poet through his song, than that the image of a great man should be marred and made mean for us by the clumsy geniality of good intentions. A true artist, and such Rossetti undoubtedly was, reveals himself so perfectly in his work, that unless a biographer has something more valuable to give us than idle anecdotes and unmeaning tales, his labour is misspent and his industry misdirected.

Bad, however, as is Mr. Knight's treatment of Rossetti's life, his treatment of Rossetti's poetry is infinitely worse. Considering the small size of the volume, and the consequently limited number of extracts, the amount of misquotation is almost incredible, and puts all recent achievements in this sphere of modern literature completely into the shade. The fine line in the first canto of *Rose Mary*:

> What glints there like a lance that flees?

appears as:

> What glints there like a *glance* that flees?

1. Sir Edmund Gosse (1849–1928), biographer and man of letters who wrote for the *Sunday Times* and introduced Ibsen to English readers.
2. This volume of humorous verse by W. S. Gilbert, of Gilbert-and-Sullivan fame, appeared in 1868.

which is very painful nonsense; in the description of that graceful
and fanciful sonnet *Autumn Idleness*, the deer are represented as
"*grazing* from hillock eaves" instead of gazing from hillock-eaves;
the opening of *Dantis Tenebrae* is rendered quite incomprehensible
by the substitution of "my" for "thy" in the second line; even such
a well-known ballad as *Sister Helen* is misquoted, and, indeed, from
the *Burden of Nineveh*, the *Blessed Damozel*, the *King's Tragedy* and
Guido Cavalcanti's lovely *ballata*, down to the *Portrait* and such
sonnets as *Love-sweetness*, *Farewell to the Glen*, and *A Match with the
Moon*, there is not one single poem that does not display some
careless error or some stupid misprint.

As for Rossetti's elaborate system of puctuation, Mr. Knight
pays no attention to it whatsoever. Indeed, he shows quite a rollick-
ing indifference to all the secrets and subtleties of style, and inserts
or removes stops in a manner that is absolutely destructive to the
lyrical beauty of the verse. The hyphen, also, so constantly employed
by Rossetti in the case of such expressions as "hillock-eaves"
quoted above, "hill-fire," "birth-hour," and the like, is almost
invariably disregarded, and by the brilliant omission of a semicolon
Mr. Knight has succeeded in spoiling one of the best stanzas in *The
Staff and Scrip*—a poem, by the way, that he speaks of as *The Staff
and the Scrip* (*sic*). After this tedious comedy of errors it seems
almost unnecessary to point out that the earliest Italian poet is not
called Ciullo *D'Alcano* (*sic*), or that *The Bothie of Toper-na-Fuosich*
(*sic*) is not the title of Clough's boisterous epic, or that *Dante and his
Cycle* (*sic*) is not the name Rossetti gave to his collection of translations; and why *Troy Town* should appear in the index as *Tory Town*
is really quite inexplicable, unless it is intended as a compliment to
Mr. Hall Caine who once dedicated, or rather tried to dedicate,
to Rossetti a lecture on the relations of poets to politics. We are
sorry, too, to find an English dramatic critic misquoting Shakespeare,
as we had always been of opinion that this was a privilege reserved
specially for our English actors.

We sincerely hope that there will soon be an end to all biographies
of this kind. They rob life of much of its dignity and its wonder,
add to death itself a new terror, and make one wish that all art
were anonymous. Nor could there have been any more unfortunate
choice of a subject for popular treatment than that to which we

owe the memoir that now lies before us. A pillar of fire to the few who knew him, and of cloud to the many who knew him not, Dante Gabriel Rossetti lived apart from the gossip and tittle-tattle of a shallow age. He never trafficked with the merchants for his soul, nor brought his wares into the market-place for the idle to gape at. Passionate and romantic though he was, yet there was in his nature something of high austerity. He loved seclusion, and hated notoriety, and would have shuddered at the idea that within a few years after his death he was to make his appearance in a series of popular biographies, sandwiched between the author of *Pickwick* and the Great Lexicographer. One man alone, the friend his verse won for him, did he desire should write his life, and it is to Mr. Theodore Watts that we, too, must look to give us the real Rossetti. It may be admitted at once that Mr. Watts's subject has for the moment been a little spoiled for him. Rude hands have touched it, and unmusical voices have made it sound almost common in our ears. Yet none the less is it for him to tell us of the marvel of this man whose art he has analysed with such exquisite insight, whose life he knows as no one else can know it, whom he so loyally loved and tended, and by whom he was so loyally beloved in turn. As for the others, the scribblers and nibblers of literature, if they indeed reverence Rossetti's memory, let them pay him the one homage he would most have valued, the gracious homage of silence. "Though you can fret me, yet you cannot play upon me," says Hamlet to his false friend, and even so might Rossetti speak to those well-intentioned mediocrities who would seem to know his stops and would sound him to the top of his compass. True, they cannot fret him now, for he has passed beyond the possibility of pain; yet they cannot play upon him either; it is not for them to pluck out the heart of his mystery.

There is, however, one feature of this book that deserves unstinted praise. Mr. Anderson's bibliography will be found of immense use by every student of Rossetti's work and influence. Perhaps Young's very powerful attack on Pre-Raphaelitism, as expounded by Mr. Ruskin (Longmans, 1857),[3] might be included, but,

3. Ruskin's defense of Pre-Raphaelitism appeared in reviews and letters written in 1851.

in all other respects, it seems quite complete, and the chronological list of paintings and drawings is really admirable. When this unfortunate "Great Writers" Series comes to an end, Mr. Anderson's bibliographies should be collected together and published in a separate volume. At present they are in a very second-rate company indeed.

*Pall Mall Gazette*, April 18, 1887.

# The Letters of a Great Woman
# [George Sand]

*Review of* Letters of George Sand, *translated and edited by Raphael Ledos de Beaufort.*

Of the many collections of letters that have appeared in this century few, if any, can rival for fascination of style and variety of incident the letters of George Sand which have recently been translated into English by M. Ledos de Beaufort. They extend over a space of more than sixty years, from 1812 to 1876, in fact, and comprise the first letters of Aurore Dupin, a child of eight years old, as well as the last letters of George Sand, a woman of seventy-two. The very early letters, those of the child and of the young married woman, possess, of course, merely a psychological interest; but from 1831, the date of Madame Dudevant's separation from her husband and her first entry into Paris life, the interest becomes universal, and the literary and political history of France is mirrored in every page.

For George Sand was an indefatigable correspondent; she longs in one of her letters, it is true, for "a planet where reading and writing are absolutely unknown," but still she had a real pleasure in letter-writing. Her greatest delight was the communication of ideas, and she is always in the heart of the battle. She discusses pauperism with Louis Napoleon in his prison at Ham, and liberty with Armand Barbes in his dungeon at Vincennes; she writes to Lamennais on philosophy, to Mazzini on socialism, to Lamartine on democracy, and to Ledru-Rollin on justice.[1] Her letters reveal

1. Armand Barbès (1809–1870), a member of the Constituent Assembly (1848), was imprisoned from 1849 to 1854, and voluntarily exiled himself upon his release.

to us not merely the life of a great novelist but the soul of a great woman, of a woman who was one with all the noblest movements of her day and whose sympathy with humanity was boundless absolutely. For the aristocracy of intellect she had always the deepest veneration, but the democracy of suffering touched her more. She preached the regeneration of mankind, not with the noisy ardour of the paid advocate, but with the enthusiasm of the true evangelist. Of all the artists of this century she was the most altruistic; she felt every one's misfortunes except her own. Her faith never left her; to the end of her life, as she tells us, she was able to believe without illusions. But the people disappointed her a little. She saw that they followed persons not principles, and for "the great man theory" George Sand had no respect. "Proper names are the enemies of principles" is one of her aphorisms.

So from 1850 her letters are more distinctly literary. She discusses modern realism with Flaubert, and play-writing with Dumas *fils*; and protests with passionate vehemence against the doctrine of *L'art pour l'art*. "Art for the sake of itself is an idle sentence," she writes; "art for the sake of truth, for the sake of what is beautiful and good, that is the creed I seek." And in a delightful letter to M. Charles Poncy she repeats the same idea very charmingly. "People say that birds sing for the sake of singing, but I doubt it. They sing their loves and happiness, and in that they are in keeping with nature. But man must do something more, and poets only sing in order to move people and to make them think." She wanted M. Poncy to be the poet of the people and, if good advice were all that had been needed, he would certainly have been the Burns of the workshop. She drew out a delightful scheme for a volume to be called *Songs of all Trades* and saw the possibilities of making

---

Félicité Robert de Lamennais (1782–1854), French priest, philosopher, and journalist, who was censured for advocating freedom in religious matters. Giuseppe Mazzini (1805–1872), Italian patriot, who with Garibaldi was a prime mover in the unification of Italy. Alphonse Marie Louis de Lamartine (1790–1869), French poet and minister of the provisional government of 1848. Alexandre Auguste Ledru-Rollin (1807–1874), also a leader of the provisional government after the 1848 revolution; he was exiled by the government of Louis Napoleon and not allowed to return to France until 1870.

handicrafts poetic. Perhaps she valued good intentions in art a little too much, and she hardly understood that art for art's sake is not meant to express the final cause of art but is merely a formula of creation; but, as she herself had scaled Parnassus, we must not quarrel at her bringing Proletarianism with her. For George Sand must be ranked among our poetic geniuses. She regarded the novel as still within the domain of poetry. Her heroes are not dead photographs; they are great possibilities. Modern novels are dissections; hers are dreams. "I make popular types," she writes, "such as I do no longer see, but such as they should and might be." For realism, in M. Zola's acceptation of the word, she had no admiration. Art to her was a mirror that transfigured truths but did not represent realities. Hence she could not understand art without personality. "I am aware," she writes to Flaubert, "that you are opposed to the exposition of personal doctrine in literature. Are you right? Does not your opposition proceed rather from a want of conviction than from a principle of aesthetics? If we have any philosophy in our brain it must needs break forth in our writings. But you, as soon as you handle literature, you seem anxious, I know not why, to be another man, the one who must disappear, who annihilates himself and is no more. What a singular mania! What a deficient taste! The worth of our productions depends entirely on our own. Besides, if we withhold our own opinions respecting the personages we create, we naturally leave the reader in uncertainty as to the opinion he should himself form of them. That amounts to wishing not to be understood, and the result of this is that the reader gets weary of us and leaves us."

She herself, however, may be said to have suffered from too dominant a personality, and this was the reason of the failure of most of her plays.

Of the drama in the sense of disinterested presentation she had no idea, and what is the strength and life-blood of her novels is the weakness of her dramatic works. But in the main she was right. Art without personality is impossible. And yet the aim of art is not to reveal personality, but to please. This she hardly recognised in her aesthetics though she realised it in her work. On literary style she has some excellent remarks. She dislikes the extravagancies of the romantic school and sees the beauty of simplicity. "Simplicity," she writes, "is the most difficult thing to secure in this world: it is the last limit of experience and the last effort of genius." She hated the slang and *argot* of Paris life, and loved the words used by the peasants in the provinces. "The provinces," she remarks, "preserve the tradition of the original tongue and create but few new words. I feel much respect for the language of the peasantry; in my estimation it is the more correct."

She thought Flaubert too much preoccupied with the sense of form, and makes these excellent observations to him—perhaps her best piece of literary criticism. "You consider the form as the aim, whereas it is but the effect. Happy expressions are only the outcome of emotion and emotion itself proceeds from a conviction. We are only moved by that which we ardently believe in." Literary schools she distrusted. Individualism was to her the keystone of art as well as of life. "Do not belong to any school: do not imitate any model," is her advice. Yet she never encouraged eccentricity. "Be correct," she writes to Eugène Pelletan,[2] "that is rarer than being eccentric, as the time goes. It is much more common to please by bad taste than to receive the cross of honour."

On the whole, her literary advice is sound and healthy. She never shrieks and she never sneers. She is the incarnation of good sense. And the whole collection of her letters is a perfect treasure-house of suggestions both on art and on politics. The manner of the translation is often rather clumsy, but the matter is always so intensely interesting that we can afford to be charitable.

*Pall Mall Gazette*, March 6, 1886.

2. Pierre Clément Eugène Pelletan (1813–1884), French politician, journalist, and miscellaneous author.

# M. Caro on George Sand

George Sand *by Elmé Marie Caro, translated by Gustave Masson, Assistant Master of Harrow School, in the "Great French Writers" Series, was published by Routledge and Sons.*

The biography of a very great man from the pen of a very ladylike writer—this is the best description we can give of M. Caro's Life of George Sand. The late Professor of the Sorbonne could chatter charmingly about culture, and had all the fascinating insincerity of an accomplished phrase-maker; being an extremely superior person he had a great contempt for democracy and its doings, but he was always popular with the Duchesses of the Faubourg,[1] as there was nothing in history or in literature that he could not explain away for their edification; having never done anything remarkable he was naturally elected a member of the Academy, and he always remained loyal to the traditions of that thoroughly respectable and thoroughly pretentious institution. In fact, he was just the sort of man who should never have attempted to write a Life of George Sand or to interpret George Sand's genius. He was too feminine to appreciate the grandeur of that large womanly nature, too much of a *dilettante* to realise the masculine force of that strong and ardent mind. He never gets at the secret of George Sand, and never brings us near to her wonderful personality. He looks on her simply as a littérateur, as a writer of pretty stories of country life and of charming, if somewhat exaggerated, romances. But George Sand was much more than this. Beautiful as are such books as *Consuelo* and *Mauprat*, *François le Champi* and *La Mare au Diable*, yet in none of them is she adequately expressed, by none of them is she adequately

1. An allusion to the old nobility, many of whom had residences on the Faubourg St-Honoré in Paris.

revealed. As Mr. Matthew Arnold said, many years ago, "We do not know George Sand unless we feel the spirit which goes through her work as a whole." With this spirit, however, M. Caro has no sympathy. Madame Sand's doctrines are antediluvian, he tells us, her philosophy is quite dead and her ideas of social regeneration are Utopian, incoherent and absurd. The best thing for us to do is to forget these silly dreams and to read *Teverino* and *Le Secrétaire Intime*. Poor M. Caro! This spirit, which he treats with such airy flippancy, is the very leaven of modern life. It is remoulding the world for us and fashioning our age anew. If it is antediluvian, it is so because the deluge is yet to come; if it is Utopian, then Utopia must be added to our geographies. To what curious straits M. Caro is driven by his violent prejudices may be estimated by the fact that he tries to class George Sand's novels with the old *Chansons de geste*, the stories of adventure characteristic of primitive literatures; whereas in using fiction as a vehicle of thought, and romance as a means of influencing the social ideals of her age, George Sand was merely carrying out the traditions of Voltaire and Rousseau, of Diderot and of Chateaubriand. The novel, says M. Caro, must be allied either to poetry or to science. That it has found in philosophy one of its strongest allies seems not to have occurred to him. In an English critic such a view might possibly be excusable. Our greatest novelists, such as Fielding, Scott and Thackeray cared little for the philosophy of their age. But coming, as it does, from a French critic, the statement seems to show a strange want of recognition of one of the most important elements of French fiction. Nor, even in the narrow limits that he has imposed upon himself, can M. Caro be said to be a very fortunate or felicitous critic. To take merely one instance out of many, he says nothing of George Sand's delightful treatment of art and the artist's life. And yet how exquisitely does she analyse each separate art and present it to us in its relation to life! In *Consuelo* she tells us of music; in *Horace* of authorship; in *Le Château des Désertes* of acting; in *Les Maîtres Mosaïstes* of mosaic work; in *Le Château de Pictordu* of portrait painting; and in *La Daniella* of the painting of landscape. What Mr. Ruskin and Mr. Browning have done for England she did for France. She invented an art literature. It is unnecessary, however, to discuss any of M. Caro's minor failings, for the whole effect of the book, so far as it attempts to portray for us the scope and character of George Sand's genius, is entirely spoiled by the false attitude assumed from the beginning, and though the dictum may seem to many harsh and exclusive, we cannot help feeling that an absolute incapacity for appreciating the spirit of a great writer is no qualification for writing a treatise on the subject.

As for Madame Sand's private life, which is so intimately connected with her art (for, like Goethe, she had to live her romances before she could write them), M. Caro says hardly anything about it. He passes it over with a modesty that almost makes one blush, and for fear of wounding the susceptibilities of those *grandes dames* whose passions M. Paul Bourget[2] analyses with such subtlety, he transforms her mother, who was a typical French *grisette*, into "a very amiable and *spirituelle* milliner"! It must be admitted that Joseph Surface[3] himself could hardly show greater tact and delicacy, though we ourselves must plead guilty to preferring Madame Sand's own description of her as an "enfant du vieux pavé de Paris."

As regards the English version, which is by M. Gustave Masson, it may be up to the intellectual requirements of the Harrow schoolboys, but it will hardly satisfy those who consider that accuracy, lucidity and ease are essential to a good translation. Its carelessness is absolutely astounding, and it is difficult to understand how a publisher like Mr. Routledge could have allowed such a piece of work to issue from his press. "Il descend avec le sourire d'un Machiavel" appears as "He descends into the smile of a Machiavell"; George Sand's remark to Flaubert about literary style, "tu la considères comme un but, elle n'est qu'un effet" is translated "you consider it an end, it is merely *an effort*"; and such a simple phrase as "ainsi le veut l'esthétique du roman" is converted into "so the aesthetes of the world would have it." "Il faudra relâcher mes économies" is "I will have to draw upon my savings," not "my economies will assuredly be relaxed"; "cassures résineuses" is not "cleavages full of rosin," and "Mme. Sand ne réussit que deux

2. Paul Bourget (1852–1935), French psychological novelist and literary critic.
3. Joseph Surface, a character in Sheridan's *School for Scandal* (1777), a type of the sanctimonious hypocrite.

fois" is hardly "Madame Sand was not twice successful." "Querelles d'école" does not mean "school disputations"; "ceux qui se font une sorte d'esthétique de l'indifférence absolue" is not "those of which the aesthetics seem to be an absolute indifference"; "chimère" should not be translated "chimera," nor "lettres inéditées" "inedited letters"; "ridicules" means absurdities, not "ridicules," and "qui pourra définir sa pensée?" is not "who can clearly despise her thought?" M. Masson comes to grief over even such a simple sentence as "elle s'étonna des fureurs qui accueillirent ce livre, ne comprenant pas que l'on haïsse un auteur à travers son oeuvre," which he translates "she was surprised at the storm which greeted this book, *not understanding that the author is hated through his work.*" Then, passing over such phrases as "substituted by religion" instead of "replaced by religion," and "vulgarisation" where "popularisation" is meant, we come to that most irritating form of translation, the literal word-for-word style. The stream "excites itself by the declivity which it obeys" is one of M. Masson's finest achievements in this *genre,* and it is an admirable instance of the influence of schoolboys on their masters. However, it would be tedious to make a complete "catalogue of slips," so we will content ourselves by saying that M. Masson's translation is not merely quite unworthy of himself, but is also quite undeserved by the public. Nowadays, the public has its feelings.

*Pall Mall Gazette,* April 14, 1888.

# The Cenci [Shelley]

*Shelley's tragedy* The Cenci *appeared in 1819; it was first acted in 1886, in the production Wilde reviews below.*

The production of *The Cenci* last week at the Grand Theatre, Islington, may be said to have been an era in the literary history of this century, and the Shelley Society deserves the highest praise and warmest thanks of all for having given us an opportunity of seeing Shelley's play under the conditions he himself desired for it. For *The Cenci* was written absolutely with a view to theatric presentation, and had Shelley's own wishes been carried out it would have been produced during his lifetime at Covent Garden, with Edmund Kean and Miss O'Neill in the principal parts. In working out his conception, Shelley had studied very carefully the aesthetics of dramatic art. He saw that the essence of the drama is disinterested presentation, and that the characters must not be merely mouthpieces for splendid poetry but must be living subjects for terror and for pity. "I have endeavoured," he says, "as nearly as possible to represent the characters as they probably were, and have sought to avoid the error of making them actuated by my own conception of right or wrong, false or true: thus under a thin veil converting names and actions of the sixteenth century into cold impersonations of my own mind. . . .

"I have avoided with great care the introduction of what is commonly called mere poetry, and I imagine there will scarcely be found a detached simile or a single isolated description, unless Beatrice's description of the chasm appointed for her father's murder should be judged to be of that nature."

He recognised that a dramatist must be allowed far greater freedom of expression than what is conceded to a poet. "In a dramatic composition," to use his own words, "the imagery and the passion should interpenetrate one another, the former being reserved simply for the full development and illustration of the latter. Imagination is as the immortal God which should assume flesh for the redemption of mortal passion. It is thus that the most remote and the most familiar imagery may alike be fit for dramatic purposes when employed in the illustration of strong feeling, which raises what is low, and levels to the apprehension that which is lofty, casting over all the shadow of its own greatness. In other respects I have written more carelessly, that is, without an over-fastidious and learned choice of words. In this respect I entirely agree with those modern critics who assert that in order to move men to true sympathy we must use the familiar language of men."

He knew that if the dramatist is to teach at all it must be by example, not by precept.

"The highest moral purpose," he remarks, "aimed at in the highest species of the drama, is the teaching the human heart, through its sympathies and antipathies, the knowledge of itself; in proportion to the possession of which knowledge every human being is wise, just, sincere, tolerant and kind. If dogmas can do more it is well: but a drama is no fit place for the enforcement of them." He fully realises that it is by a conflict between our artistic sympathies and our moral judgment that the greatest dramatic effects are produced. "It is in the restless and anatomising casuistry with which men seek the justification of Beatrice, yet feel that she has done what needs justification; it is in the superstitious horror with which they contemplate alike her wrongs and their revenge, that the dramatic character of what she did and suffered consists."

In fact no one has more clearly understood than Shelley the mission of the dramatist and the meaning of the drama.

And yet I hardly think that the production of *The Cenci*, its absolute presentation on the stage, can be said to have added anything to its beauty, its pathos, or even its realism. Not that the principal actors were at all unworthy of the work of art they interpreted; Mr. Hermann Vezin's Cenci was a noble and magnificent performance; Miss Alma Murray stands now in the very first rank of our English actresses as a mistress of power and pathos; and Mr. Leonard Outram's Orsino was most subtle and artistic; but that *The*

*Cenci* needs for the production of its perfect effect no interpretation at all. It is, as we read it, a complete work of art—capable, indeed, of being acted, but not dependent on theatric presentation; and the impression produced by its exhibition on the stage seemed to me to be merely one of pleasure at the gratification of an intellectual curiosity of seeing how far Melpomene could survive the wagon of Thespis.

In producing the play, however, the members of the Shelley Society were merely carrying out the poet's own wishes, and they are to be congratulated on the success of their experiment—a success due not to any gorgeous scenery or splendid pageant, but to the excellence of the actors who aided them.

*Dramatic Review*, May 15, 1886.

# Mr. Swinburne's Last Volume

*Review of* Poems and Ballads, *Third Series, by Algernon Charles Swinburne.*

Mr. Swinburne once set his age on fire by a volume of very perfect and very poisonous poetry. Then he became revolutionary and pantheistic, and cried out against those that sit in high places both in heaven and on earth. Then he invented Marie Stuart and laid upon us the heavy burden of *Bothwell.* Then he retired to the nursery and wrote poems about children of a somewhat over-subtle character. He is now extremely patriotic, and manages to combine with his patriotism a strong affection for the Tory party. He has always been a great poet. But he has his limitations, the chief of which is, curiously enough, the entire lack of any sense of limit. His song is nearly always too loud for his subject. His magnificent rhetoric, nowhere more magnificent than in the volume that now lies before us, conceals rather than reveals. It has been said of him, and with truth, that he is a master of language, but with still greater truth it may be said that Language is his master. Words seem to dominate him. Alliteration tyrannises over him. Mere sound often becomes his lord. He is so eloquent that whatever he touches becomes unreal.

Let us turn to the poem on the Armada:

The wings of the south-west wind are widened; the breath of his
  fervent lips,
More keen than a sword's edge, fiercer than fire, falls full on the
  plunging ships.
The pilot is he of the northward flight, their stay and their steersman
  he;
A helmsman clothed with the tempest, and girdled with strength to
  constrain the sea.

And the host of them trembles and quails, caught fast in his hand as a
    bird in the toils;
For the wrath and the joy that fulfil him are mightier than man's,
    whom he slays and spoils.
And vainly, with heart divided in sunder, and labour of wavering will,
The lord of their host takes counsel with hope if haply their star
    shine still.

Somehow we seem to have heard all this before. Does it come
from the fact that of all the poets who ever lived Mr. Swinburne is
the one who is the most limited in imagery? It must be admitted that
he is so. He has wearied us with his monotony. "Fire" and the "Sea"
are the two words ever on his lips. We must confess also that this
shrill singing—marvellous as it is—leaves us out of breath. Here is a
passage from a poem called *A Word with the Wind*:

Be the sunshine bared or veiled, the sky superb or shrouded,
    Still the waters, lax and languid, chafed and foiled,
Keen and thwarted, pale and patient, clothed with fire or clouded,
    Vex their heart in vain, or sleep like serpents coiled.
Thee they look for, blind and baffled, wan with wrath and weary,
    Blown for ever back by winds that rock the bird:
Winds that seamews breast subdue the sea, and bid the dreary
    Waves be weak as hearts made sick with hope deferred.
Let the clarion sound from westward, let the south bear token
    How the glories of thy godhead sound and shine:
Bid the land rejoice to see the land-wind's broad wings broken,
    Bid the sea take comfort, bid the world be thine.

Verse of this kind may be justly praised for the sustained strength
and vigour of its metrical scheme. Its purely technical excellence is
extraordinary. But is it more than an oratorical *tour de force*? Does
it really convey much? Does it charm? Could we return to it again
and again with renewed pleasure? We think not. It seems to us
empty.

Of course, we must not look to these poems for any revelation of
human life. To be at one with the elements seems to be Mr. Swinburne's aim. He seeks to speak with the breath of wind and wave.
The roar of the fire is ever in his ears. He puts his clarion to the lips
of Spring and bids her blow, and the Earth wakes from her dreams

and tells him her secret. He is the first lyric poet who has tried to make an absolute surrender of his own personality, and he has succeeded. We hear the song, but we never know the singer. We never even get near to him. Out of the thunder and splendour of words he himself says nothing. We have often had man's interpretation of Nature; now we have Nature's interpretation of man, and she has curiously little to say. Force and Freedom form her vague message. She deafens us with her clangours.

But Mr. Swinburne is not always riding the whirlwind and calling out of the depths of the sea. Romantic ballads in Border dialect have not lost their fascination for him, and this last volume contains some very splendid examples of this curious artificial kind of poetry. The amount of pleasure one gets out of dialect is a matter entirely of temperament. To say "mither" instead of "mother" seems to many the acme of romance. There are others who are not quite so ready to believe in the pathos of provincialisms. There is, however, no doubt of Mr. Swinburne's mastery over the form, whether the form be quite legitimate or not. *The Weary Wedding* has the concentration and colour of a great drama, and the quaintness of its style lends it something of the power of a grotesque. The ballad of *The Witch-Mother*, a mediaeval Medea who slays her children because her lord is faithless, is worth reading on account of its horrible simplicity. *The Bride's Tragedy*, with its strange refrain of

> In, in, out and in,
> Blaws the wind and whirls the whin:

The *Jacobite's Exile*—

> O lordly flow the Loire and Seine,
>   And loud the dark Durance:
> But bonnier shine the braes of Tyne
>   Than a' the fields of France;
> And the waves of Till that speak sae still
>   Gleam goodlier where they glance:

*The Tyneside Widow* and *A Reiver's Neck-verse* are all poems of fine imaginative power, and some of them are terrible in their fierce intensity of passion. There is no danger of English poetry narrowing itself to a form so limited as the romantic ballad in dialect. It is of too vital a growth for that. So we may welcome Mr. Swinburne's masterly experiments with the hope that things which are inimitable will not be imitated. The collection is completed by a few poems on children, some sonnets, a threnody on John William Inchbold, and a lovely lyric entitled *The Interpreters*.

> In human thought have all things habitation;
> > Our days
> Laugh, lower, and lighten past, and find no station
> > That stays.
>
> But thought and faith are mightier things than time
> > Can wrong,
> Made splendid once by speech, or made sublime
> > By song.
>
> Remembrance, though the tide of change that rolls
> > Wax hoary,
> Gives earth and heaven, for song's sake and the soul's,
> > Their glory.

Certainly, "for song's sake" we should love Mr. Swinburne's work, cannot, indeed, help loving it, so marvellous a music-maker is he. But what of the soul? For the soul we must go elsewhere.

*Pall Mall Gazette,* June 27, 1889.

# The Gospel According to Walt Whitman

*Review of* November Boughs *by Walt Whitman.*

"No one will get at my verses who insists upon viewing them as a literary performance . . . or as aiming mainly toward art and aestheticism." "*Leaves of Grass* . . . has mainly been the outcropping of my own emotional and other personal nature—an attempt, from first to last, to put *a Person*, a human being (myself, in the latter half of the nineteenth century in America,) freely, fully and truly on record. I could not find any similar personal record in current literature that satisfied me." In these words Walt Whitman gives us the true attitude we should adopt towards his work, having, indeed, a much saner view of the value and meaning of that work than either his eloquent admirers or noisy detractors can boast of possessing. His last book, *November Boughs*, as he calls it, published in the winter of the old man's life, reveals to us, not indeed a soul's tragedy, for its last note is one of joy and hope, and noble and unshaken faith in all that is fine and worthy of such faith, but certainly the drama of a human soul, and puts on record with a simplicity that has in it both sweetness and strength the record of his spiritual development, and of the aim and motive both of the manner and the matter of his work. His strange mode of expression is shown in these pages to have been the result of deliberate and self-conscious choice. The "barbaric yawp" which he sent over "the roofs of the world" so many years ago, and which wrung from Mr. Swinburne's lip such lofty panegyric in song and such loud clamorous censure in prose, appears here in what will be to many an entirely new light. For in his very rejection of art Walt Whitman is an artist. He tried to produce a certain effect by certain means and he succeeded. There is much method in what many have termed his madness, too much method, indeed, some may be tempted to fancy.

In the story of his life, as he tells it to us, we find him at the age of sixteen beginning a definite and philosophical study of literature:

> Summers and falls, I used to go off, sometimes for a week at a stretch, down in the country, or to Long Island's seashores—there, in the presence of outdoor influences, I went over thoroughly the Old and New Testaments, and absorb'd (probably to better advantage for me than in any library or indoor room—it makes such difference *where* you read) Shakespere, Ossian, the best translated versions I could get of Homer, Eschylus, Sophocles, the old German Nibelungen, the ancient Hindoo poems, and one or two other masterpieces, Dante's among them. As it happen'd, I read the latter mostly in an old wood. The *Iliad* . . . I read first thoroughly on the peninsula of Orient, northeast end of Long Island, in a shelter'd hollow of rock and sand, with the sea on each side. (I have wonder'd since why I was not overwhelm'd by those mighty masters. Likely because I read them, as described, in the full presence of Nature, under the sun, with the far-spreading landscape and vistas, or the sea rolling in.)

Edgar Allan Poe's amusing bit of dogmatism that, for our occasions and our day, "there can be no such thing as a long poem," fascinated him. "The same thought had been haunting my mind before," he said, "but Poe's argument . . . work'd the sum out, and proved it to me," and the English translation of the Bible seems to have suggested to him the possibility of a poetic form which, while retaining the spirit of poetry, would still be free from the trammels of rhyme and of a definite metrical system. Having thus, to a certain degree, settled upon what one might call the "technique" of Whitmanism, he began to brood upon the nature of that spirit which was to give life to the strange form. The central point of the poetry of the future seemed to him to be necessarily "an identical body and soul, a personality," in fact, which personality, he tells us frankly, "after many considerations and ponderings I deliberately settled should be myself." However, for the true creation and revealing of this personality, at first only dimly felt, a new stimulus was needed. This came from the Civil War. After describing the many dreams and passions of his boyhood and early manhood, he goes on to say:

> These, however, and much more might have gone on and come to naught (almost positively would have come to naught,) if a sudden,

vast, terrible, direct and indirect stimulus for new and national de-
clamatory expression had not been given to me. It is certain, I say, that
although I had made a start before, only from the occurrence of the
Secession War, and what it show'd me as by flashes of lightning, with
the emotional depths it sounded and arous'd (of course, I don't mean in
my own heart only, I saw it just as plainly in others, in millions)—that
only from the strong flare and provocation of that war's sights and
scenes the final reasons-for-being of an autochthonic and passionate
song definitely came forth.

I went down to the war fields of Virginia . . . lived thenceforward in
camp—saw great battles and the days and nights afterward—partook
of all the fluctuations, gloom, despair, hopes again arous'd, courage
evoked—death readily risk'd—*the cause*, too—along and filling those
agonistic and lurid following years , , , the real parturition years . . . of
this henceforth homogeneous Union. Without those three or four years
and the experiences they gave, *Leaves of Grass* would not now be existing.

Having thus obtained the necessary stimulus for the quickening
and awakening of the personal self, some day to be endowed with
universality, he sought to find new notes of song, and, passing beyond
the mere passion for expression, he aimed at "Suggestiveness" first.

I round and finish little, if anything; and could not, consistently
with my scheme. The reader will have his or her part to do, just as much
as I have had mine. I seek less to state or display any theme or thought,
and more to bring you, reader, into the atmosphere of the theme or
thought—there to pursue your own flight.

Another "impetus-word" is Comradeship, and other "word-
signs" are Good Cheer, Content and Hope. Individuality, especially,
he sought for:

I have allow'd the stress of my poems from beginning to end to bear
upon American individuality and assist it—not only because that is a
great lesson in Nature, amid all her generalising laws, but as counter-
poise to the leveling tendencies of Democracy—and for other reasons.
Defiant of ostensible literary and other conventions, I avowedly chant
"the great pride of man in himself," and permit it to be more or less a
*motif* of nearly all my verse. I think this pride indispensable to an
American. I think it not inconsistent with obedience, humility, def-
erence, and self-questioning.

A new theme also was to be found in the relation of the sexes, conceived in a natural, simple and healthy form, and he protests against poor Mr. William Rossetti's attempt to Bowdlerise and expurgate his song.[1]

> From another point of view *Leaves of Grass* is avowedly the song of Sex and Amativeness, and even Animality—though meanings that do not usually go along with these words are behind all, and will duly emerge; and all are sought to be lifted into a different light and atmosphere. Of this feature, intentionally palpable in a few lines, I shall only say the espousing principle of those lines so gives breath to my whole scheme that the bulk of the pieces might as well have been left unwritten were those lines omitted. . . .
>
> Universal as are certain facts and symptoms of communities . . . there is nothing so rare in modern conventions and poetry as their normal recognizance. Literature is always calling in the doctor for consultation and confession, and always giving evasions and swathing suppressions in place of that "heroic nudity" on which only a genuine diagnosis . . . can be built. And in respect to editions of *Leaves of Grass* in time to come (if there should be such) I take occasion now to confirm those lines with the settled convictions and deliberate renewals of thirty years, and to hereby prohibit, as far as word of mine can do so, any elision of them.

But beyond all these notes and moods and motives is the lofty spirit of a grand and free acceptance of all things that are worthy of existence. He desired, he says, "to formulate a poem whose every thought or fact should directly or indirectly be or connive at an implicit belief in the wisdom, health, mystery, beauty of every process, every concrete object, every human or other existence, not only consider'd from the point of view of all, but of each." His two final utterances are that "really great poetry is always . . . the result of a national spirit, and not the privilege of a polish'd and select few"; and that "the strongest and sweetest songs yet remain to be sung."

1. The selections from Whitman edited and published by William M. Rossetti in 1868 in London established the poet's reputation in England much sooner than at home; but this was because Rossetti had omitted the sexual poems which had offended the prudish tastes of mid-century Americans and which would have equally repelled Victorians.

Such are the views contained in the opening essay *A Backward Glance O'er Travel'd Roads*, as he calls it; but there are many other essays in this fascinating volume, some on poets such as Burns and Lord Tennyson, for whom Walt Whitman has a profound admiration; some on old actors and singers, the elder Booth, Forrest, Alboni and Mario[2] being his special favourites; others on the native Indians on the Spanish element in American nationality, on Western slang, on the poetry of the Bible, and on Abraham Lincoln. But Walt Whitman is at his best when he is analysing his own work and making schemes for the poetry of the future. Literature, to him, has a distinctly social aim. He seeks to build up the masses by "building up grand individuals." And yet literature itself must be preceded by noble forms of life. "The best literature is always the result of something far greater than itself—not the hero but the portrait of the hero. Before there can be recorded history or poem there must be the transaction." Certainly, in Walt Whitman's views there is a largeness of vision, a healthy sanity and a fine ethical purpose. He is not to be placed with the professional littérateurs of his country, Boston novelists, New York poets and the like. He stands apart, and the chief value of his work is in its prophecy, not in its performance. He has begun a prelude to larger themes. He is the herald to a new era. As a man he is the precursor of a fresh type. He is a factor in the heroic and spiritual evolution of the human being. If Poetry has passed him by, Philosophy will take note of him.

*Pall Mall Gazette*, January 25, 1889.

2. Junius Brutus Booth (1796–1852), American actor and father of Edwin Booth, John Wilkes Booth, and Junius Brutus Booth; Edwin Forrest (1906–1872), American actor; Marietta Alboni (1826–1894), Italian operatic contralto; and Giovanni Matteo Mario (1810–1883), Italian operatic tenor.

# Some Literary Notes [on Yeats]

"The various collectors of Irish folk-lore," says Mr. W. B. Yeats in his charming little book *Fairy and Folk Tales of the Irish Peasantry*, "have, from our point of view, one great merit, and from the point of view of others, one great fault."

They have made their work literature rather than science, and told us of the Irish peasantry rather than of the primitive religion of mankind, or whatever else the folk-lorists are on the gad after. To be considered scientists they should have tabulated all their tales in forms like grocers' bills—item the fairy king, item the queen. Instead of this they have caught the very voice of the people, the very pulse of life, each giving what was most noticed in his day. Croker and Lover, full of the ideas of harum-scarum Irish gentility, saw everything humorised. The impulse of the Irish literature of their time came from a class that did not—mainly for political reasons—take the populace seriously, and imagined the country as a humorist's Arcadia; its passion, its gloom, its tragedy, they knew nothing of. What they did was not wholly false; they merely magnified an irresponsible type, found oftenest among boatmen, carmen, and gentlemen's servants, into the type of a whole nation, and created the stage Irishman. The writers of 'Forty-eight, and the famine combined, burst their bubble. Their work had the dash as well as the shallowness of an ascendant and idle class, and in Croker is touched everywhere with beauty—a gentle Arcadian beauty. Carleton, a peasant born, has in many of his stories, . . . more especially in his ghost stories, a much more serious way with him, for all his humour. Kennedy, an old bookseller in Dublin, who seems to have had a something of genuine belief in the fairies, comes next in time. He has far less literary faculty, but is wonderfully accurate, giving often the very words the stories were told in. But the best book since Croker is Lady Wilde's *Ancient Legends*. The humour has all given way to pathos and tenderness. We have here the innermost heart of the Celt in the moments he has grown to love through years of persecution, when, cushioning himself about with dreams, and hearing fairy-songs in the twilight, he ponders on the soul and on the dead. Here is the Celt, only it is the Celt dreaming.

Into a volume of very moderate dimensions, and of extremely moderate price, Mr. Yeats has collected together the most characteristic of our Irish folk-lore stories, grouping them together according to subject. First come *The Trooping Fairies*. The peasants say that these are "fallen angels who were not good enough to be saved, nor bad enough to be lost"; but the Irish antiquarians see in them "the gods of pagan Ireland," who, "when no longer worshipped and fed with offerings, dwindled away in the popular imagination, and now are only a few spans high." Their chief occupations are feasting, fighting, making love, and playing the most beautiful music. "They have only one industrious person amongst them, the *lepra-caun*—the shoemaker." It is his duty to repair their shoes when they wear them out with dancing. Mr. Yeats tells us that "near the village of Ballisodare is a little woman who lived amongst them seven years. When she came home she had no toes—she had danced them off." On May Eve, every seventh year, they fight for the harvest, for the best ears of grain belong to them. An old man informed Mr. Yeats that he saw them fight once, and that they tore the thatch off a house. "Had anyone else been near they would merely have seen a great wind whirling everything into the air as it passed." When the wind drives the leaves and straws before it, "that is the fairies, and the peasants take off their hats and say 'God bless them.'" When they are gay, they sing. Many of the most beautiful tunes of Ireland "are only their music, caught up by eavesdroppers." No prudent peasant would hum *The Pretty Girl Milking the Cow* near a fairy rath, "for they are jealous, and do not like to hear their songs on clumsy mortal lips." Blake once saw a fairy's funeral. But this, as Mr. Yeats points out, must have been an English fairy, for the Irish fairies never die; they are immortal.

Then come *The Solitary Fairies*, amongst whom we find the little *Lepracaun* mentioned above. He has grown very rich, as he possesses all the treasure-crocks buried in war-time. In the early part of this century, according to Croker, they used to show in Tipperary a little shoe forgotten by the fairy shoemaker. Then there are two rather disreputable little fairies—the *Cluricaun*, who gets intoxicated in gentlemen's cellars, and the Red Man, who plays unkind practical jokes. "The *Fear-Gorta* (Man of Hunger) is an emaciated phantom that goes through the land in famine time, begging an alms and bringing good luck to the giver." The *Water-sheerie* is "own brother to the English Jack-o'-Lantern." "*The Leanhaun Shee* (fairy mistress) seeks the love of mortals. If they refuse, she must be their slave; if they consent, they are hers, and can only escape by finding another to take their place. The fairy lives on their life, and they waste away. Death is no escape from her. She is the Gaelic muse, for she gives inspiration to those she persecutes. The Gaelic poets die young, for she is restless, and will not let them remain long on earth." The *Pooka* is essentially an animal spirit, and some have considered him the forefather of Shakespeare's "Puck." He lives on solitary mountains and among old ruins "grown monstrous with much solitude," and "is of the race of the nightmare." "He has many shapes—is now a horse, . . . now a goat, now an eagle. Like all spirits, he is only half in the world of form." The *banshee* does not care much for our democratic levelling tendencies; she loves only old families, and despises the *parvenu* or the *nouveau riche*. When more than one banshee is present, and they wail and sing in chorus, it is for the death of some holy or great one. An omen that sometimes accompanies the banshee is ". . . an immense black coach, mounted by a coffin, and drawn by headless horses driven by a *Dullahan*." A *Dullahan* is the most terrible thing in the world. In 1807 two of the sentries stationed outside St. James's Park saw one climbing the railings, and died of fright. Mr. Yeats suggests that they are possibly "descended from that Irish giant who swam across the Channel with his head in his teeth."

Then come the stories of ghosts, of saints and priests, and of giants. The ghosts live in a state intermediary between this world and the next. They are held there by some earthly longing or affection, or some duty unfulfilled, or anger against the living; they are those who are too good for hell, and too bad for heaven. Sometimes they "take the forms of insects, especially of butterflies." The author of the *Parochial Survey of Ireland* "heard a woman say to a child who was chasing a butterfly, 'How do you know it is not the soul of your grandfather?' On November eve they are abroad, and dance with the fairies." As for the saints and priests, "there are no martyrs in the stories." That ancient chronicler Giraldus Cambrensis[1] "taunted the Archbishop of Cashel, because no one in Ireland had received the crown of martyrdom. 'Our people may be barbarous,' the prelate answered, 'but they have never lifted their hands against God's saints; but now that a people have come amongst us who know how to make them (it was just after the English invasion), we shall have martyrs plentifully.' " The giants were the old pagan heroes of Ireland, who grew bigger and bigger, just as the gods grew smaller and smaller. The fact is they did not wait for offerings; they took them *vi et armis*.

Some of the prettiest stories are those that cluster round *Tir-na-n-Og*. This is the Country of the Young, "for age and death have not found it; neither tears nor loud laughter have gone near it." "One man has gone there and returned. The bard, Oisen, who wandered away on a white horse, moving on the surface of the foam with his fairy Niamh, lived there three hundred years, and then returned looking for his comrades. The moment his foot touched the earth his three hundred years fell on him, and he was bowed double, and his beard swept the ground. He described his sojourn in the Land of Youth to Patrick before he died." Since then, according to Mr. Yeats, "many have seen it in many places; some in the depths of lakes, and have heard rising therefrom a vague sound of bells; more have seen it far off on the horizon, as they peered out from the western cliffs. Not three years ago a fisherman imagined that he saw it."

Mr. Yeats has certainly done his work very well. He has shown great critical capacity in his selection of the stories, and his little introductions are charmingly written. It is delightful to come across a collection of purely imaginative work, and Mr. Yeats has a very quick instinct in finding out the best and the most beautiful things in Irish folklore. I am also glad to see that he has not confined himself entirely to prose, but has included Allingham's[2] lovely poem on *The Fairies*:

1. Giraldus Cambrensis (ca. 1146–ca. 1220), British historian and ecclesiastic, who served as chaplain to King Henry II and accompanied Prince John on his expedition to Ireland.
2. William Allingham (1824–1889), Irish poet and editor of *Fraser's Magazine* (1874–1879).

Up the airy mountain,
   Down the rushy glen,
We daren't go a-hunting
   For fear of little men;
Wee folk, good folk,
   Trooping all together;
Green jacket, red cap,
   And white owl's feather!

Down along the rocky shore
   Some make their home,
They live on crispy pancakes
   Of yellow tide-foam;
Some in the reeds
   Of the black mountain lake,
With frogs for their watch-dogs
   All night awake.

High on the hill-top
   The old King sits;
He is now so old and gray
   He's nigh lost his wits.
With a bridge of white mist
   Columbkill he crosses,
On his stately journeys
   From Slieveleague to Rosses;
Or going up with music,
   On cold starry nights,
To sup with the Queen
   Of the gay Northern Lights.

All lovers of fairy tales and folklore should get this little book. *The Horned Women, The Priest's Soul,*[3] and *Teig O'Kane,* are really marvellous in their way; and, indeed, there is hardly a single story that is not worth reading and thinking over.

*Woman's World,* February, 1889.

3. The article carried here the footnote "From Lady Wilde's *Ancient Legends of Ireland*"—the reviewer's reference to his mother's book. Lady Wilde (1824–1896) was a poetess (as "Speranza"), later an Irish folklorist, and even later one of the more famous London hostesses.

# Three New Poets [Yeats and Others]

*The review of Yeats's* The Wanderings of Oisin and Other Poems *was followed by reviews of two other books of poetry, neither of any significance, although one of the poets was Richard Le Gallienne.*

Books of poetry by young writers are usually promissory notes that are never met. Now and then, however, one comes across a volume that is so far above the average that one can hardly resist the fascinating temptation of recklessly prophesying a fine future for its author. Such a book Mr. Yeats's *Wanderings of Oisin* certainly is. Here we find nobility of treatment and nobility of subject-matter, delicacy of poetic instinct and richness of imaginative resource. Unequal and uneven much of the work must be admitted to be. Mr. Yeats does not try to "out-baby" Wordsworth, we are glad to say; but he occasionally succeeds in "out-glittering" Keats, and, here and there, in his book we come across strange crudities and irritating conceits. But when he is at his best he is very good. If he has not the grand simplicity of epic treatment, he has at least something of the largeness of vision that belongs to the epical temper. He does not rob of their stature the great heroes of Celtic mythology. He is very naïve and very primitive and speaks of his giants with the air of a child. Here is a characteristic passage from the account of Oisin's return from the Island of Forgetfulness:

And I rode by the plains of the sea's edge, where all is barren and
    grey,
Grey sands on the green of the grasses and over the dripping trees,
Dripping and doubling landward, as though they would hasten away
Like an army of old men longing for rest from the moan of the seas.

Long fled the foam-flakes around me, the winds fled out of the vast,
Snatching the bird in secret, nor knew I, embosomed apart,
When they froze the cloth on my body like armour riveted fast,
For Remembrance, lifting her leanness, keened in the gates of my
    heart.

Till fattening the winds of the morning, an odour of new-mown hay
Came, and my forehead fell low, and my tears like berries fell down;
Later a sound came, half lost in the sound of a shore far away,
From the great grass-barnacle calling, and later the shore-winds
    brown.***[1]

In one or two places the music is faulty, the construction is
sometimes too involved, and the word "populace" in the last line
is rather infelicitous; but, when all is said, it is impossible not to feel
in these stanzas the presence of the true poetic spirit. * * *

*Pall Mall Gazette,* July 12, 1889.

1. Wilde quotes considerably more from the poem, perhaps as a device to fill
additional space; however, it was useful mass-circulation exposure for young
Yeats.

# English Poetesses

England has given to the world one great poetess, Elizabeth Barrett Browning. By her side Mr. Swinburne would place Miss Christina Rossetti, whose New Year hymn he describes as so much the noblest of sacred poems in our language, that there is none which comes near it enough to stand second. "It is a hymn," he tells us, "touched as with the fire, and bathed as in the light of sun-beams, tuned as to chords and cadences of refluent sea-music beyond reach of harp and organ, large echoes of the serene and sonorous tides of heaven." Much as I admire Miss Rossetti's work, her subtle choice of words, her rich imagery, her artistic naïveté, wherein curious notes of strangeness and simplicity are fantastically blended together, I cannot but think that Mr. Swinburne has, with noble and natural loyalty, placed her on too lofty a pedestal. To me, she is simply a very delightful artist in poetry. This is indeed something so rare that when we meet it we cannot fail to love it, but it is not everything. Beyond it and above it are higher and more sunlit heights of a song, a larger vision, and an ampler air, a music at once more passionate and more profound, a creative energy that is born of the spirit, a winged rapture that is born of the soul, a force and fervour of mere utterance that has all the wonder of the prophet, and not a little of the consecration of the priest.

Mrs. Browning is unapproachable by any woman who has ever touched lyre or blown through reed since the days of the great Aeolian poetess. But Sappho, who, to the antique world was a pillar of flame, is to us but a pillar of shadow. Of her poems, burnt with other most precious work by a Byzantine Emperor and by Roman Pope, only a few fragments remain. Possibly they lie mouldering in the scented darkness of an Egyptian tomb, clasped in the withered hands of some long-dead lover. Some Greek monk at Athos may even now be poring over an ancient manuscript, whose crabbed characters conceal lyric or ode by her whom the Greeks spoke of as "the Poetess" just as they termed Homer "the Poet," who was to them the tenth Muse, the flower of the Graces, the child of Eros, and the pride of Hellas—Sappho, with the sweet voice, the bright, beautiful eyes, the dark hyacinth-coloured hair. But, practically, the work of the marvellous singer of Lesbos is entirely lost to us.

We have a few rose-leaves out of her garden, that is all. Literature nowadays survives marble and bronze, but in old days, in spite of the Roman poet's noble boast, it was not so. The fragile clay vases of the Greeks still keep for us pictures of Sappho, delicately painted in black and red and white; but of her song we have only the echo of an echo.

Of all the women of history, Mrs. Browning is the only one that we could name in any possible or remote conjunction with Sappho.

Sappho was undoubtedly a far more flawless and perfect artist. She stirred the whole antique world more than Mrs. Browning ever stirred our modern age. Never had Love such a singer. Even in the few lines that remain to us the passion seems to scorch and burn. But, as unjust Time, who has crowned her with the barren laurels of fame, has twined with them the dull poppies of oblivion, let us turn from the mere memory of a poetess to one whose song still remains to us as an imperishable glory to our literature; to her who heard the cry of the children from dark mine and crowded factory, and made England weep over its little ones; who, in the feigned sonnets from the Portuguese, sang of the spiritual mystery of Love, and of the intellectual gifts that Love brings to the soul; who had faith in all that is worthy, and enthusiasm for all that is great, and pity for all that suffers; who wrote the *Vision of Poets* and *Casa Guidi Windows* and *Aurora Leigh*.

As one, to whom I owe my love of poetry no less than my love of country, has said of her:

> Still on our ears
> The clear "Excelsior" from a woman's lip
> Rings out across the Apennines, although
> The woman's brow lies pale and cold in death

With all the mighty marble dead in Florence.
For while great songs can stir the hearts of men,
Spreading their full vibrations through the world
In ever-widening circles till they reach
The Throne of God, and song becomes a prayer,
And prayer brings down the liberating strength
That kindles nations to heroic deeds,
She lives—the great-souled poetess who saw
From Casa Guidi windows Freedom dawn
On Italy, and gave the glory back
In sunrise hymns to all Humanity!

She lives indeed, and not alone in the heart of Shakespeare's England, but in the heart of Dante's Italy also. To Greek literature she owed her scholarly culture, but modern Italy created her human passion for Liberty. When she crossed the Alps she became filled with a new ardour, and from that fine, eloquent mouth, that we can still see in her portraits, broke forth such a noble and majestic outburst of lyrical song as had not been heard from woman's lips for more than two thousand years. It is pleasant to think that an English poetess was to a certain extent a real factor in bringing about that unity of Italy that was Dante's dream, and if Florence drove her great singer into exile, she at least welcomed within her walls the later singer that England had sent to her.

If one were asked the chief qualities of Mrs. Browning's work, one would say, as Mr. Swinburne said of Byron's its sincerity and its strength. Faults it, of course, possesses. "She would rhyme moon to table," used to be said of her in jest; and certainly no more monstrous rhymes are to be found in all literature than some of those we come across in Mrs. Browning's poems. But her ruggedness was never the result of carelessness. It was deliberate, as her letters to Mr. Horne[1] show very clearly. She refused to sandpaper her muse. She disliked facile smoothness and artificial polish. In her very rejection of art she was an artist. She intended to produce a certain effect by certain means, and she succeeded; and her indifference to

1. Richard Henry Horne (1803–1884), poet and miscellaneous writer, who collaborated with Elizabeth Barrett on the essays *A New Spirit of the Age* (1844).

complete assonance in rhyme often gives a splendid richness to her verse, and brings into it a pleasurable element of surprise.

In philosophy she was a Platonist, in politics an Opportunist. She attached herself to no particular party. She loved the people when they were king-like, and kings when they showed themselves to be men. Of the real value and motive of poetry she had a most exalted idea. "Poetry," she says, in the preface of one of her volumes, "has been as serious a thing to me as life itself; and life has been a very serious thing. There has been no playing at skittles for me in either. I never mistook pleasure for the final cause of poetry, nor leisure for the hour of the poet. I have done my work so far, not as mere hand and head work apart from the personal being, but as the completest expression of that being to which I could attain."

It certainly is her completest expression, and through it she realises her fullest perfection. "The poet," she says elsewhere, "is at once richer and poorer than he used to be; he wears better broadcloth, but speaks no more oracles." These words give us the keynote to her view of the poet's mission. He was to utter Divine oracles, to be at once inspired prophet and holy priest; and as such we may, I think, without exaggeration, conceive her. She was a Sibyl delivering a message to the world, sometimes through stammering lips, and once at least with blinded eyes, yet always with the true fire and fervour of lofty and unshaken faith, always with the great raptures of a spiritual nature, the high ardours of an impassioned soul. As we read her best poems we feel that, though Apollo's shrine be empty and the bronze tripod overthrown, and the vale of Delphi desolate, still the Pythia is not dead. In our own age she has sung for us, and this land gave her new birth. Indeed, Mrs. Browning is the wisest of the Sibyls, wiser even than that mighty figure whom Michael Angelo has painted on the roof of the Sistine Chapel at Rome, poring over the scroll of mystery, and trying to decipher the secrets of Fate; for she realised that, while knowledge is power, suffering is part of knowledge.

To her influence, almost as much as to the higher education of women, I would be inclined to attribute the really remarkable awakening of woman's song that characterises the latter half of our century in England. No country has ever had so many poetesses at once. Indeed, when one remembers that the Greeks had only nine muses, one is sometimes apt to fancy that we have too many. And yet the work done by women in the sphere of poetry is really of a very high standard of excellence. In England we have always been prone to under-rate the value of tradition in literature. In our eagerness to find a new voice and a fresh mode of music, we have forgotten how beautiful Echo may be. We look first for individuality and personality, and these are, indeed, the chief characteristics of the masterpieces of our literature, either in prose or verse; but deliberate culture and a study of the best models, if united to an artistic temperament and a nature susceptible of exquisite impressions, may produce much that is admirable, much that is worthy of praise. It would be quite impossible to give a complete catalogue of all the women who since Mrs. Browning's day have tried lute and lyre. Mrs. Pfeiffer, Mrs. Hamilton King, Mrs. Augusta Webster, Graham Tomson, Miss Mary Robinson, Jean Ingelow, Miss May Kendall, Miss Nesbit, Miss May Probyn, Mrs. Craik, Mrs. Meynell, Miss Chapman, and many others have done really good work in poetry, either in the grave Dorian mode of thoughtful and intellectual verse, or in the light and graceful forms of old French song, or in the romantic manner of antique ballad, or in that "moment's monument," as Rossetti called it, the intense and concentrated sonnet. Occasionally one is tempted to wish that the quick, artistic faculty that women undoubtedly possess developed itself somewhat more in prose and somewhat less in verse. Poetry is for our highest moods, when we wish to be with the gods, and in our poetry nothing but the very best should satisfy us; but prose is for our daily bread, and the lack of good prose is one of the chief blots on our culture. French prose, even in the hands of the most ordinary writers, is always readable, but English prose is detestable. We have a few, a very few, masters, such as they are. We have Carlyle, who should not be imitated; and Mr. Pater, who, through the subtle perfection of his form, is inimitable absolutely; and Mr. Froude, who is useful; and Matthew Arnold, who is a model; and Mr. George Meredith, who is a warning; and Mr. Lang, who is the divine amateur; and Mr. Stevenson, who is the humane artist; and Mr. Ruskin, whose rhythm and colour and fine rhetoric and marvellous music of words are entirely unattainable. But the general prose that one reads in magazines and in newspapers is terribly dull and cumbrous, heavy in movement and uncouth or exaggerated in expression. Possibly some day our women of letters will apply themselves more definitely to prose.

Their light touch, and exquisite ear, and delicate sense of balance and proportion would be of no small service to us. I can fancy women bringing a new manner into our literature.

However, we have to deal here with women as poetesses, and it is interesting to note that, though Mrs. Browning's influence undoubtedly contributed very largely to the development of this new song-movement, if I may so term it, still there seems to have been never a time during the last three hundred years when the women of this kingdom did not cultivate, if not the art, at least the habit, of writing poetry.

Who the first English poetess was I cannot say. I believe it was the Abbess Juliana Berners, who lived in the fifteenth century; but I have no doubt that Mr. Freeman would be able at a moment's notice to produce some wonderful Saxon or Norman poetess, whose works cannot be read without a glossary, and even with its aid are completely unintelligible. For my own part, I am content with the Abbess Juliana, who wrote enthusiastically about hawking; and after her I would mention Anne Askew, who in prison and on the eve of her fiery martyrdom wrote a ballad that has, at any rate, a pathetic and historical interest. Queen Elizabeth's "most sweet and sententious ditty" on Mary Stuart is highly praised by Puttenham, a contemporary critic, as an example of "Exargasia, or the Gorgeous in Literature," which somehow seems a very suitable epithet for such a great Queen's poems. The term she applies to the unfortunate Queen of Scots, "the daughter of debate," has, of course, long since passed into literature. The Countess of Pembroke, Sir Philip Sidney's sister, was much admired as a poetess in her day.

In 1613 the "learned, virtuous, and truly noble ladie," Elizabeth Carew, published a *Tragedie of Marian, the Faire Queene of Jewry*, and a few years later the "noble ladie Diana Primrose" wrote *A Chain of Pearl*, which is a panegyric on the "peerless graces" of Gloriana. Mary Morpeth, the friend and admirer of Drummond of Hawthornden;

Lady Mary Wroth, to whom Ben Jonson dedicated *The Alchemist*; and the Princess Elizabeth the sister of Charles I, should also be mentioned.

After the Restoration women applied themselves with still greater ardour to the study of literature and the practice of poetry. Margaret, Duchess of Newcastle, was a true woman of letters, and some of her verses are extremely pretty and graceful. Mrs. Aphra Behn was the first Englishwoman who adopted literature as a regular profession. Mrs. Katharine Philips, according to Mr. Gosse, invented sentimentality. As she was praised by Dryden and mourned by Cowley, let us hope she may be forgiven. Keats came across her poems at Oxford when he was writing *Endymion*, and found in one of them "a most delicate fancy of the Fletcher kind"; but I fear nobody reads the Matchless Orinda now. Of Lady Winchelsea's *Nocturnal Reverie* Wordsworth said that, with the exception of Pope's *Windsor Forest*, it was the only poem of the period intervening between *Paradise Lost* and Thomson's *Seasons* that contained a single new image of external nature. Lady Rachel Russell, who may be said to have inaugurated the letter-writing literature of England; Eliza Haywood, who is immortalized by the badness of her work, and has a niche in *The Dunciad*; and the Marchioness of Wharton, whose poems Waller said he admired, are very remarkable types, the finest of them being, of course, the first named, who was a woman of heroic mould and of a most noble dignity of nature.

Indeed, though the English poetesses up to the time of Mrs. Browning cannot be said to have produced any work of absolute genius, they are certainly interesting figures, fascinating subjects for study. Amongst them we find Lady Mary Wortley Montague, who had all the caprice of Cleopatra, and whose letters are delightful reading; Mrs. Centlivre, who wrote one brilliant comedy; Lady Anne Barnard, whose *Auld Robin Gray* was described by Sir Walter Scott as "worth all the dialogues Corydon and Phillis have together spoken from the days of Theocritus downwards," and is certainly a very beautiful and touching poem; Esther Vanhomrigh and Hester Johnson, the Vanessa and the Stella of Dean Swift's life; Mrs. Thrale, the friend of the great lexicographer; the worthy Mrs. Barbauld; the excellent Mrs. Hannah More; the industrious

Joanna Baillie; the admirable Mrs. Chapone, whose *Ode to Solitude* always fills me with the wildest passion for society, and who will at least be remembered as the patroness of the establishment at which Becky Sharp was educated; Miss Anna Seward, who was called "The Swan of Lichfield"; poor L. E. L., whom Disraeli described in one of his clever letters to his sister as "the personification of Brompton—pink satin dress, white satin shoes, red cheeks, snub nose, and her hair *à la* Sappho"; Mrs. Ratcliffe, who introduced the romantic novel, and has consequently much to answer for; the beautiful Duchess of Devonshire, of whom Gibbon said that she was "made for something better than a Duchess"; the two wonderful sisters, Lady Dufferin and Mrs. Norton; Mrs. Tighe, whose *Psyche* Keats read with pleasure; Constantia Grierson, a marvellous blue-stocking in her time; Mrs. Hemans; pretty, charming "Perdita," who flirted alternately with poetry and the Prince Regent, played divinely in the *Winter's Tale*, was brutally attacked by Gifford, and has left us a pathetic little poem on the Snowdrop; and Emily Brontë, whose poems are instinct with tragic power, and seem often on the verge of being great.

Old fashions in literature are not so pleasant as old fashions in dress. I like the costume of the age of powder better than the poetry of the age of Pope. But if one adopts the historical standpoint—and this is, indeed, the only standpoint from which we can ever form a fair estimate of work that is not absolutely of the highest order—we cannot fail to see that many of the English poetesses who preceded Mrs. Browning were women of no ordinary talent, and that if the majority of them looked upon poetry simply as a department of *belles lettres*, so in most cases did their contemporaries. Since Mrs. Browning's day our woods have become full of singing birds, and I venture to ask them to apply themselves more to prose and less to song, it is not that I like poetical prose, but that I love the prose of poets.

*Queen*, December 8, 1888.

# Political Socialists

*Review of* Chants of Labour: A Song-Book of the People, *edited by Edward Carpenter (1844-1929), a disciple of Thoreau and Whitman, and poet, socialist, and essayist.*

Mr. Stopford Brooke[1] said some time ago that Socialism and the socialistic spirit would give our poets nobler and loftier themes for song, would widen their sympathies and enlarge the horizon of their vision and would touch, with the fire and fervour of a new faith, lips that had else been silent, hearts that but for this fresh gospel had been cold. What Art gains from contemporary events is always a fascinating problem and a problem that is not easy to solve. It is, however, certain that Socialism starts well equipped. She has her poets and her painters, her art lecturers and her cunning designers, her powerful orators and her clever writers. If she fails it will not be for lack of expression. If she succeeds her triumph will not be a triumph of mere brute force. The first thing that strikes one, as one looks over the list of contributors to Mr. Edward Carpenter's *Chants of Labour*, is the curious variety of their several occupations, the wide differences of social position that exist between them, and the strange medley of men whom a common passion has for the moment united. The editor is a "Science lecturer"; he is followed by a draper and a porter; then we have two late Eton masters and then two boot-makers; and these are, in their turn, succeeded by an ex-Lord Mayor of Dublin, a bookbinder, a photographer, a steel-worker and an authoress. On one page we have a journalist, a draughtsman and a music-teacher: and on another a Civil servant, a machine fitter, a medical student, a cabinet-maker and a minister of the Church of Scotland. Certainly, it is no ordinary movement

1. Stopford Brooke (1832–1916) clergyman, critic, biographer, and anthologist.

that can bind together in close brotherhood men of such dissimilar pursuits, and when we mention that Mr. William Morris is one of the singers, and that Mr. Walter Crane[2] has designed the cover and frontispiece of the book, we cannot but feel that, as we pointed out before, Socialism starts well equipped.

As for the songs themselves, some of them, to quote from the editor's preface, are "purely revolutionary, others are Christian in tone; there are some that might be called merely material in their tendency, while many are of a highly ideal and visionary character." This is, on the whole, very promising. It shows that Socialism is not going to allow herself to be trammelled by any hard and fast creed or to be stereotyped into an iron formula. She welcomes many and multiform natures. She rejects none and has room for all. She has the attraction of a wonderful personality and touches the heart of one and the brain of another, and draws this man by his hatred of injustice, and his neighbour by his faith in the future, and a third, it may be, by his love of art or by his wild worship of a lost and buried past. And all of this is well. For, to make men Socialists is nothing, but to make Socialism human is a great thing.

They are not of any very high literary value, these poems that have been so dexterously set to music. They are meant to be sung, not to be read. They are rough, direct and vigorous, and the tunes are stirring and familiar. Indeed, almost any mob could warble them with ease. The transpositions that have been made are rather amusing. *'Twas in Trafalgar Square* is set to the tune of *'Twas in Trafalgar's Bay; Up, Ye People!* a very revolutionary song by Mr. John Gregory, boot-maker, with a refrain of

> Up, ye People! or down into your graves!
> Cowards ever will be slaves!

is to be sung to the tune of *Rule, Britannia!* the old melody of *The Vicar of Bray* is to accompany the new *Ballade of Law and Order*— which, however, is not a ballade at all—and to the air of *Here's to the Maiden of Bashful Fifteen* the democracy of the future is to thunder forth one of Mr. T. D. Sullivan's most powerful and pathetic

2. Walter Crane (1845–1915), painter and illustrator, was at first identified with the Pre-Raphaelites and later with the arts and crafts movement of William Morris.

lyrics. It is clear that the Socialists intend to carry on the musical education of the people simultaneously with their education in political science and, here as elsewhere, they seem to be entirely free from any narrow bias or formal prejudice. Mendelssohn is followed by Moody and Sankey; the *Wacht am Rhein* stands side by side with the *Marseillaise*; *Lillibulero*, a chorus from *Norma*, *John Brown* and an air from Beethoven's *Ninth Symphony* are all equally delightful to them. They sing the National Anthem in Shelley's version and chant William Morris's *Voice of Toil* to the flowing numbers of *Ye Banks and Braes of Bonny Doon*. Victor Hugo talks somewhere of the terrible cry of "Le Tigre Populaire," but it is evident from Mr. Carpenter's book that should the Revolution ever break out in England we shall have no inarticulate roar but, rather, pleasant glees and graceful part-songs. The change is certainly for the better. Nero fiddled while Rome was burning—at least, inaccurate historians say he did; but it is for the building up of an eternal city that the Socialists of our day are making music, and they have complete confidence in the art instincts of the people.

> They say that the people are brutal—
>   That their instincts of beauty are dead—
> Were it so, shame on those who condemn them
>   To the desperate struggle for bread.
> But they lie in their throats when they say it,
>   For the people are tender at heart,
> And a wellspring of beauty lies hidden
>   Beneath their life's fever and smart,

is a stanza from one of the poems in this volume, and the feeling expressed in these words is paramount everywhere. The Reformation gained much from the use of popular hymn-tunes, and the Socialists seem determined to gain by similar means a similar hold upon the people. However, they must not be too sanguine about the result. The walls of Thebes rose up to the sound of music, and Thebes was a very dull city indeed.

*Pall Mall Gazette*, February 15, 1889.

# Some Literary Notes
# [The New Obscurity in Poetry]

*This selection covered a number of minor poets, quoting liberally from them, but Wilde's major points were made in the opening paragraphs extracted here.*

Miss Caroline Fitz Gerald's volume of poems, *Venetia Victrix*, is dedicated to Mr. Robert Browning, and in the poem that gives its title to the book it is not difficult to see traces of Mr. Browning's influence. *Venetia Victrix* is a powerful psychological study of a man's soul, a vivid presentation of a terrible, fiery-coloured moment in a marred and incomplete life. It is sometimes complex and intricate in expression, but then the subject itself is intricate and complex. Plastic simplicity of outline may render for us the visible aspect of life; it is different when we come to deal with those secrets which self-consciousness alone contains, and which self-consciousness itself can but half reveal. Action takes place in the sunlight, but the soul works in the dark.

There is something curiously interesting in the marked tendency of modern poetry to become obscure. Many critics, writing with their eyes fixed on the masterpieces of past literature, have ascribed this tendency to wilfulness and to affectation. Its origin is rather to be found in the complexity of the new problems, and in the fact that self-consciousness is not yet adequate to explain the contents of the Ego. In Mr. Browning's poems, as in life itself which has suggested, or rather necessitated, the new method, thought seems to proceed not on logical lines, but on lines of passion. The unity of the individual is being expressed through its inconsistencies and its contradictions. In a strange twilight man is seeking for himself, and when he has found his own image, he cannot understand it. Objective forms of art, such as sculpture and the drama, sufficed one for the perfect presentation of life; they can no longer so suffice. * * *

*Woman's World*, May, 1889.

# II. ON SHAKESPEARE

# Shakespeare on Scenery

I have often heard people wonder what Shakespeare would say, could he see Mr. Irving's production of his *Much Ado About Nothing*, or Mr. Wilson Barrett's[1] setting of his *Hamlet*. Would he take pleasure in the glory of the scenery and the marvel of the colour? Would he be interested in the Cathedral of Messina, and the battlements of Elsinore? Or would he be indifferent, and say the play, and the play only, is the thing?

Speculations like these are always pleasurable, and in the present case happen to be profitable also. For it is not difficult to see what Shakespeare's attitude would be; not difficult, that is to say, if one reads Shakespeare himself, instead of reading merely what is written about him.

Speaking, for instance, directly, as the manager of a London theatre, through the lips of the chorus in *Henry V*, he complains of the smallness of the stage on which he has to produce the pageant of a big historical play, and of the want of scenery which obliges him to cut out many of its most picturesque incidents, apologises for the scanty number of supers who had to play the soldiers, and for the shabbiness of the properties, and, finally, expresses his regret at being unable to bring on real horses.

In the *Midsummer Night's Dream*, again, he gives us a most amusing picture of the straits to which theatrical managers of his day were reduced by the want of proper scenery. In fact, it is impossible to read him without seeing that he is constantly protesting against the two special limitations of the Elizabethan stage—the lack of suitable scenery, and the fashion of men playing women's parts, just as he protests against other difficulties with which managers of theatres have still to contend, such as actors who do

1. Wilson Barrett (1846–1904), actor, playwright (*The Sign of the Cross*), and theater manager.

115

not understand their words; actors who miss their cues; actors who overact their parts; actors who mouth; actors who gag; actors who play to the gallery, and amateur actors.

And, indeed, a great dramatist, as he was, could not but have felt very much hampered at being obliged continually to interrupt the progress of a play in order to send on some one to explain to the audience that the scene was to be changed to a particular place on the entrance of a particular character, and after his exit to somewhere else; that the stage was to represent the deck of a ship in a storm, or the interior of a Greek temple, or the streets of a certain town, to all of which inartistic devices Shakespeare is reduced, and for which he always amply apologises. Besides this clumsy method, Shakespeare had two other substitutes for scenery— the hanging out of a placard, and his descriptions. The first of these could hardly have satisfied his passion for picturesqueness and his feeling for beauty, and certainly did not satisfy the dramatic critic of his day. But as regards the description, to those of us who look on Shakespeare not merely as a playwright but as a poet, and who enjoy reading him at home just as much as we enjoy seeing him acted, it may be a matter of congratulation that he had not at his command such skilled machinists as are in use now at the Princess's and at the Lyceum. For had Cleopatra's barge, for instance, been a structure of canvas and Dutch metal, it would probably have been painted over or broken up after the withdrawal of the piece, and, even had it survived to our own day, would, I am afraid, have become extremely shabby by this time. Whereas now the beaten gold of its poop is still bright, and the purple of its sails still beautiful; its silver oars are not tired of keeping time to the music of the flutes they follow, nor the Nereid's flower-soft hands of touching its silken tackle; the mermaid still lies at its helm, and still on its deck stand the boys with their coloured fans. Yet lovely as all Shakespeare's descriptive passages are, a description is in its essence undramatic. Theatrical audiences are far more impressed by what they look at than by what they listen to; and the modern dramatist, in having the surroundings of his play visibly presented to the audience when the curtain rises, enjoys an advantage for which Shakespeare often expresses his desire. It is true that Shakespeare's descriptions are not what descriptions are in modern plays—accounts of what the audience can observe for themselves; they are the imaginative method by which he creates in the mind of the spectators the image of that which he desires them to see. Still, the quality of the drama is action. It is always dangerous to pause for picturesqueness. And the introduction of self-explanatory scenery enables the modern method to be far more direct, while the loveliness of form and colour which it gives us, seems to me often to create an artistic temperament in the audience, and to produce that joy in beauty for beauty's sake, without which the great masterpieces of art can never be understood, to which, and to which only, are they ever revealed.

To talk of the passion of a play being hidden by the paint, and of sentiment being killed by scenery, is mere emptiness and folly of words. A noble play, nobly mounted, gives us double artistic pleasure. The eye as well as the ear is gratified, and the whole nature is made exquisitely receptive of the influence of imaginative work. And as regards a bad play, have we not all seen large audiences lured by the loveliness of scenic effect into listening to rhetoric posing as poetry, and to vulgarity doing duty for realism? Whether this be good or evil for the public I will not here discuss, but it is evident that the playwright, at any rate, never suffers.

Indeed, the artist who really has suffered through the modern mounting of plays is not the dramatist at all, but the scene-painter proper. He is rapidly being displaced by the stage-carpenter. Now and then, at Drury Lane, I have seen beautiful old front cloths let down, as perfect as pictures some of them, and pure painter's work, and there are many which we all remember at other theatres, in front of which some dialogue was reduced to graceful dumb-show through the hammer and tin-tacks behind. But as a rule the stage is overcrowded with enormous properties, which are not merely far more expensive and cumbersome than scene-paintings, but far less beautiful, and far less true. Properties kill perspective. A painted door is more like a real door than a real door is itself, for the proper conditions of light and shade can be given to it; and the excessive use of built up structures always makes the stage too glaring, for as they have to be lit from behind, as well as from the front, the gas-jets become the absolute light of the scene instead of the means merely by which we perceive the conditions of light and shadow which the painter has desired to show us.

So, instead of bemoaning the position of the playwright, it were better for the critics to exert whatever influence they may possess towards restoring the scene-painter to his proper position as an artist, and not allowing him to be built over by the property man, or hammered to death by the carpenter. I have never seen any reason myself why such artists as Mr. Beverley, Mr. Walter Hann, and Mr. Telbin should not be entitled to become Academicians. They have certainly as good a claim as have many of those R.A.'s whose total inability to paint we can see every May for a shilling.

And lastly, let those critics who hold up for our admiration the simplicity of the Elizabethan Stage, remember that they are lauding a condition of things against which Shakespeare himself, in the spirit of a true artist, always strongly protested.

*Dramatic Review*, March 14, 1885.

# *Hamlet* at the Lyceum

It sometimes happens that at a *première* in London the least enjoyable part of the performance is the play. I have seen many audiences more interesting than the actors, and have often heard better dialogue in the *foyer* than I have on the stage. At the Lyceum, however, this is rarely the case, and when the play is a play of Shakespeare's, and among its exponents are Mr. Irving and Miss Ellen Terry,[1] we turn from the gods in the gallery and from the goddesses in the stalls, to enjoy the charm of the production, and to take delight in the art. The lions are behind the footlights and not in front of them when we have a noble tragedy nobly acted. And I have rarely witnessed such enthusiasm as that which greeted on last Saturday night the two artists I have mentioned. I would like, in fact, to use the word ovation, but a pedantic professor has recently informed us, with the Batavian buoyancy of misapplied learning, that this expression is not to be employed except when a sheep has been sacrificed. At the Lyceum last week I need hardly say nothing so dreadful occurred. The only inartistic incident of the evening was the hurling of a bouquet from a box at Mr. Irving while he was engaged in pourtraying the agony of Hamlet's death, and the pathos

1. Born John Henry Brodribb, Sir Henry Irving (1838–1905) was one of the last of the great English actor-managers, dominating the English stage the last thirty years of his life with the great contemporary and classic rhetorical roles. Among his prestigious, yet controversial, roles were Hamlet, King Lear, Shylock, and Henry VIII, while he also played the leads in now forgotten plays of his era, such as *The Bells, Becket, The Lady of Lyons,* and *Madame Sans-Gêne.* His most famous partnership, on and off stage, was with Ellen Terry (1847–1928), who shared leading roles with him from 1878 until 1902, accompanying him on his American tours and playing in revivals of Shakespeare as well as Victorian dramas. Her most lasting fame may rest in her lengthy correspondence with Bernard Shaw, who wrote his Lady Cecily role in *Captain Brassbound's Conversion* for her. Four of her lectures on Shakespeare were published in 1931, the same year in which the Shaw-Terry letters were published.

of his parting with Horatio. The Dramatic College might take up the
education of spectators as well as that of players, and teach people
that there is a proper moment for the throwing of flowers as well as
a proper method.

As regards Mr. Irving's own performance, it has been already so
elaborately criticised and described, from his business with the
supposed pictures in the closet scene down to his use of "peacock"
for "paddock," that little remains to be said; nor, indeed, does a
Lyceum audience require the interposition of the dramatic critic
in order to understand or to appreciate the Hamlet of this great
actor. I call him a great actor because he brings to the interpretation
of a work of art the two qualities which we in this century so much
desire, the qualities of personality and of perfection. A few years
ago it seemed to many, and perhaps rightly, that the personality
overshadowed the art. No such criticism would be fair now. The
somewhat harsh angularity of movement and faulty pronunciation
have been replaced by exquisite grace of gesture and clear precision
of word, where such precision is necessary. For delightful as good
elocution is, few things are so depressing as to hear a passionate
passage recited instead of being acted. The quality of a fine performance is its life more than its learning, and every word in a play
has a musical as well as an intellectual value, and must be made
expressive of a certain emotion. So it does not seem to me that in all
parts of a play perfect pronunciation is necessarily dramatic. When
the words are "wild and whirling," the expression of them must be
wild and whirling also. Mr. Irving, I think, manages his voice with
singular art; it was impossible to discern a false note or wrong
intonation in his dialogue or his soliloquies, and his strong dramatic
power, his realistic power as an actor, is as effective as ever. A great
critic at the beginning of this century said that Hamlet is the most
difficult part to personate on the stage, that it is like the attempt to
"embody a shadow." I cannot say that I agree with this idea.
Hamlet seems to me essentially a good acting part, and in Mr.
Irving's performance of it there is that combination of poetic grace
with absolute reality which is so eternally delightful. Indeed, if the
words easy and difficult have any meaning at all in matters of art,
I would be inclined to say that Ophelia is the more difficult part.

She has, I mean, less material by which to produce her effects. She is the occasion of the tragedy, but she is neither its heroine nor its chief victim. She is swept away by circumstances, and gives the opportunity for situation, of which she is not herself the climax, and which she does not herself command. And of all the parts which Miss Terry has acted in her brilliant career, there is none in which her infinite powers of pathos and her imaginative and creative faculty are more shown than in her Ophelia. Miss Terry is one of those rare artists who needs for her dramatic effect no elaborate dialogue, and for whom the simplest words are sufficient. "I love you not," says Hamlet, and all that Ophelia answers is, "I was the more deceived." These are not very grand words to read, but as Miss Terry gave them in acting they seemed to be the highest possible expression of Ophelia's character. Beautiful, too, was the quick remorse she conveyed by her face and gesture the moment she had lied to Hamlet and told him her father was at home. This I thought a masterpiece of good acting, and her mad scene was wonderful beyond all description. The secrets of Melpomene are known to Miss Terry as well as the secrets of Thalia. As regards the rest of the company there is always a high standard at the Lyceum, but some particular mention should be made of Mr. Alexander's brilliant performance of Laertes. Mr. Alexander has a most effective presence, a charming voice, and a capacity for wearing lovely costumes with ease and elegance. Indeed, in the latter respect his only rival was Mr. Norman Forbes, who played either Guildenstern or Rosencrantz very gracefully. I believe one of our budding Hazlitts is preparing a volume to be entitled "Great Guildensterns and Remarkable Rosencrantzes," but I have never been able myself to discern any difference between these two charac- ters. They are, I think, the only characters Shakespeare has not cared to individualise. Whichever of the two, however, Mr. Forbes acted, he acted it well. Only one point in Mr. Alexander's perform- ance seemed to me open to question, that was his kneeling during the whole of Polonius's speech. For this I see no necessity at all, and it makes the scene look less natural than it should—gives it, I mean, too formal an air. However, the performance was most spirited and gave great pleasure to every one. Mr. Alexander is an artist from whom much will be expected, and I have no doubt he will give us much that is fine and noble. He seems to have all the qualifications for a good actor.

There is just one other character I should like to notice. The First Player seemed to me to act far too well. He should act very badly. The First Player, besides his position in the dramatic evolution of the tragedy, is Shakespeare's caricature of the ranting actor of his day, just as the passage he recites is Shakespeare's own parody on the dull plays of some of his rivals. The whole point of Hamlet's advice to the players seems to me to be lost unless the Player himself has been guilty of the fault which Hamlet reprehends, unless he has sawn the air with his hand, mouthed his lines, torn his passion to tatters, and out-Heroded Herod. The very sensibility which Hamlet notices in the actor, such as his real tears and the like, is not the quality of a good artist. The part should be played after the manner of a provincial tragedian. It is meant to be a satire, and to play it well is to play it badly. The scenery and costumes were excellent with the exception of the King's dress, which was coarse in colour and tawdry in effect. And the Player Queen should have come in boy's attire to Elsinore.

However, last Saturday night was not a night for criticism. The theatre was filled with those who desired to welcome Mr. Irving back to his own theatre, and we were all delighted at his re-appearance among us. I hope that some time will elapse before he and Miss Terry cross again that disappointing Atlantic Ocean.

*Dramatic Review*, May 9, 1885.

# *Henry the Fourth* at Oxford

I have been told that the ambition of every Dramatic Club is to act *Henry IV*. I am not surprised. The spirit of comedy is as fervent in this play as is the spirit of chivalry; it is an heroic pageant as well as an heroic poem, and like most of Shakespeare's historical dramas it contains an extraordinary number of thoroughly good acting parts, each of which is absolutely individual in character, and each of which contributes to the evolution of the plot.

Rumour, from time to time, has brought in tidings of a proposed production by the banks of the Cam, but it seems at the last moment *Box and Cox*[1] has always had to be substituted in the bill.

To Oxford belongs the honour of having been the first to present on the stage this noble play, and the production which I saw last week was in every way worthy of that lovely town, that mother of sweetness and of light. For, in spite of the roaring of the young lions at the Union, and the screaming of the rabbits in the home of the vivisector, in spite of Keble College, and the tramways, and the sporting prints, Oxford still remains the most beautiful thing in England, and nowhere else are life and art so exquisitely blended, so perfectly made one. Indeed, in most other towns art has often to present herself in the form of a reaction against the sordid ugliness of ignoble lives, but at Oxford she comes to us as an exquisite flower born of the beauty of life and expressive of life's joy. She finds her home by the Isis as once she did by the Ilissus; the Magdalen walks and the Magdalen cloisters are as dear to her as were ever the silver olives of Colonus and the golden gateway of the house of Pallas: she covers with fanlike tracery the vaulted entrance to Christ Church Hall, and looks out from the windows of Merton;

---

1. A play (1847) by John M. Morton about two men by the names of Box and Cox who occupy the same room, though neither knows it, one working in the daytime and the other having a night job.

her feet have stirred the Cumnor cowslips, and she gathers fritillaries in the river-fields. To her the clamour of the schools and the dulness of the lecture-room are a weariness and a vexation of spirit; she seeks not to define virtue, and cares little for the categories; she smiles on the swift athlete whose plastic grace has pleased her, and rejoices in the young Barbarians at their games; she watches the rowers from the reedy bank and gives myrtle to her lovers, and laurel to her poets, and rue to those who talk wisely in the street; she makes the earth lovely to all who dream with Keats; she opens high heaven to all who soar with Shelley; and turning away her head from pedant, proctor and Philistine, she has welcomed to her shrine a band of youthful actors, knowing that they have sought with much ardour for the stern secret of Melpomene, and caught with much gladness the sweet laughter of Thalia. And to me this ardour and this gladness were the two most fascinating qualities of the Oxford performance, as indeed they are qualities which are necessary to any fine dramatic production. For without quick and imaginative observation of life the most beautiful play becomes dull in presentation, and what is not conceived in delight by the actor can give no delight at all to others.

I know that there are many who consider that Shakespeare is more for the study than for the stage. With this view I do not for a moment agree. Shakespeare wrote the plays to be acted, and we have no right to alter the form which he himself selected for the full expression of his work. Indeed, many of the beauties of that work can be adequately conveyed to us only through the actor's art. As I sat in the Town Hall of Oxford the other night, the majesty of the mighty lines of the play seemed to me to gain new music from the clear young voices that uttered them, and the ideal grandeur of the heroism to be made more real to the spectators by the chivalrous bearing, the noble gesture and the fine passion of its exponents. Even the dresses had their dramatic value. Their archaeological accuracy gave us, immediately on the rise of the curtain, a perfect picture of the time. As the knights and nobles moved across the stage in the flowing robes of peace and in the burnished steel of battle, we needed no dreary chorus to tell us in what age or land the play's action was passing, for the fifteenth century in all the dignity and grace of its apparel was living actually before us, and the delicate harmonies of colour struck from the first a dominant note of beauty which added to the intellectual realism of archaeology the sensuous charm of art.

As for individual actors, Mr. Mackinnon's Prince Hal was a most gay and graceful performance, lit here and there with charming touches of princely dignity and of noble feeling. Mr. Coleridge's Falstaff was full of delightful humour, though perhaps at times he did not take us sufficiently into his confidence. An audience looks at a tragedian, but a comedian looks at his audience. However, he gave much pleasure to every one, and Mr. Bourchier's Hotspur was really most remarkable. Mr. Bourchier has a fine stage presence, a beautiful voice, and produces his effects by a method as dramatically impressive as it is artistically right. Once or twice he seemed to me to spoil his last line by walking through it. The part of Harry Percy is one full of climaxes which must not be let slip. But still there was always a freedom and spirit in his style which was very pleasing, and his delivery of the colloquial passages I thought excellent, notably of that in the first act:

> What d' ye call the place?
> A plague upon 't—it is in Gloucestershire;
> 'Twas where the madcap duke his uncle kept,
> His uncle York;

lines by the way in which Kemble made a great effect. Mr. Bourchier has the opportunity of a fine career on the English stage, and I hope he will take advantage of it. Among the minor parts in the play Glendower, Mortimer and Sir Richard Vernon were capitally acted, Worcester was a performance of some subtlety, Mrs. Woods was a charming Lady Percy, and Lady Edward Spencer Churchill, as Mortimer's wife, made us all believe that we understood Welsh. Her dialogue and her song were most pleasing bits of artistic realism which fully accounted for the Celtic chair at Oxford.

But though I have mentioned particular actors, the real value of the whole representation was to be found in its absolute unity, in its delicate sense of proportion, and in that breadth of effect which is to be got only by the most careful elaboration of detail. I have rarely seen a production better stage-managed. Indeed, I hope that the University will take some official notice of this delightful work of art. Why should not degrees be granted for good acting? Are they not given to those who misunderstand Plato and who mistranslate Aristotle? And should the artist be passed over? No. To Prince Hal, Hotspur and Falstaff, D.C.L.'s should be gracefully offered. I feel sure they would be gracefully accepted. To the rest of the company the crimson or the sheep-skin hood might be assigned *honoris causa* to the eternal confusion of the Philistine, and the rage of the industrious and the dull. Thus would Oxford confer honour on herself, and the artist be placed in his proper position. However, whether or not Convocation recognises the claims of culture, I hope that the Oxford Dramatic Society will produce every summer for us some noble play like *Henry IV*. For, in plays of this kind, plays which deal with bygone times, there is always this peculiar charm, that they combine in one exquisite presentation the passions that are living with the picturesqueness that is dead. And when we have the modern spirit given to us in an antique form, the very remoteness of that form can be made a method of increased realism. This was Shakespeare's own attitude towards the ancient world, this is the attitude we in this century should adopt towards his plays, and with a feeling akin to this it seemed to me that these brilliant young Oxonians were working. If it was so, their aim is the right one. For while we look to the dramatist to give romance to realism, we ask of the actor to give realism to romance.

*Dramatic Review*, May 23, 1885.

# *As You Like It* at Coombe House

In Théophile Gautier's first novel, that golden book of spirit and sense, that holy writ of beauty, there is a most fascinating account of an amateur performance of *As You Like It* in the large orangery of a French country house. Yet, lovely as Gautier's description is, the real presentation of the play last week at Coombe seemed to me lovelier still, for not merely were there present in it all those elements of poetry and picturesqueness which *le maître impeccable* so desired, but to them was added also the exquisite charm of the open woodland and the delightful freedom of the open air. Nor indeed could the Pastoral Players have made a more fortunate selection of a play. A tragedy under the same conditions would have been impossible. For tragedy is the exaggeration of the individual, and nature thinks nothing of dwarfing a hero by a holly bush, and reducing a heroine to a mere effect of colour. The subtleties also of facial expressions are in the open air almost entirely lost; and while this would be a serious defect in the presentation of a play which deals immediately with psychology, in the case of a comedy, where the situations predominate over the characters, we do not feel it nearly so much; and Shakespeare himself seems to have clearly recognised this difference, for while he had *Hamlet* and *Macbeth* always played by artificial light he acted *As You Like It* and the rest of his comedies *en plein jour*.

The condition then under which this comedy was produced by Lady Archibald Campbell and Mr. Godwin[1] did not place any great limitations on the actor's art, and increased tenfold the value of the play as a picture. Through an alley of white hawthorn and

---

1. Edward William Godwin (1833–1886), architect and theatrical designer, lived with Ellen Terry from 1868 to 1875, while she was technically still married to artist G. F. Watts. Two children were born of the relationship, Edith and Gordon Craig.

gold laburnum we passed into the green pavilion that served as the theatre, the air sweet with odour of the lilac and with the blackbird's song; and when the curtain fell into its trench of flowers, and the play commenced, we saw before us a real forest, and we knew it to be Arden. For with whoop and shout, up through the rustling fern came the foresters trooping, the banished Duke took his seat beneath the tall elm, and as his lords lay around him on the grass, the rich melody of Shakespeare's blank verse began to reach our ears. And all through the performance this delightful sense of joyous woodland life was sustained, and even when the scene was left empty for the shepherd to drive his flock across the sward, or for Rosalind to school Orlando in love-making, far away we could hear the shrill halloo of the hunter, and catch now and then the faint music of some distant horn. One distinct dramatic advantage was gained by the *mise en scène*. The abrupt exits and entrances, which are necessitated on the real stage by the inevitable limitations of space, were in many cases done away with, and we saw the characters coming gradually towards us through brake and underwood, or passing away down the slope till they were lost in some deep recess of the forest; the effect of distance thus gained being largely increased by the faint wreaths of blue mist that floated at times across the background. Indeed I never saw an illustration at once so perfect and so practical of the aesthetic value of smoke.

As for the players themselves, the pleasing naturalness of their method harmonised delightfully with their natural surroundings. Those of them who were amateurs were too artistic to be stagey, and those who were actors too experienced to be artificial. The humorous sadness of Jaques, that philosopher in search of sensation, found a perfect exponent in Mr. Hermann Vezin. Touchstone has been so often acted as a low comedy part that Mr. Elliott's rendering of the swift sententious fool was a welcome change, and a more graceful and winning Phebe than Mrs. Plowden, a more tender Celia than Miss Schletter, a more realistic Audrey than Miss Fulton, I have never seen. Rosalind suffered a good deal through the omission of the first act; we saw, I mean, more of the saucy boy than we did of the noble girl; and through the *persiflage* always told, the poetry was often lost; still Miss Calhoun gave much pleasure;

and Lady Archibald Campbell's Orlando was a really remarkable performance. Too melancholy some seemed to think it. Yet is not Orlando lovesick? Too dreamy, I heard it said. Yet Orlando is a poet. And even admitting that the vigour of the lad who tripped up the Duke's wrestler was hardly sufficiently emphasised, still in the low music of Lady Archibald Campbell's voice, and in the strange beauty of her movements and gestures, there was a wonderful fascination, and the visible presence of romance quite consoled me for the possible absence of robustness. Among the other characters should be mentioned Mr. Claude Ponsonby's First Lord, Mr. De Cordova's Corin (a bit of excellent acting), and the Silvius of Mr. Webster.

As regards the costumes the colour scheme was very perfect. Brown and green were the dominant notes, and yellow was most artistically used. There were, however, two distinct discords. Touchstone's motley was far too glaring, and the crude white of Rosalind's bridal raiment in the last act was absolutely displeasing. A contrast may be striking but should never be harsh. And lovely in colour as Mrs. Plowden's dress was, a sort of panegyric on a pansy, I am afraid that in Shakespeare's Arden there were no Chelsea China Shepherdesses, and I am sure that the romance of Phebe does not need to be intensified by any reminiscences of porcelain. Still, *As You Like It* has probably never been so well mounted, nor costumes worn with more ease and simplicity. Not the least charming part of the whole production was the music, which was under the direction of the Rev. Arthur Batson. The boys' voices were quite exquisite, and Mr. Walsham sang with much spirit.

On the whole the Pastoral Players are to be warmly congratulated on the success of their representation, and to the artistic sympathies of Lady Archibald Campbell, and the artistic knowledge of Mr. Godwin, I am indebted for a most delightful afternoon. Few things are so pleasurable as to be able by an hour's drive to exchange Piccadilly for Parnassus.

*Dramatic Review*, June 6, 1885.

# *Twelfth Night* at Oxford

On Saturday last the new theatre at Oxford was opened by the University Dramatic Society. The play selected was Shakespeare's delightful comedy of *Twelfth Night*, a play eminently suitable for performance by a club, as it contains so many good acting parts. Shakespeare's tragedies may be made for a single star, but his comedies are made for a galaxy of constellations. In the first he deals with the pathos of the individual, in the second he gives us a picture of life. The Oxford undergraduates, then, are to be congratulated on the selection of the play, and the result fully justified their choice. Mr. Bourchier as Festa the clown was easy, graceful and joyous, as fanciful as his dress and as funny as his bauble. The beautiful songs which Shakespeare has assigned to this character were rendered by him as charmingly as they were dramatically. To act singing is quite as great an art as to sing. Mr. Letchmere Stuart was a delightful Sir Andrew, and gave much pleasure to the audience. One may hate the villains of Shakespeare, but one cannot help loving his fools. Mr. Macpherson was, perhaps, hardly equal to such an immortal part as that of Sir Toby Belch, though there was much that was clever in his performance. Mr. Lindsay threw new and unexpected light on the character of Fabian, and Mr. Clark's Malvolio was a most remarkable piece of acting. What a difficult part Malvolio is! Shakespeare undoubtedly meant us to laugh all through at the pompous steward, and to join in the practical joke upon him, and yet how impossible not to feel a good deal of sympathy with him! Perhaps in this century we are too altruistic to be really artistic. Hazlitt says somewhere that poetical justice is done him in the uneasiness which Olivia suffers on account of her mistaken attachment to Orsino, as her insensibility to the violence of the Duke's passion is atoned for by the discovery of Viola's concealed love for him; but it is difficult not to feel Malvolio's treatment is unnecessarily harsh. Mr. Clark, however, gave a very clever rendering, full of subtle touches. If I ventured on a bit of advice, which I feel most reluctant to do, it would be to the effect that while one should always study the method of a great artist, one should never imitate his manner. The manner of an artist is essentially individual, the method of an artist is absolutely universal. The first is personality, which no one should copy; the second is perfection, which all should aim at. Miss Arnold was a most sprightly Maria, and Miss Farmer a dignified Olivia; but as Viola Mrs. Bewicke was hardly successful. Her manner was too boisterous and her method too modern. Where there is violence there is no Viola, where there is no illusion there is no Illyria, and where there is no style there is no Shakespeare. Mr. Higgins looked the part of Sebastian to perfection, and some of the minor characters were excellently played by Mr. Adderley, Mr. King-Harman, Mr. Coningsby Disraeli and Lord Albert Osborne. On the whole, the performance reflected much credit on the Dramatic Society; indeed, its excellence was such that I am led to hope that the University will some day have a theatre of its own, and that proficiency in scene-painting will be regarded as a necessary qualification for the Slade Professorship. On the stage, literature returns to life and archaeology becomes art. A fine theatre is a temple where all the muses may meet, a second Parnassus, and the dramatic spirit, though she has long tarried at Cambridge, seems now to be migrating to Oxford.

> Thebes did her green unknowing youth engage;
> She chooses Athens in her riper age.

*Dramatic Review*, February 20, 1886.

# The Truth of Masks

In many of the somewhat violent attacks that have recently been made on that splendour of mounting which now characterises our Shakespearian revivals in England, it seems to have been tacitly assumed by the critics that Shakespeare himself was more or less indifferent to the costume of his actors, and that, could he see Mrs. Langtry's[1] production of *Antony and Cleopatra*, he would probably say that the play, and the play only, is the thing, and that everything else is leather and prunella. While, as regards any historical accuracy in dress, Lord Lytton,[2] in an article in the *Nineteenth Century*, has laid it down as a dogma of art that archaeology is entirely out of place in the presentation of any of Shakespeare's plays, and the attempt to introduce it one of the stupidest pedantries of an age of prigs.

Lord Lytton's position I shall examine later on; but, as regards the theory that Shakespeare did not busy himself much about the costume-wardrobe of his theatre, anybody who cares to study Shakespeare's method will see that there is absolutely no dramatist of the French, English, or Athenian stage who relies so much for his illusionist effects on the dress of his actors as Shakespeare does himself.

Knowing how the artistic temperament is always fascinated by beauty of costume, he constantly introduces into his plays masques

1. Lily Langtry (1852–1929), English actress, was a daughter of the Dean of the Channel Isle of Jersey, resulting in her later nickname, "the Jersey Lily." A well-known society beauty and intimate friend of the Prince of Wales (later Edward VII), she shocked Londoners by going on the stage in 1881 as Kate Hardcastle in *She Stoops to Conquer*. One of her most famous roles was Rosalind in *As You Like It*.
2. Edward Robert Bulwer-Lytton (1831–1891), was the first Earl of Lytton and son of novelist-playwright Lord Lytton (Edward Bulwer-Lytton, 1803–1873). Although his earldom was a reward for diplomatic services, notably as Governor-General of India, he was known equally well at home as a poet and litterateur under the pen name of Owen Meredith.

and dances, purely for the sake of the pleasure which they give the eye; and we have still his stage-directions for the three great processions in *Henry the Eighth*, directions which are characterised by the most extraordinary elaborateness of detail down to the collars of S.S. and the pearls in Anne Boleyn's hair. Indeed it would be quite easy for a modern manager to reproduce these pageants absolutely as Shakespeare had them designed; and so accurate were they that one of the Court officials of the time, writing an account of the last performance of the play at the Globe Theatre to a friend, actually complains of their realistic character, notably of the production on the stage of the Knights of the Garter in the robes and insignia of the order, as being calculated to bring ridicule on the real ceremonies; much in the same spirit in which the French Government, some time ago, prohibited that delightful actor, M. Christian, from appearing in uniform, on the plea that it was prejudicial to the glory of the army that a colonel should be carica-tured. And elsewhere the gorgeousness of apparel which distinguished the English stage under Shakespeare's influence was attacked by the contemporary critics, not as a rule, however, on the grounds of the democratic tendencies of realism, but usually on those moral grounds which are always the last refuge of people who have no sense of beauty.

The point, however, which I wish to emphasise is, not that Shakespeare appreciated the value of lovely costumes in adding picturesqueness to poetry, but that he saw how important costume is as a means of producing certain dramatic effects. Many of his plays, such as *Measure for Measure, Twelfth Night, The Two Gentlemen of Verona, All's Well That Ends Well, Cymbeline*, and others, depend for their illusion on the character of the various dresses worn by the hero or the heroine; the delightful scene in *Henry the Sixth*, on the modern miracles of healing by faith, loses all its point unless Gloster is in black and scarlet; and the *dénoûment* of the *Merry Wives of Windsor* hinges on the colour of Anne Page's gown. As for the uses Shakespeare makes of disguises the instances are almost numberless. Posthumus hides his passion under a peasant's garb, and Edgar his pride beneath an idiot's rags; Portia wears the apparel of a lawyer, and Rosalind is attired in "all points as a man"; the cloak-bag of Pisanio changes Imogen to the youth Fidele; Jessica flees from from her father's house in boy's dress, and Julia ties up her yellow hair in fantastic love-knots, and dons hose and doublet; Henry the Eighth woos his lady as a shepherd, and Romeo his as a pilgrim; Prince Hal and Poins appear first as footpads in buckram suits, and then in white aprons and leather jerkins as the waiters in a tavern; and as for Falstaff, does he not come on as a highwayman, as an old woman, as Herne the Hunter, and as the clothes going to the laundry?

Nor are the examples of the employment of costume as a mode of intensifying dramatic situation less numerous. After slaughter of Duncan, Macbeth appears in his night-gown as if aroused from sleep; Timon ends in rags the play he had begun in splendour; Richard flatters the London citizens in a suit of mean and shabby armour, and, as soon as he has stepped in blood to the throne, marches through the streets in crown and George and Garter; the climax of *The Tempest* is reached when Prospero, throwing off his enchanter's robes, sends Ariel for his hat and rapier, and reveals himself as the great Italian Duke; the very Ghost in *Hamlet* changes his mystical apparel to produce different effects; and as for Juliet, a modern playwright would probably have lain her out in her shroud, and made the scene a scene of horror merely, but Shakespeare arrays her in rich and gorgeous raiment, whose loveliness makes the vault "a feasting presence full of light," turns the tomb into a bridal chamber, and gives the cue and motive for Romeo's speech of the triumph of Beauty over Death.

Even small details of dress, such as the colour of a major-domo's stockings, the pattern on a wife's handkerchief, the sleeve of a young soldier, and a fashionable woman's bonnets, become in Shakespeare's hands points of actual dramatic importance, and by some of them the action of the play in question is conditioned absolutely. Many other dramatists have availed themselves of costume as a method of expressing directly to the audience the character of a person on his entrance, though hardly so brilliantly as Shakespeare has done in the case of the dandy Parolles, whose dress, by the way, only an archaeologist can understand; the fun of a master and servant exchanging coats in presence of the audience, of shipwrecked sailors squabbling over the division of a lot of fine clothes, and of a tinker dressed up like a duke while he is in his cups, may be regarded as part of that great career which costume has always played in comedy from the time of Aristophanes down to Mr. Gilbert; but nobody from the mere details of apparel and adornment has ever drawn such irony of contrast, such immediate and tragic effect, such pity and such pathos, as Shakespeare himself. Armed cap-à-pie, the dead King stalks on the battlements of Elsinore because all is not right with Denmark; Shylock's Jewish gaberdine is part of the stigma under which that wounded and embittered nature writhes; Arthur begging for his life can think of no better plea than the handkerchief he had given Hubert—

> "Have you the heart? when your head did but ache,
> I knit my handkerchief about your brows,
> (The best I had, a princess wrought it me)
> And I did never ask it you again";

and Orlando's blood-stained napkin strikes the first sombre note in that exquisite woodland idyll, and shows us the depth of feeling that underlies Rosalind's fanciful wit and wilful jesting.

> "Last night 'twas on my arm; I kissed it;
> I hope it be not gone to tell my lord
> That I kiss aught but he,"

says Imogen, jesting on the loss of the bracelet which was already on its way to Rome to rob her of her husband's faith; the little Prince passing to the Tower plays with the dagger in his uncle's girdle; Duncan sends a ring to Lady Macbeth on the night of his own murder, and the ring of Portia turns the tragedy of the merchant into a wife's comedy. The great rebel York dies with a paper crown on his head; Hamlet's black suit is a kind of colour-motive in the piece, like the mourning of the Chimène in the Cid; and the climax of Antony's speech is the production of Caesar's cloak:—

> "I remember
> The first time ever Caesar put it on.
> 'Twas on a summer's evening, in his tent,
> The day he overcame the Nervii:—

> Look, in this place ran Cassius' dagger through:
> See what a rent the envious Casca made:
> Through this the well-beloved Brutus stabbed. . . .
> Kind souls, what, weep you when you but behold
> Our Caesar's vesture wounded?"

The flowers which Ophelia carries with her in her madness are as pathetic as the violets that blossom on a grave; the effect of Lear's wandering on the heath is intensified beyond words by his fantastic attire; and when Cloten, stung by the taunt of that simile which his sister draws from her husband's raiment, arrays himself in that husband's very garb to work upon her the deed of shame, we feel that there is nothing in the whole of modern French realism, nothing even in *Thérèse Raquin*, that masterpiece of horror, which for terrible and tragic significance can compare with this strange scene in *Cymbeline*.[3]

In the actual dialogue also some of the most vivid passages are those suggested by costume. Rosalind's

> "Dost thou think, though I am caparisoned like a man, if have a doublet and hose in my disposition?"

Constance's

> "Grief fills the place of my absent child,
> Stuffs out his vacant garments with his form";

and the quick sharp cry of Elizabeth—

> "Ah! cut my lace asunder!"—

are only a few of the many examples one might quote. One of the finest effects I have ever seen on the stage was Salvini,[4] in the last act of *Lear*, tearing the plume from Kent's cap and applying it to Cordelia's lips when he came to the line,

> "This feather stirs; she lives!"

---

3. *Thérèse Raquin* (1873), was a "slice of life" play by Emile Zola, dramatized from his novel of the same title.

4. Tommaso Salvini (1829–1916), Italian actor famous for his portrayals of Shakespearian roles, notably Othello, Lear, and Macbeth. He once played Othello to the Iago of Edwin Booth.

Mr. Booth, whose Lear had many noble qualities of passion, plucked, I remember, some fur from his archaeologically-incorrect ermine for the same business; but Salvini's was the finer effect of the two, as well as the truer. And those who saw Mr. Irving in the last act of *Richard the Third* have not, I am sure, forgotten how much the agony and terror of his dream was intensified, by contrast, through the calm and quiet that preceded it, and the delivery of such lines as

> "What, is my beaver easier than it was?
> And all my armour laid into my tent?
> Look that my staves be sound and not too heavy"—

lines which had a double meaning for the audience, remembering the last words which Richard's mother called after him as he was marching to Bosworth:—

> "Therefore take with thee my most grievous curse,
> Which in the day of battle tire thee more
> Than all the complete armour that thou wear'ot."

As regards the resources which Shakespeare had at his disposal, it is to be remarked that, while he more than once complains of the smallness of the stage on which he has to produce big historical plays, and of the want of scenery which obliges him to cut out many effective open-air incidents, he always writes as a dramatist who had at his disposal a most elaborate theatrical wardrobe, and who could rely on the actors taking pains about their make-up. Even now it is difficult to produce such a play as the *Comedy of Errors*; and to the picturesque accident of Miss Ellen Terry's brother resembling herself we owe the opportunity of seeing *Twelfth Night* adequately performed. Indeed, to put any play of Shakespeare's on the stage, absolutely as he himself wished it to be done, requires the services of a good property-man, a clever wig-maker, a costumier with a sense of colour and a knowledge of textures, a master of the methods of making-up, a fencing-master, a dancing-master, and an artist to direct personally the whole production. For he is most careful to tell us the dress and appearance of each character. "Racine abhorre la réalité," says Auguste Vacquerie somewhere;

"il ne daigne pas s'occuper de son costume. Si l'on s'en rapportait aux indications du poète, Agamemnon serait vêtu d'un sceptre et Achille d'une épée."[5] But with Shakespeare it is very different. He gives us directions about the costumes of Perdita, Florizel, Autolycus, the Witches in *Macbeth*, and the apothecary in *Romeo and Juliet*, several elaborate descriptions of his fat knight, and a detailed account of the extraordinary garb in which Petruchio is to be married. Rosalind, he tells us, is tall, and is to carry a spear and a little dagger; Celia is smaller, and is to paint her face brown so as to look sunburnt. The children who play at fairies in Windsor Forest are to be dressed in white and green—a compliment, by the way, to Queen Elizabeth, whose favourite colours they were—and in white, with green garlands and gilded vizors, the angels are to come to Katharine in Kimbolton. Bottom is in homespun, Lysander is distinguished from Oberon by his wearing an Athenian dress, and Launce has holes in his boots. The Duchess of Gloucester stands in a white sheet with her husband in mourning beside her. The motley of the Fool, the scarlet of the Cardinal, and the French lilies broidered on the English coats, are all made occasion for jest or taunt in the dialogue. We know the patterns on the Dauphin's armour and the Pucelle's sword, the crest on Warwick's helmet and the colour of Bardolph's nose. Portia has golden hair, Phoebe is black-haired, Orlando has chestnut curls, and Sir Andrew Aguecheek's hair hangs like flax on a distaff, and won't curl at all. Some of the characters are stout, some lean, some straight, some hunchbacked, some fair, some dark, and some are to blacken their faces. Lear has a white beard, Hamlet's father a grizzled, and Benedick is to shave his in the course of the play. Indeed, on the subject of stage beards Shakespeare is quite elaborate; tells us of the many different colours in use, and gives a hint to actors always to see that their own are properly tied on. There is a dance of reapers in rye-straw hats, and of rustics in hairy coats like satyrs; a masque of Amazons, a masque of Russians, and a classical masque; several immortal scenes over a weaver in an ass's head, a riot over

5. "Racine loathes reality; he does not deign to bother about his dress. If you paid attention to the poet's own instructions, Agamemnon would be clad in a scepter and Achilles in a sword."

the colour of a coat which it takes the Lord Mayor of London to quell, and a scene between an infuriated husband and his wife's milliner about the slashing of a sleeve.

As for the metaphors Shakespeare draws from dress, and the aphorisms he makes on it, his hits at the costume of his age, particularly at the ridiculous size of the ladies' bonnets, and the many descriptions of the *mundus muliebris* [women's world], from the song of Autolycus in the *Winter's Tale* down to the account of the Duchess of Milan's gown in *Much Ado About Nothing*, they are far too numerous to quote; though it may be worth while to remind people that the whole of the Philosophy of Clothes is to be found in Lear's scene with Edgar—a passage which has the advantage of brevity and style over the grotesque wisdom and somewhat mouthing metaphysics of *Sartor Resartus*. But I think that from what I have already said it is quite clear that Shakespeare was very much interested in costume. I do not mean in that shallow sense by which it has been concluded from his knowledge of deeds and daffodils that he was the Blackstone and Paxton of the Elizabethan age; but that he saw that costume could be made at once impressive of a certain effect on the audience and expressive of certain types of character, and is one of-the essential factors of the means which a true illusionist has at his disposal. Indeed to him the deformed figure of Richard was of as much value as Juliet's loveliness; he sets the serge of the radical beside the silks of the lord, and sees the stage effects to be got from each: he has as much delight in Caliban as he has in Ariel, in rags as he has in cloth of gold, and recognises the artistic beauty of ugliness.

The difficulty Ducis[6] felt about translating *Othello* in consequence of the importance given to such a vulgar thing as a handkerchief, and his attempt to soften its grossness by making the Moor reiterate "Le bandeau! le bandeau!" may be taken as an example of the difference between *la tragédie philosophique* and the drama of real life; and the introduction for the first time of the word *mouchoir* at the Théâtre Français was an era in that romantic-realistic movement

6. Jean François Ducis (1733–1816), French dramatist known primarily for his adaptations of Shakespeare to the French stage, including *Hamlet, Romeo and Juliet, King Lear, Macbeth, King John,* and *Othello.*

of which Hugo is the father and M. Zola the *enfant terrible*, just as the classicism of the earlier part of the century was emphasised by Talma's[7] refusal to play Greek heroes any longer in a powdered periwig—one of the many instances, by the way, of that desire for archaeological accuracy in dress which has distinguished the great actors of our age.

In criticising the importance given to money in *La Comédie Humaine*, Théophile Gautier says that Balzac may claim to have invented a new hero in fiction, *le héros métallique*. Of Shakespeare it may be said that he was the first to see the dramatic value of doublets, and that a climax may depend on a crinoline.

The burning of the Globe Theatre—an event due, by the way, to the results of the passion for illusion that distinguished Shakespeare's stage-management—has unfortunately robbed us of many important documents; but in the inventory, still in existence, of the costume-wardrobe of a London theatre in Shakespeare's time, there are mentioned particular costumes for cardinals, shepherds, kings, clowns, friars, and fools; green coats for Robin Hood's men, and a green gown for Maid Marian; a white and gold doublet for Henry the Fifth, and a robe for Longshanks; besides surplices, copes, damask gowns, gowns of cloth of gold and of cloth of silver, taffeta gowns, calico gowns, velvet coats, satin coats, frieze coats, jerkins of yellow leather and of black leather, red suits, grey suits, French Pierrot suits, a robe "for to goo invisibell," which seems inexpensive at £3, 10s., and four incomparable fardingales—all of which show a desire to give every character an appropriate dress. There are also entries of Spanish, Moorish and Danish costumes, of helmets, lances, painted shields, imperial crowns, and papal tiaras, as well as of costumes for Turkish Janissaries, Roman Senators, and all the gods and goddesses of Olympus, which evidence a good deal of archaeological research on the part of the manager of the theatre. It is true that there is a mention of a bodice for Eve, but probably the *donnée* of the play was after the Fall.

Indeed, anybody who cares to examine the age of Shakespeare will see that archaeology was one of its special characteristics. After

7. François Joseph Talma (1763–1826), French actor whose playing in the Ducis adaptation of *Othello* was mainly responsible for its success.

that revival of the classical forms of architecture which was one of the notes of the Renaissance, and the printing at Venice and elsewhere of the masterpieces of Greek and Latin literature, had come naturally an interest in the ornamentation and costume of the antique world. Nor was it for the learning that they could acquire, but rather for the loveliness that they might create, that the artists studied these things. The curious objects that were being constantly brought to light by excavations were not left to moulder in a museum, for the contemplation of a callous curator, and the *ennui* of a policeman bored by the absence of crime. They were used as motives for the production of a new art, which was to be not beautiful merely, but also strange.

Infessura tells us that in 1485 some workmen digging on the Appian Way came across an old Roman sarcophagus inscribed with the name "Julia, daughter of Claudius." On opening the coffer they found within its marble womb the body of a beautiful girl of about fifteen years of age, preserved by the embalmer's skill from corruption and the decay of time. Her eyes were half open, her hair rippled round her in crisp curling gold, and from her lips and cheek the bloom of maidenhood had not yet departed. Borne back to the Capitol, she became at once the centre of a new cult, and from all parts of the city crowded pilgrims to worship at the wonderful shrine, till the Pope fearing lest those who had found the secret of beauty in a Pagan tomb might forget what secrets Judaea's rough and rockhewn sepulchre contained, had the body conveyed away by night, and in secret buried. Legend though it may be, yet the story is none the less valuable as showing us the attitude of the Renaissance towards the antique world. Archaeology to them was not a mere science for the antiquarian; it was a means by which they could touch the dry dust of antiquity into the very breath and beauty of life, and fill with the new wine of romanticism forms that else had been old and outworn. From the pulpit of Niccola Pisano down to Mantegna's "Triumph of Caesar," and the service Cellini designed for King Francis, the influence of this spirit can be traced; nor was it confined merely to the immobile arts—the arts of arrested movement—but its influence was to be seen also in the great Graeco-Roman masques which were the constant amusement of the gay courts of the

time, and in the public pomps and processions with which the citizens
of big commercial towns were wont to greet the princes that chanced
to visit them; pageants, by the way, which were considered so important that large prints were made of them and published—a fact which
is a proof of the general interest at the time in matters of such kind.

And this use of archaeology in shows, so far from being a bit of
priggish pedantry, is in every way legitimate and beautiful. For the
stage is not merely the meeting-place of all the arts, but is also the
return of art to life. Sometimes in an archaeological novel the use of
strange and obsolete terms seems to hide the reality beneath the
learning, and I dare say that many of the readers of *Notre Dame de
Paris* have been much puzzled over the meaning of such expressions
as *la casaque à mahoitres, les voulgiers, le gallimard taché d'encre, les
craaquiniers,*[8] and the like; but with the stage how different it is!
The ancient world wakes from its sleep, and history moves as a
pageant before our eyes, without obliging us to have recourse to
a dictionary or an encyclopaedia for the perfection of our enjoyment.
Indeed, there is not the slightest necessity that the public should
know the authorities for the mounting of any piece. From such
materials, for instance, as the disk of Theodosius, materials with
which the majority of people are probably not very familiar,
Mr. E. W. Godwin, one of the most artistic spirits of this century
in England, created the marvellous loveliness of the first act of
*Claudian,* and showed us the life of Byzantium in the fourth century,
not by a dreary lecture and a set of grimy casts, not by a novel
which requires a glossary to explain it, but by the visible presentation
before us of all the glory of that great town. And while the costumes
were true to the smallest points of colour and design, yet the details
were not assigned that abnormal importance which they must
necessarily be given in a piecemeal lecture, but were subordinated
to the rules of lofty composition and the unity of artistic effect. Mr.
Symonds, speaking of that great picture of Mantegna's, now in
Hampton Court, says that the artist has converted an antiquarian
motive into a theme for melodies of line. The same could have been
said with equal justice of Mr. Godwin's scene. Only the foolish

8. Cloak with padded sleeves, halberdiers, pen box stained with ink, sailors of
carracks.

called it pedantry, only those who would neither look nor listen
spoke of the passion of the play being killed by its paint. It was in
reality a scene not merely perfect in its picturesqueness, but absolutely dramatic also, getting rid of any necessity for tedious descriptions, and showing us, by the colour and character of Claudian's
dress, and the dress of his attendants, the whole nature and life of
the man, from what school of philosophy he affected, down to what
horses he backed on the turf.

And indeed archaeology is only really delightful when transfused
into some form of art. I have no desire to underrate the services
of laborious scholars, but I feel that the use Keats made of
Lemprière's Dictionary is of far more value to us than Professor
Max Müller's[9] treatment of the same mythology as a disease of
language. Better *Endymion* than any theory, however sound, or, as
in the present instance, unsound, of an epidemic among adjectives!
And who does not feel that the chief glory of Piranesi's[10] book on
Vases is that it gave Keats the suggestion for his "Ode on a Grecian
Urn"? Art, and art only, can make archaeology beautiful; and
the theatric art can use it most directly and most vividly, for it can
combine in one exquisite presentation the illusion of actual life with
the wonder of the unreal world. But the sixteenth century was not
merely the age of Vitruvius; it was the age of Vecellio also.[11] Every

9. Friedrich Max Müller (1823–1900), German poet and scholar who became
(1854) Taylorian Professor of Modern European Languages at Oxford, and afterwards curator of the Bodleian Library.

10. Gianbattista Piranesi (1720–1778), an artist who did not particularly apply
himself to the theater, although his magnificent designs of dark prisons and sunlit,
columned courtyards were paradoxically both inspired by contemporary stage
settings and themselves the source of inspiration for others.

11. Vitruvius Pollio was a first-century B.C. Roman architect and engineer, the
rediscovery of whose works in the late fifteenth century stimulated study of the
classical stage, leading to treatises on methods of changing scenery, construction of
playhouses, and stage lighting. The first complete edition of Vitruvius, prepared by
Sulpicio da Veroli, appeared in print in 1486.

The program notes to the 1850 revival of *The Merchant of Venice* at the Princess's
Theatre inform the playgoer that "the costumes and customs are represented as
existing about the year 1600, when Shakespeare wrote the play. The dresses are
chiefly selected from a work by Cesare Vecellio, entitled '*Degli Habiti Antichi e
Moderne di diverse Parti del Mondo*. In Venetia, 1590' as well as from other sources to
be found in the British Museum."

nation seems suddenly to have become interested in the dress of its neighbours. Europe began to investigate its own clothes, and the amount of books published on national costumes is quite extraordinary. At the beginning of the century the *Nuremberg Chronicle,* with its two thousand illustrations, reached its fifth edition, and before the century was over seventeen editions were published of Munster's *Cosmography.* Besides these two books there were also the works of Michael Colyns, of Hans Weigel, of Amman,[12] and of Vecellio himself, all of them well illustrated, some of the drawings in Vecellio being probably from the hand of Titian.[13]

Nor was it merely from books and treatises that they acquired their knowledge. The development of the habit of foreign travel, the increased commercial intercourse between countries, and the frequency of diplomatic missions, gave every nation many opportunities of studying the various forms of contemporary dress. After the departure from England, for instance, of the ambassadors from the Czar, the Sultan and the Prince of Morocco, Henry the Eighth and his friends gave several masques in the strange attire of their visitors. Later on London saw, perhaps too often, the sombre splendour of the Spanish Court, and to Elizabeth came envoys from all lands, whose dress, Shakespeare tells us, had an important influence on English costume.

And the interest was not confined merely to classical dress, or the dress of foreign nations; there was also a good deal of research, amongst theatrical people especially, into the ancient costume of England itself: and when Shakespeare, in the prologue to one of his plays, expresses his regret at being unable to produce helmets of the period, he is speaking as an Elizabethan manager and not merely as an Elizabethan poet. At Cambridge, for instance, during his day, a play of *Richard the Third* was performed, in which the actors

12. Josse Amman (d. 1591), artist whose print of a sixteenth-century procession, now in the British Museum, was used as a basis for the costume designs for the opening scene of the *Merchant of Venice* production at the Princess's Theatre in 1850.

13. Titian's real name was Tiziano Vecellio. The similarity of his name to that of his contemporary Cesare Vecellio may have prompted Wilde's suggestion that Titian was responsible for some of Cesare Vecellio's drawings of costumes, but these were probably executed after Titian's death in 1576, for the book of costume drawings appeared in 1590.

were attired in real dresses of the time, procured from the great collection of historical costume in the Tower, which was always open to the inspection of managers, and sometimes placed at their disposal. And I cannot help thinking that this performance must have been far more artistic, as regards costume, than Garrick's mounting of Shakespeare's own play on the subject, in which he himself appeared in a nondescript fancy dress, and everybody else in the costume of the time of George the Third, Richmond especially being much admired in the uniform of a young guardsman.

For what is the use to the stage of that archaeology which has so strangely terrified the critics, but that it, and it alone, can give us the architect and apparel suitable to the time in which the action of the play passes? It enables us to see a Greek dressed like a Greek, and an Italian like an Italian; to enjoy the arcades of Venice and the balconies of Verona; and, if the play deals with any of the great eras in our country's history, to contemplate the age in its proper attire, and the king in his habit as he lived. And I wonder, by the way, what Lord Lytton would have said some time ago, at the Princess's Theatre, had the curtain risen on his father's Brutus reclining in a Queen Anne chair, attired in a flowing wig and a flowered dressing-gown, a costume which in the last century was considered peculiarly appropriate to an antique Roman! For in those halcyon days of the drama no archaeology troubled the stage, or distressed the critics, and our inartistic grandfathers sat peaceably in a stifling atmosphere of anachronisms, and beheld with the calm complacency of the age of prose an Iachimo in powder and patches, a Lear in lace ruffles, and a Lady Macbeth in a large crinoline. I can understand archaeology being attacked on the ground of its excessive realism, but to attack it as pedantic seems to be very much beside the mark. However, to attack it for any reason is foolish; one might just as well speak disrespectfully of the equator. For archaeology, being a science, is neither good nor bad, but a fact simply. Its value depends entirely on how it is used, and only an artist can use it. We look to the archaeologist for the materials, to the artist for the method.

In designing the scenery and costumes for any of Shakespeare's plays, the first thing the artist has to settle is the best date for the drama. This should be determined by the general spirit of the play, more than by any actual historical references which may occur in it. Most *Hamlets* I have seen were placed far too early. *Hamlet* is essentially a scholar of the Revival of Learning; and if the allusion to the recent invasion of England by the Danes puts it back to the ninth century, the use of foils brings it down much later. Once, however, that the date has been fixed, then the archaeologist is to supply us with the facts which the artist is to convert into effects.

It has been said that the anachronisms in the plays themselves show us that Shakespeare was indifferent to historical accuracy, and a great deal of capital has been made out of Hector's indiscreet quotation from Aristotle. Upon the other hand, the anachronisms are really few in number, and not very important, and, had Shakespeare's attention been drawn to them by a brother artist, he would probably have corrected them. For, though they can hardly be called blemishes, they are certainly not the great beauties of his work; or, at least, if they are, their anachronistic charm cannot be emphasised unless the play is accurately mounted according to its proper date. In looking at Shakespeare's plays as a whole, however, what is really remarkable is their extraordinary fidelity as regards his personages and his plots. Many of his *dramatis personae* are people who had actually existed, and some of them might have been seen in real life by a portion of his audience. Indeed the most violent attack that was made on Shakespeare in his time was for his supposed caricature of Lord Cobham. As for his plots, Shakespeare constantly draws them either from authentic history, or from the old ballads and traditions which served as history to the Elizabethan public, and which even now no scientific historian would dismiss as absolutely untrue. And not merely did he select fact instead of fancy as the basis of much of his imaginative work, but he always gives to each play the general character, the social atmosphere in a word, of the age in question. Stupidity he recognises as being one of the permanent characteristics of all European civilisations; so he sees no difference between a London mob of his own day and a Roman mob of pagan days, between a silly watchman in Messina and a silly Justice of the Peace in Windsor. But when he deals with higher characters, with those exceptions of each age

which are so fine that they become its types, he gives them absolutely
the stamp and seal of their time. Virgilia is one or those Roman
wives on whose tomb was written "Domi mansit, lanam fecit,"[14] as
surely as Juliet is the romantic girl of the Renaissance. He is even
true to the characteristics of race. Hamlet has all the imagination and
irresolution of the Northern nations, and the Princess Katharine is
as entirely French as the heroine of *Divorçons*.[15] Harry the Fifth is a
pure Englishman, and Othello a true Moor.

Again when Shakespeare treats of the history of England from
the fourteenth to the sixteenth centuries, it is wonderful how careful
he is to have his facts perfectly right—indeed he follows Holinshed
with curious fidelity. The incessant wars between France and
England are described with extraordinary accuracy down to the
names of the besieged towns, the ports of landing and embarkation,
the sites and dates of the battles, the titles of the commanders on
each side, and the lists of the killed and wounded. And as regards
the Civil Wars of the Roses we have many elaborate genealogies of
the seven sons of Edward the third; the claims of the rival Houses
of York and Lancaster to the throne are discussed at length; and
if the English aristocracy will not read Shakespeare as a poet, they
should certainly read him as a sort of early Peerage. There is hardly
a single title in the Upper House, with the exception of course of
the uninteresting titles assumed by the law lords, which does not
appear in Shakespeare along with many details of family history,
creditable and discreditable. Indeed if it be really necessary that
the School Board children should know all about the Wars of the
Roses, they could learn their lessons just as well out of Shakespeare
as out of shilling primers, and learn them, I need not say, far more
pleasurably. Even in Shakespeare's own day this use of his plays
was recognised. "The historical plays teach history to those who
cannot read it in the chronicles," says Heywood in a tract about
the stage, and yet I am sure that sixteenth-century chronicles were
much more delightful reading than nineteenth-century primers are.

Of course the aesthetic value of Shakespeare's plays does not, in

14. "She remained at home and spun wool."
15. *Divorçons* was a farcical play by Sardou and De Najac, produced in Paris in
1880.

the slightest degree, depend on their facts, but on their Truth, and Truth is independent of facts always, inventing or selecting them at pleasure. But still Shakespeare's use of facts is a most interesting part of his method of work, and shows us his attitude towards the stage, and his relations to the great art of illusion. Indeed he would have been very much surprised at any one classing his plays with "fairy tales," as Lord Lytton does; for one of his aims was to create for England a national historical drama, which should deal with incidents with which the public was well acquainted, and with heroes that lived in the memory of a people. Patriotism, I need hardly say, is not a necessary quality of art; but it means, for the artist, the substitution of a universal for an individual feeling, and for the public the presentation of a work of art in a most attractive and popular form. It is worth noticing that Shakespeare's first and last successes were both historical plays.

It may be asked, what has this to do with Shakespeare's attitude towards costume? I answer that a dramatist who laid such stress on historical accuracy of fact would have welcomed historical accuracy of costume as a most important adjunct to his illusionist method. And I have no hesitation in saying that he did so. The reference to helmets of the period in the prologue to *Henry the Fifth* may be considered fanciful, though Shakespeare must have often seen

> "The very casque
> That did affright the air at Agincourt,"

where it still hangs in the dusky gloom of Westminster Abbey, along with the saddle of that "imp of fame," and the dinted shield with its torn blue velvet lining and its tarnished lilies of gold; but the use of military tabards in *Henry the Sixth* is a bit of pure archaeology, as they were not worn in the sixteenth century; and the King's own tabard, I may mention, was still suspended over his tomb in St. George's Chapel, Windsor, in Shakespeare's day. For, up to the time of the unfortunate triumph of the Philistines in 1645, the chapels and cathedrals of England were the great national museums of archaeology, and in them was kept the armour and attire of the heroes of English history. A good deal was of course preserved in the Tower, and even in Elizabeth's day tourists were brought there to see such curious relics of the past as Charles Brandon's huge lance, which is still, I believe, the admiration of our country visitors; but the cathedrals and churches were, as a rule, selected as the most suitable shrines for the reception of the historic antiquities. Canterbury can still show us the helm of the Black Prince, Westminster the robes of our kings, and in old St. Paul's the very banner that had waved on Bosworth field was hung up by Richmond himself.

In fact, everywhere that Shakespeare turned in London, he saw the apparel and appurtenances of past ages, and it is impossible to doubt that he made use of his opportunities. The employment of lance and shield, for instance, in actual warfare, which is so frequent in his plays, is drawn from archaeology, and not from the military accoutrements of his day; and his general use of armour in battle was not a characteristic of his age, a time when it was rapidly disappearing before firearms. Again, the crest on Warwick's helmet, of which such a point is made in *Henry the Sixth*, is absolutely correct in a fifteenth-century play when crests were generally worn, but would not have been so in a play of Shakespeare's own time, when feathers and plumes had taken their place—a fashion which, as he tells us in *Henry the Eighth*, was borrowed from France. For the historical plays, then, we may be sure that archaeology was employed, and as for the others I feel certain that it was the case also. The appearance of Jupiter on his eagle, thunderbolt in hand, of Juno with her peacocks, and of Iris with her many-coloured bow; the Amazon masque and the masque of the Five Worthies, may all be regarded as archaeological; and the vision which Posthumus sees in prison of Sicilius Leonatus—"an old man, attired like a warrior, leading an ancient matron"—is clearly so. Of the "Athenian dress" by which Lysander is distinguished from Oberon I have already spoken; but one of the most marked instances is in the case of the dress of Coriolanus, for which Shakespeare goes directly to Plutarch. That historian, in his Life of the great Roman, tells us of the oak-wreath with which Caius Marcius was crowned, and of the curious kind of dress in which, according to ancient fashion, he had to canvass his electors; and on both of these points he enters into long disquisitions, investigating the origin and meaning of the old customs. Shakespeare, in the spirit of the true artist, accepts the facts of the antiquarian and converts them into dramatic and picturesque effects: indeed the gown of humility, the "woolvish gown," as Shakespeare calls it, is the central note of the play. There are other cases I might quote, but this one is quite sufficient for my purpose; and it is evident from it at any rate that, in mounting a play in the accurate costume of the time, according to the best authorities, we are carrying out Shakespeare's own wishes and method.

Even if it were not so, there is no more reason that we should continue any imperfections which may be supposed to have characterised Shakespeare's stage-mounting than that we should have Juliet played by a young man, or give up the advantage of changeable scenery. A great work of dramatic art should not merely be made expressive of modern passion by means of the actor, but should be presented to us in the form most suitable to the modern spirit. Racine produced his Roman plays in Louis Quatorze dress on a stage crowded with spectators; but we require different conditions for the enjoyment of his art. Perfect accuracy of detail, for the sake of perfect illusion, is necessary for us. What we have to see is that the details are not allowed to usurp the principal place. They must be subordinate always to the general motive of the play. But subordination in art does not mean disregard of truth; it means conversion of fact into effect, and assigning to each detail its proper relative value.

> "Les petits détails d'histoire et de vie domestique (says Hugo) doivent être scrupuleusement étudiés et reproduits par le poète, mais uniquement comme des moyens d'accroître la réalité de l'ensemble, et de faire pénétrer jusque dans les coins les plus obscurs de l'oeuvre cette vie générale et puissante au milieu de laquelle les personnages sont plus vrais, et les catastrophes, par conséquent, plus poignantes. Tout doit être subordonne à ce but. L'Homme sur le premier plan, le reste au fond." [16]

16. "The little details of history and of home life must be scrupulously studied and reproduced by the poet, but solely as a way of adding to the reality of the whole and of filling the most obscure corners of the work with that powerful general life, in the midst of which the characters are more real and consequently the disasters more moving. Everything must be subordinated to this goal. Man in the foreground, the rest in the background."

This passage is interesting as coming from the first great French dramatist who employed archaeology on the stage, and whose plays, though absolutely correct in detail, are known to all for their passion, not for their pedantry—for their life, not for their learning. It is true that he has made certain concessions in the case of the employment of curious or strange expressions. Ruy Blas talks of M. de Priego as "sujet du roi" instead of "noble du roi," and Angelo Malipieri speaks of "la croix rouge" instead of "la croix de gueules." But they are concessions made to the public, or rather to a section of it. "J'en offre ici toute mes excuses aux spectateurs intelligents," he says in a note to one of the plays; "espérons qu'un jour un seigneur vénitien pourra dire tout bonnement sans péril son blason sur le théâtre. C'est un progrès qui viendra."[17] And, though the description of the crest is not couched in accurate language, still the crest itself was accurately right. It may, of course, be said that the public do not notice these things; upon the other hand, it should be remembered that Art has no other aim but her own perfection, and proceeds simply by her own laws, and that the play which Hamlet describes as being caviare to the general is a play he highly praises. Besides, in England, at any rate, the public have undergone a transformation; there is far more appreciation of beauty now than there was a few years ago; and though they may not be familiar with the authorities and archaeological data for what is shown to them, still they enjoy whatever loveliness they look at. And this is the important thing. Better to take pleasure in a rose than to put its root under a microscope. Archaeological accuracy is merely a condition of illusionist stage effect; it is not its quality. And Lord Lytton's proposal that the dresses should merely be beautiful without being accurate is founded on a misapprehension of the nature of costume, and of its value on the stage. This value is twofold, picturesque and dramatic; the former depends on the colour of the dress, the latter on its design and character. But so interwoven are the two that, whenever in our own day historical accuracy has been disregarded, and the various dresses in a play

17. "I offer here all my apologies to intelligent spectators; let us hope that one day a Venetian nobleman will be able to mention his coat of arms on the stage quite simply without endangering himself. It is an improvement that will come."

taken from different ages, the result has been that the stage has been turned into that chaos of costume, that caricature of the centuries, the Fancy Dress Ball, to the entire ruin of all dramatic and picturesque effect. For the dresses of one age do not artistically harmonise with the dresses of another; and, as far as dramatic value goes, to confuse the costumes is to confuse the play. Costume is a growth, an evolution, and a most important, perhaps the most important, sign of the manners, customs and mode of life of each century. The Puritan dislike of colour, adornment and grace in apparel was part of the great revolt of the middle classes against Beauty in the seventeenth century. A historian who disregarded it would give us a most inaccurate picture of the time, and a dramatist who did not avail himself of it would miss a most vital element in producing an illusionist effect. The effeminacy of dress that characterised the reign of Richard the Second was a constant theme of contemporary authors. Shakespeare, writing two hundred years after, makes the king's fondness for gay apparel and foreign fashions a point in the play, from John of Gaunt's reproaches down to Richard's own speech in the third act on his deposition from the throne. And that Shakespeare examined Richard's tomb in Westminster Abbey seems to me certain from York's speech:—

> "See, see, King Richard doth himself appear
> As doth the blushing discontented sun
> From out the fiery portal of the east,
> When he perceives the envious clouds are bent
> To dim his glory."

For we can still discern on the King's robe his favourite badge—the sun issuing from a cloud. In fact, in every age the social conditions are so exemplified in costume, that to produce a sixteenth-century play in fourteenth-century attire, or *vice versa*, would make the performance seem unreal because untrue. And, valuable as beauty of effect on the stage is, the highest beauty is not merely comparable with absolute accuracy of detail, but really dependent on it. To invent an entirely new costume is almost impossible except in burlesque or extravaganza, and as for combining the dress of different centuries into one, the experiment would be dangerous,

and Shakespeare's opinion of the artistic value of such a medley may
be gathered from his incessant satire of the Elizabethan dandies for
imagining that they were well dressed because they got their
doublets in Italy, their hats in Germany, and their hose in France.
And it should be noted that the most lovely scenes that have been
produced on our stage have been those that have been characterised
by perfect accuracy, such as Mr. and Mrs. Bancroft's eighteenth-
century revivals at the Haymarket, Mr. Irving's superb production
of *Much Ado About Nothing*, and Mr. Barrett's *Claudian*. Besides, and
this is perhaps the most complete answer to Lord Lytton's theory,
it must be remembered that neither in costume nor in dialogue is
beauty the dramatist's primary aim at all. The true dramatist aims
first at what is characteristic, and no more desires that all his personages should be beautifully attired than he desires that they should
all have beautiful natures or speak beautiful English. The true dramatist, in fact, shows us life under the conditions of art, not art in the
form of life. The Greek dress was the loveliest dress the world has
ever seen, and the English dress of the last century one of the most
monstrous; yet we cannot costume a play by Sheridan as we would
costume a play by Sophokles. For, as Polonius says in his excellent
lecture, a lecture to which I am glad to have the opportunity of
expressing my obligations, one of the first qualities of apparel is its
expressiveness. And the affected style of dress in the last century
was the natural characteristic of a society of affected manners and
affected conversation—a characteristic which the realistic dramatist
will highly value down to the smallest detail of accuracy, and the
materials for which he can get only from archaeology.

But it is not enough that a dress should be accurate; it must be
also appropriate to the stature and appearance of the actor, and
to his supposed condition, as well as to his necessary action in the
play. In Mr. Hare's production of *As You Like It* at the St. James's
Theatre, for instance, the whole point of Orlando's complaint that
he is brought up like a peasant, and not like a gentleman, was
spoiled by the gorgeousness of his dress, and the splendid apparel
worn by the banished Duke and his friends was quite out of place.
Mr. Lewis Wingfield's explanation that the sumptuary laws of the
period necessitated their doing so, is, I am afraid, hardly sufficient.

Outlaws, lurking in a forest and living by the chase, are not very likely to care much about ordinances of dress. They were probably attired like Robin Hood's men, to whom, indeed, they are compared in the course of the play. And that their dress was not that of wealthy noblemen may be seen by Orlando's words when he breaks in upon them. He mistakes them for robbers, and is amazed to find that they answer him in courteous and gentle terms. Lady Archibald Campbell's production, under Mr. E. W. Godwin's direction, of the same play in Coombe Wood was, as regards mounting, far more artistic. At least it seemed so to me. The Duke and his companions were dressed in serge tunics, leathern jerkins, high boots and gauntlets, and wore bycocket hats and hoods. And as they were playing in a real forest, they found, I am sure, their dresses extremely convenient. To every character in the play was given a perfectly appropriate attire, and the brown and green of their costumes harmonised exquisitely with the ferns through which they wandered, the trees beneath which they lay, and the lovely English landscape that surrounded the Pastoral Players. The perfect naturalness of the scene was due to the absolute accuracy and appropriateness of everything that was worn. Nor could archaeology have been put to a severer test, or come out of it more triumphantly. The whole production showed once for all that, unless a dress is archaeologically correct, and artistically appropriate, it always looks unreal, unnatural, and theatrical in the sense of artificial.

Nor, again, is it enough that there should be accurate and appropriate costumes of beautiful colours; there must be also beauty of colour on the stage as a whole, and as long as the background is painted by one artist, and the foreground figures independently designed by another, there is the danger of a want of harmony in the scene as a picture. For each scene the colour-scheme should be settled as absolutely as for the decoration of a room, and the textures which it is proposed to use should be mixed and re-mixed in every possible combination, and what is discordant removed. Then, as regards the particular kinds of colours, the stage is often made too glaring, partly through the excessive use of hot, violent reds, and partly through the costumes looking too new. Shabbiness, which in modern life is merely the tendency of the lower orders towards tone, is not without its artistic value, and modern colours are often much improved by being a little faded. Blue also is too frequently used: it is not merely a dangerous colour to wear by gaslight, but it is really difficult in England to get a thoroughly good blue. The fine Chinese blue, which we all so much admire, takes two years to dye, and the English public will not wait so long for a colour. Peacock blue, of course, has been employed on the stage, notably at the Lyceum, with great advantage; but all attempts at a good light blue, or good dark blue, which I have seen have been failures. The value of black is hardly appreciated; it was used effectively by Mr. Irving in *Hamlet* as the central note of the composition, but as a tone-giving neutral its importance is not recognised. And this is curious, considering the general colour of the dress of a century in which, as Baudelaire says, "Nous célébrons tous quelque enterrement."[18] The Archaeologist of the future will probably point to this age as a time when the beauty of black was understood; but I hardly think that, as regards stage-mounting or house decoration, it really is. Its decorative value is, of course, the same as that of white or gold; it can separate and harmonise colours. In modern plays the black frock coat of the hero becomes important in itself, and should be given a suitable background. But it rarely is. Indeed the only good background for a play in modern dress which I have ever seen was the dark grey and cream-white scene of the first act of the *Princesse Georges*[19] in Mrs. Langtry's production. As a rule, the hero is smothered in *bric-à-brac* and palm-trees, lost in the gilded abyss of Louis Quatorze furniture, or reduced to a mere midge in the midst of marqueterie; whereas the background should always be kept as a background, and colour subordinated to effect. This, of course, can only be done when there is one single mind directing the whole production. The facts of art are diverse, but the essence of artistic effect is unity. Monarchy, Anarchy and Republicanism may contend for the government of nations; but a theatre should be in the power of a cultured despot. There may be division of labour, but there must be no division of mind. Whoever

18. "We are all dressed for some funeral."

19. *Princesse Georges* was a French play of anonymous authorship, produced at the Princess's on January 20, 1885.

understands the costume of an age understands of necessity its architecture and its surroundings also, and it is easy to see from the chairs of a century whether it was a century of crinolines or not. In fact, in art there is no specialism, and a really artistic production should bear the impress of one master, and one master only, who not merely should design and arrange everything, but should have complete control over the way in which each dress is to be worn.

Mademoiselle Mars, in the first production of *Hernani*,[20] absolutely refused to call her lover *"Mon Lion!"* unless she was allowed to wear a little fashionable *toque* then much in vogue on the Boulevards; and many young ladies on our own stage insist to the present day on wearing stiff starched petticoats under Greek dresses, to the entire ruin of all delicacy of line and fold; but these wicked things should not be allowed. And there should be far more dress rehearsals than there are now. Actors such as Mr. Forbes-Robertson, [21] Mr. Conway, Mr. George Alexander, and others, not to mention older artists, can move with ease and elegance in the attire of any century; but there are not a few who seem dreadfully embarrassed about their hands if they have no side pockets, and who always wear their dresses as if they were costumes. Costumes of course, they are to the designer; but dresses they should be to those that wear them. And it is time that a stop should be put to the idea, very prevalent on the stage, that the Greeks and Romans always went about bareheaded in the open air—a mistake the Elizabethan managers did not fall into, for they gave hoods as well as gowns to their Roman senators.

More dress rehearsals would also be of value in explaining to the

20. Anne Françoise Hippolyte Mars (1779–1847) was a French actress who began her long and glorious career in child roles and continued as leading lady in comedies by Molière and Beaumarchais, romantic dramas by Dumas and Hugo, and "modern" comedies by Scribe.

*Hernani*, a romantic, rhetorical melodrama by Victor Hugo, was produced in Paris in 1830, sparking a revolution in emotional playwriting and a first-night riot in the theater.

21. Sir Johnston Forbes-Robertson (1853–1937), English actor-manager famous for his interpretations of Shakespeare, notably Hamlet and Buckingham (*Henry VIII*). Shaw wrote the Caesar role in his *Caesar and Cleopatra* for him, but he never played it.

actors that there is a form of gesture and movement that is not merely appropriate to each style of dress, but really conditioned by it. The extravagant use of the arms in the eighteenth century, for instance, was the necessary result of the large hoop, and the solemn dignity of Burleigh owed as much to his ruff as to his reason. Besides until an actor is at home in his dress, he is not at home in his part.

Of the value of beautiful costume in creating an artistic temperament in the audience, and producing that joy in beauty for beauty's sake without which the great masterpieces of art can never be understood, I will not here speak; though it is worth while to notice how Shakespeare appreciated that side of the question in the production of his tragedies, acting them always by artificial light, and in a theatre hung with black; but what I have tried to point out is that archaeology is not a pedantic method, but a method of artistic illusion, and that costume is a means of displaying character without description, and of producing dramatic situations and dramatic effects. And I think it is a pity that so many critics should have set themselves to attack one of the most important movements on the modern stage before that movement has at all reached its proper perfection. That it will do so, however, I feel as certain as that we shall require from our dramatic critics in the future higher qualifications than that they can remember Macready or have seen Benjamin Webster: we shall require them indeed, that they cultivate a sense of beauty. *Pour être plus difficile, la tâche n'en est que plus glorieuse.*[22] And if they will not encourage, at least they must not oppose, a movement of which Shakespeare of all dramatists would have most approved, for it has the illusion of truth for its method, and the illusion of beauty for its result. Not that I agree with everything that I have said in this essay. There is much with which I entirely disagree. The essay simply represents an artistic standpoint, and in aesthetic criticism attitude is everything. For in art there is no such thing as a universal truth. A Truth in art is that whose contradictory is also true. And just as it is only in art-criticism, and through it, that we can apprehend the Platonic theory of ideas, so it is only in art-criticism, and through it, that we can realise Hegel's

22. The task is only the more glorious for being more difficult.

system of contraries. The truths of metaphysics are the truths of masks.

First published in *Nineteenth Century*, XVII (May 1885), 800–818, under the title "Shakespeare and Stage Design." Reprinted in revised and augmented form in *Intentions* (London, 1891), pp. 217–258.

# Rosencrantz and Guildenstern

*Extracted from* De Profundis, *Robert Ross's title for a letter Wilde wrote to Lord Alfred Douglas from Reading Prison between January and March, 1897. On the day Wilde left Prison he gave it to Ross for delivery to Douglas, but Ross instead sent a typed copy he had made. In 1905, five years after Wilde's death, Ross—then literary executor of the Wilde estate—published an incomplete version of the letter. In 1909 he gave the manuscript to the British Museum with the proviso that it be sealed for fifty years. During that period several inaccurate versions were published, including a long, book-sized text by Vyvyan Holland, Wilde's surviving son. Not until 1962 was the complete text published, in* The Letters of Oscar Wilde, *edited by Rupert Hart-Davis. The text of this extract follows the 1962 definitive version.*

*The thesis of the extract, expressed pointedly in both its first and last lines, is central to Tom Stoppard's witty drama of 1966–1967,* Rosencrantz and Guildenstern Are Dead, *a* Hamlet *played from the perspective of the Wittenberg school chums.*

There is no error more common that that of thinking that those who are the causes or occasions of great tragedies share in the feelings suitable to the tragic mood: no error more fatal then expecting it of them. The martyr in his "shirt of flame"[1] may be looking on the face of God, but to him who is piling the faggots or loosening the logs for the blast the whole scene is no more than the slaying of an ox is to the butcher, or the felling of a tree to the charcoal-burner in the forest, or the fall of a flower to one who is mowing down the grass with a scythe. Great passions are for the great of soul, and great events can be seen only by those who are on a level with them.

1. Wilde quotes Alexander Smith's *A Life of Drama*, scene ii. [Rupert Hart-Davis]

I know of nothing in all Drama more incomparable from the point of view of Art, or more suggestive in its subtlety of observation, than Shakespeare's drawing of Rosencrantz and Guildenstern. They are Hamlet's college friends. They have been his companions. They bring with them memories of pleasant days together. At the moment when they come across him in the play he is staggering under the weight of a burden intolerable to one of his temperament. The dead have come armed out of the grave to impose on him a mission at once too great and too mean for him. He is a dreamer, and he is called upon to act. He has the nature of the poet and he is asked to grapple with the common complexities of cause and effect, with life in its practical realisation, of which he knows nothing, not with life in its ideal essence, of which he knows much. He has no conception of what to do, and his folly is to feign folly. Brutus used madness as a cloak to conceal the sword of his purpose, the dagger of his will,[2] but to Hamlet madness is a mere mask for the hiding of weakness. In the making of mows and jests he sees a chance of delay. He keeps playing with action, as an artist plays with a theory. He makes himself the spy of his proper actions, and listening to his own words knows them to be but "words, words, words." Instead of trying to be the hero of his own history, he seeks to be the spectator of his own tragedy. He disbelieves in everything, including himself, and yet his doubt helps him not, as it comes not from scepticism but from a divided will.

Of all this, Guildenstern and Rosencrantz realise nothing. They bow and smirk and smile, and what the one says the other echoes with sicklier iteration. When at last, by means of the play within the play and the puppets in their dalliance, Hamlet "catches the conscience" of the King, and drives the wretched man in terror from his throne, Guildenstern and Rosencrantz see no more in his conduct than a rather painful breach of court-etiquette. That is as far as they can attain to in "the contemplation of the spectacle of life with appropriate emotions."[3] They are close to his very secret

2. Junius Brutus, who expelled Tarquin, last King of Rome (and thus not the more famous Brutus associated with Julius Caesar). [Rupert Hart-Davis]

3. Probably a reference to a line by Walter Pater in an essay on Wordsworth. After quoting Wordsworth on "the operations of the elements and the appearances

and know nothing of it. Nor would there be any use in telling them. They are the little cups that can hold so much and no more. Towards the close it is suggested that, caught in a cunning springe set for another, they have met, or may meet with a violent and sudden death. But a tragic ending of this kind, though touched by Hamlet's humour with something of the surprise and justice of comedy, is really not for such as they. They never die. Horatio who, in order to "report Hamlet and his cause aright to the unsatisfied,"

> Absents him from felicity a while
> And in this harsh world draws his breath in pain,

dies, though not before an audience, and leaves no brother. But Guildenstern and Rosencrantz are as immortal as Angelo and Tartuffe, and should rank with them. They are what modern life has contributed to the antique ideal of friendship. He who writes a new *De Amicitia*[4] must find a niche for them and praise them in Tusculan prose. They are types fixed for all time. To censure them would show a lack of appreciation. They are merely out of their sphere: that is all. In sublimity of soul there is no contagion. High thoughts and high emotions are by their very existence isolated. What Ophelia herself could not understand was not to be realised by "Guildenstern and gentle Rosencrantz," by "Rosencrantz and gentle Guildenstern."

*De Profundis*, in *The Letters of Oscar Wilde*, ed. Rupert Hart-Davis (London: Hart-Davis, 1962), pp. 504-505.

---

of the visible universe, on storm and sunshine, on the revolutions of the seasons, on cold and heat, on loss of friends and kindred, on injuries and resentments, on gratitude and hope, on fear and sorrow," Pater observes, "To witness this spectacle with appropriate emotions is the aim of all culture." [Rupert Hart-Davis]

4. Cicero's treatise on the nature of friendship (44 B.C.).

# III.  ON AESTHETICS AND THE CRITIC

# The Decay of Lying
## An Observation

*In 1885 and 1886 Wilde's sons Cyril and Vyvyan were born. Their father obviously was using their names in order to speak for himself in the following selection.*

### A Dialogue

PERSONS: *Cyril and Vivian.*    SCENE: *the library of a country house in Nottinghamshire.*

CYRIL (*coming in through the open window from the terrace*): My dear Vivian, don't coop yourself up all day in the library. It is a perfectly lovely afternoon. The air is exquisite. There is a mist upon the woods, like the purple bloom upon a plum. Let us go and lie on the grass and smoke cigarettes and enjoy Nature.

VIVIAN: Enjoy Nature! I am glad to say that I have entirely lost that faculty. People tell us that Art makes us love Nature more than we loved her before; that it reveals her secrets to us; and that after a careful study of Corot and Constable we see things in her that had escaped our observation. My own experience is that the more we study Art, the less we care for Nature. What Art really reveals to us is Nature's lack of design, her curious crudities, her extraordinary monotony, her absolutely unfinished condition. Nature has good intentions, of course, but, as Aristotle once said, she cannot carry them out. When I look at a landscape I cannot help seeing all its defects. It is fortunate for us, however, that Nature is so imperfect, as otherwise we should have had no art at all. Art is our spirited protest, our gallant attempt to teach Nature her proper place. As for the infinite variety of Nature, that is a pure myth. It is not to be found in Nature herself. It resides in

165

the imagination, or fancy, or cultivated blindness of the man who looks at her.

CYRIL: Well, you need not look at the landscape. You can lie on the grass and smoke and talk.

VIVIAN: But Nature is so uncomfortable. Grass is hard and lumpy and damp, and full of dreadful black insects. Why, even Morris's poorest workman could make you a more comfortable seat than the whole of Nature can. Nature pales before the furniture of "the street which from Oxford has borrowed its name," as the poet you love so much once vilely phrased it. I don't complain. If nature had been comfortable, mankind would never have invented architecture, and I prefer houses to the open air. In a house we all feel of the proper proportions. Everything is subordinated to us, fashioned for our use and our pleasure. Egotism itself, which is so necessary to a proper sense of human dignity, is entirely the result of indoor life. Out of doors one becomes abstract and impersonal. One's individuality absolutely leaves one. And then Nature is so indifferent, so unappreciative. Whenever I am walking in the park here, I always feel that I am no more to her than the cattle that browse on the slope, or the burdock that blooms in the ditch. Nothing is more evident than that Nature hates Mind. Thinking is the most unhealthy thing in the world, and people die of it just as they die of any other disease. Fortunately, in England at any rate, thought is not catching. Our splendid physique as a people is entirely due to our national stupidity. I only hope we shall be able to keep this great historic bulwark of our happiness for many years to come; but I am afraid that we are beginning to be over-educated; at least everybody who is incapable of learning has taken to teaching —that is really what our enthusiasm for education has come to. In the meantime, you had better go back to your wearisome uncomfortable Nature, and leave me to correct my proofs.

CYRIL: Writing an article! That is not very consistent after what you have just said.

VIVIAN: Who wants to be consistent? The dullard and the doctrinaire, the tedious people who carry out their principles to the bitter end of action, to the *reductio ad absurdum* of practice. Not I. Like Emerson, I write over the door of my library the word

"Whim." Besides, my article is really a most salutary and valuable warning. If it is attended to, there may be a new Renaissance of Art.

CYRIL: What is the subject?

VIVIAN: I intend to call it "The Decay of Lying: A Protest."

CYRIL: Lying! I should have thought that our politicians kept up that habit.

VIVIAN: I assure you that they do not. They never rise beyond the level of misrepresentation, and actually condescend to prove, to discuss, to argue. How different from the temper of the true liar, with his frank, fearless statements, his superb irresponsibility, his healthy, natural disdain of proof of any kind! After all, what is a fine lie? Simply that which is its own evidence. If a man is sufficiently unimaginative to produce evidence in support of a lie, he might just as well speak the truth at once. No, the politicians won't do. Something may, perhaps, be urged on behalf of the Bar. The mantle of the Sophist has fallen on its members. Their feigned ardours and unreal rhetoric are delightful. They can make the worse appear the better cause, as though they were fresh from Leontine schools, and have been known to wrest from reluctant juries triumphant verdicts of acquittal for their clients, even when those clients, as often happens, were clearly and unmistakably innocent. But they are briefed by the prosaic, and are not ashamed to appeal to precedent. In spite of their endeavours, the truth will out. Newspapers, even, have degenerated. They may now be absolutely relied upon. One feels it as one wades through their columns. It is always the unreadable that occurs. I am afraid that there is not much to be said in favour of either the lawyer or the journalist. Besides, what I am pleading for is Lying in art. Shall I read you what I have written? It might do you a great deal of good.

CYRIL: Certainly, if you give me a cigarette. Thanks. By the way, what magazine do you intend it for?

VIVIAN: For the *Retrospective Review*.[1] I think I told you that the elect had revived it.

CYRIL: Whom do you mean by "the elect"?

VIVIAN: Oh, The Tired Hedonists, of course. It is a club to which

1. A journal facetiously invented for the occasion.

I belong. We are supposed to wear faded roses in our button-holes when we meet, and to have a sort of cult for Domitian.[2] I am afraid you are not eligible. You are too fond of simple pleasures.

CYRIL: I should be black-balled on the ground of animal spirits, I suppose?

VIVIAN: Probably. Besides, you are a little too old. We don't admit anybody who is of the usual age.

CYRIL: Well, I should fancy you are all a good deal bored with each other.

VIVIAN: We are. That is one of the objects of the club. Now, if you promise not to interrupt too often, I will read you my article.

CYRIL: You will find me all attention.

VIVIAN (*reading in a very clear voice*): "THE DECAY OF LYING: A PROTEST.—One of the chief causes that can be assigned for the curiously commonplace character of most of the literature of our age is undoubtedly the decay of Lying as an art, a science, and a social pleasure. The ancient historians gave us delightful fiction in the form of fact; the modern novelist presents us with dull facts under the guise of fiction. The Blue-Book is rapidly becoming his ideal both for method and manner. He has his tedious *document humain*, his miserable little *coin de la création* into which he peers with his microscope. He is to be found at the Librairie Nationale, or at the British Museum, shamelessly reading up his subject. He has not even the courage of other people's ideas, but insists on going directly to life for everything, and ultimately, between encyclopaedias and personal experience, he comes to the ground, having drawn his types from the family circle or from the weekly washer-woman, and having acquired an amount of useful information from which never, even in his most meditative moments, can he thoroughly free himself.

"The loss that results to literature in general from this false ideal of our time can hardly be overestimated. People have a careless way of talking about a 'born liar,' just as they talk about a 'born poet.' But in both cases they are wrong. Lying and poetry

2. "Cult for Domitian" is very likely a suggestion of philistinism, for Domitian (Titus Flavius Domitianus), who lived from 51 A.D. to 96 A.D., was the cruel, suspicious Roman emperor who banished philosophers and literati.

are arts—arts, as Plato saw, not unconnected with each other—and they require the most careful study, the most disinterested devotion. Indeed, they have their technique, just as the more material arts of painting and sculpture have their subtle secrets of form and colour, their craft-mysteries, their deliberate artistic methods. As one knows the poet by his fine music, so one can recognise the liar by his rich rhythmic utterance, and in neither case will the casual inspiration of the moment suffice. Here, as elsewhere, practice must precede perfection. But in modern days while the fashion of writing poetry has become far too common, and should, if possible, be discouraged, the fashion of lying has almost fallen into disrepute. Many a young man starts in life with a natural gift for exaggeration which, if nurtured in congenial and sympathetic surroundings, or by the imitation of the best models, might grow into something really great and wonderful. But, as a rule, he comes to nothing. He either falls into careless habits of accuracy——"

CYRIL: My dear fellow!

VIVIAN: Please don't interrupt in the middle of a sentence. "He either falls into careless habits of accuracy, or takes to frequenting the society of the aged and the well-informed. Both things are equally fatal to his imagination, as indeed they would be fatal to the imagination of anybody, and in a short time he develops a morbid and unhealthy faculty of truth-telling, begins to verify all statements made in his presence, has no hesitation in contradicting people who are much younger than himself, and often ends by writing novels which are so life-like that no one can possibly believe in their probability. This is no isolated instance that we are giving. It is simply one example out of many; and if something cannot be done to check, or at least to modify, our monstrous worship of facts, Art will become sterile and beauty will pass away from the land.

"Even Mr. Robert Louis Stevenson, that delightful master of delicate and fanciful prose, is tainted with this modern vice, for we know positively no other name for it. There is such a thing as robbing a story of its reality by trying to make it too true, and *The Black Arrow* is so inartistic as not to contain a single anachronism to boast of, while the transformation of Dr. Jekyll reads dangerously like an experiment out of the *Lancet*. As for Mr. Rider Haggard,[3] who really has, or had once, the makings of a perfectly magnificent liar, he is now so afraid of being suspected of genius that when he does tell us anything marvellous, he feels bound to invent a personal reminiscence, and to put it into a footnote as a kind of cowardly corroboration. Nor are our other novelists much better. Mr. Henry James writes fiction as if it were a painful duty, and wastes upon mean motives and imperceptible 'points of view' his neat literary style, his felicitous phrases, his swift and caustic satire. Mr. Hall Caine, it is true, aims at the grandiose, but then he writes at the top of his voice. He is so loud that one cannot hear what he says. Mr. James Payn is an adept in the art of concealing what is not worth finding. He hunts down the obvious with the enthusiasm of a short-sighted detective. As one turns over the pages, the suspense of the author becomes almost unbearable. The horses of Mr. William Black's phaeton do not soar towards the sun. They merely frighten the sky at evening into violent chromo-lithographic effects. On seeing them approach, the peasants take refuge in dialect. Mrs. Oliphant prattles pleasantly about curates, lawn-tennis parties, domesticity, and other wearisome things. Mr. Marion Crawford has immolated himself upon the altar of local colour. He is like the lady in the French comedy who keeps talking about *le beau ciel d'Italie*. Besides, he has fallen into the bad habit of uttering moral platitudes. He is always telling us that to be good is to be good, and that to be bad is to be wicked. At times he is almost edifying. *Robert Elsmere* is of course a masterpiece—a masterpiece of the *genre ennuyeux*, the one form of literature that the English people seems thoroughly to enjoy. A thoughtful young friend of ours once told us that it reminded him of the sort of conversation that goes on at a meat tea in the house of a serious Nonconformist family, and we

3. Sir Henry Rider Haggard (1856–1925), English novelist best known for such tales of romance and adventure as *King Solomon's Mines* (1886) and *Allan Quatermain* (1887). Other authors mentioned below are James Payn (1830–1898), English poet, novelist, and editor of *Chambers's Journal* and the *Cornhill Magazine*; Margaret Oliphant (1828–1897), English novelist best known for her novels titled collectively the *Chronicles of Carlingford*; Francis Marion Crawford (1854–1909), expatriate American romantic novelist; and Mrs. Humphry Ward (1851–1920), novelist granddaughter of Thomas Arnold of Rugby.

can quite believe it. Indeed, it is only in England that such a book could be produced. England is the home of lost ideas. As for that great and daily increasing school of novelists for whom the sun always rises in the East-End, the only thing that can be said about them is that they find life crude, and leave it raw.

"In France, though nothing so deliberately tedious as *Robert Elsmere* had been produced, things are not much better. M. Guy de Maupassant, with his keen mordant irony and his hard vivid style, strips life of the few poor rags that still cover her, and shows us foul sore and festering wound. He writes lurid little tragedies in which everybody is ridiculous; bitter comedies at which one cannot laugh for very tears. M. Zola, true to the lofty principle that he lays down in one of his pronunciamentos on literature, *L'homme de génie n'a jamais d'esprit*, is determined to show that, if he has not got genius, he can at least be dull. And how well he succeeds! He is not without power. Indeed, at times, as in *Germinal*, there is something almost epic in his work. But his work is entirely wrong from beginning to end, and wrong not on the ground of morals, but on the ground of art. From any ethical standpoint it is just what it should be. The author is perfectly truthful, and describes things exactly as they happen. What more can any moralist desire? We have no sympathy at all with the moral indignation of our time against M. Zola. It is simply the indignation of Tartuffe on being exposed. But from the standpoint of art, what can be said in favour of the author of *L'Assommoir*, *Nana* and *Pot-Bouille*? Nothing. Mr. Ruskin once described the characters in George Eliot's novels as being like the sweepings of a Pentonville omnibus, but M. Zola's characters are much worse. They have their dreary vices, and their drearier virtues. The record of their lives is absolutely without interest. Who cares what happens to them? In literature we require distinction, charm, beauty and imaginative power. We don't want to be harrowed and disgusted with an account of the doings of the lower orders. M. Daudet is better. He has wit, a light touch and an amusing style. But he has lately committed literary suicide. Nobody can possibly care for Delobelle with his *Il faut lutter pour l'art*, or for Valmajour with his eternal refrain about the nightingale, or for the poet in *Jack* with his *mots cruels*, now that we have learned from

*Vingt Ans de ma Vie littéraire* that these characters were taken directly from life. To us they seem to have suddenly lost all their vitality, all the few qualities they ever possessed. The only real people are the people who never existed, and if a novelist is base enough to go to life for his personages he should at least pretend that they are creations, and not boast of them as copies. The justification of a character in a novel is not that other persons are what they are, but that the author is what he is. Otherwise the novel is not a work of art. As for M. Paul Bourget, the master of the *roman psycologique*, he commits the error of imagining that the men and women of modern life are capable of being infinitely analysed for an innumerable series of chapters. In point of fact what is interesting about people in good society—and M. Bourget rarely moves out of the Faubourg St. Germain, except to come to London—is the mask that each one of them wears, not the reality that lies behind the mask. It is a humiliating confession, but we are all of us made out of the same stuff. In Falstaff there is something of Hamlet, in Hamlet there is not a little of Falstaff. The fat knight has his moods of melancholy, and the young prince his moments of coarse humour. Where we differ from each other is purely in accidentals: in dress, manner, tone of voice, religious opinions, personal appearance, tricks of habit and the like. The more one analyses people, the more all reasons for analysis disappear. Sooner or later one comes to that dreadful universal thing called human nature. Indeed, as anyone who has ever worked among the poor knows only too well, the brotherhood of man is no mere poet's dream, it is a most depressing and humiliating reality; and if a writer insists upon analysing the upper classes, he might just as well write of match-girls and coster-mongers at once." However, my dear Cyril, I will not detain you any further just here. I quite admit that modern novels have many good points. All I insist on is that, as a class, they are quite unreadable.

CYRIL: That is certainly a very grave qualification, but I must say that I think you are rather unfair in some of your strictures. I like *The Deemster*, and *The Daughter of Heth*, and *Le Disciple*, and *Mr. Isaacs*, and as for *Robert Elsmere*,[4] I am quite devoted to it. Not that

4. Currently popular novels by, respectively, Hall Caine, Rider Haggard, Paul Bourget, Marion Crawford, and Mrs. Humphry Ward.

I can look upon it as a serious work. As a statement of the problems that confront the earnest Christian it is ridiculous and antiquated. It is simply Arnold's *Literature and Dogma* with the literature left out. It is as much behind the age as Paley's *Evidences,* or Colenso's method of Biblical exegesis.[5] Nor could anything be less impressive than the unfortunate hero gravely heralding a dawn that rose long ago, and so completely missing its true significance that he proposes to carry on the business of the old firm under the new name. On the other hand, it contains several clever caricatures, and a heap of delightful quotations, and Green's philosophy very pleasantly sugars the somewhat bitter pill of the author's fiction. I also cannot help expressing my surprise that you have said nothing about the two novelists whom you are always reading, Balzac and George Meredith. Surely they are realists, both of them?

VIVIAN: Ah! Meredith! Who can define him? His style is chaos illumined by flashes of lightning. As a writer he has mastered everything except language: as a novelist he can do everything, except tell a story: as an artist he is everything except articulate. Somebody in Shakespeare—Touchstone, I think—talks about a man who is always breaking his shins over his own wit, and it seems to me that this might serve as the basis for a criticism of Meredith's method. But whatever he is, he is not a realist. Or rather I would say that he is a child of realism who is not on speaking terms with his father. By deliberate choice he has made himself a romanticist. He has refused to bow the knee to Baal, and after all, even if the man's fine spirit did not revolt against the noisy assertions of realism, his style would be quite sufficient of itself to keep life at a respectful distance. By its means he has planted round his garden a hedge full of thorns, and red with wonderful roses. As for Balzac, he was a most remarkable combination of the artistic temperament with the scientific spirit. The latter he bequeathed to his disciples. The former was entirely his own. The difference between such a book as M. Zola's *L'Assommoir* and Balzac's *Illusions Perdues* is the difference

5. These men and their writings were all concerned with the problems of biblical interpretation that were the subject of controversy during the Victorian era and that were also the concern of Mrs. Ward's novel, which created an enormous stir when it was published in 1888.

between unimaginative realism and imaginative reality. "All Balzac's characters," said Baudelaire, "are gifted with the same ardour of life that animated himself. All his fictions are as deeply coloured as dreams. Each mind is a weapon loaded to the muzzle with will. The very scullions have genius." A steady course of Balzac reduces our living friends to shadows, and our acquaintances to the shadows of shades. His characters have a kind of fervent fiery-coloured existence. They dominate us, and defy scepticism. One of the greatest tragedies of my life is the death of Lucien de Rubempré. It is a grief from which I have never been able completely to rid myself. It haunts me in my moments of pleasure. I remember it when I laugh. But Balzac is no more a realist than Holbein was. He created life, he did not copy it. I admit, however, that he set far too high a value on modernity of form, and that, consequently, there is no book of his that, as an artistic masterpiece, can rank with *Salammbô* or *Esmond*, or *The Cloister and the Hearth*, or the *Vicomte de Bragelonne*.[6]

CYRIL: Do you object to modernity of form, then?

VIVIAN: Yes. It is a huge price to pay for a very poor result. Pure modernity of form is always somewhat vulgarising. It cannot help being so. The public imagine that, because they are interested in their immediate surroundings, Art should be interested in them also, and should take them as her subject-matter. But the mere fact that they are interested in these things makes them unsuitable subjects for Art. The only beautiful things, as somebody once said, are the things that do not concern us. As long as a thing is useful or necessary to us, or affects us in any way, either for pain or for pleasure, or appeals strongly to our sympathies, or is a vital part of the environment in which we live, it is outside the proper sphere of art. To art's subject-matter we should be more or less indifferent. We should, at any rate, have no preferences, no prejudices, no partisan feeling of any kind. It is exactly because Hecuba is nothing to us that her sorrows are such an admirable motive for a tragedy. I do not know anything in the whole history of literature sadder than the artistic career of Charles Reade. He wrote one beautiful book, *The*

6. Historical novels by, respectively, Flaubert, Thackeray, Charles Reade, and Dumas *pere*.

*Cloister and the Hearth,* a book as much above *Romola* as *Romola* is above *Daniel Deronda,* and wasted the rest of his life in a foolish attempt to be modern, to draw public attention to the state of our convict prisons, and the management of our private lunatic asylums. Charles Dickens was depressing enough in all conscience when he tried to arouse our sympathy for the victims of the poor-law administration; but Charles Reade, an artist, a scholar, a man with a true sense of beauty, raging and roaring over the abuses of contemporary life like a common pamphleteer or a sensational journalist, is really a sight for the angels to weep over. Believe me, my dear Cyril, modernity of form and modernity of subject-matter are entirely and absolutely wrong. We have mistaken the common livery of the age for the vesture of the Muses, and spend our days in the sordid streets and hideous suburbs of our vile cities when we should be out on the hillside with Apollo. Certainly we are a degraded race, and have sold our birthright for a mess of facts.

CYRIL: There is something in what you say, and there is no doubt that whatever amusement we may find in reading a purely modern novel, we have rarely any artistic pleasure in re-reading it. And this is perhaps the best rough test of what is literature and what is not. If one cannot enjoy reading a book over and over again, there is no use reading it at all. But what do you say about the return to Life and Nature? This is the panacea that is always being recommended to us.

VIVIAN: I will read you what I say on that subject. The passage comes later on in the article, but I may as well give it to you now:—

"The popular cry of our time is 'Let us return to Life and Nature; they will recreate Art for us, and send the red blood coursing through her veins; they will shoe her feet with swiftness and make her hand strong.' But, alas! we are mistaken in our amiable and well-meaning efforts. Nature is always behind the age. And as for Life, she is the solvent that breaks up Art, the enemy that lays waste her house."

CYRIL: What do you mean by saying that Nature is always behind the age?

VIVIAN: Well, perhaps that is rather cryptic. What I mean is this. If we take Nature to mean natural simple instinct as opposed to self-conscious culture, the work produced under this influence is always old-fashioned, antiquated, and out of date. One touch of Nature may make the whole world kin, but two touches of Nature will destroy any work of Art. If, on the other hand, we regard Nature as the collection of phenomena external to man, people only discover in her what they bring to her. She has no suggestions of her own. Wordsworth went to the lakes, but he was never a lake poet. He found in stones the sermons he had already hidden there. He went moralising about the district, but his good work was produced when he returned, not to Nature but to poetry. Poetry gave him "Laodamia," and the fine sonnets, and the great Ode such as it is. Nature gave him "Martha Ray" and "Peter Bell," and the address to Mr. Wilkinson's spade.

CYRIL: I think that view might be questioned. I am rather inclined to believe in "the impulse from a vernal wood," though of course the artistic value of such an impulse depends entirely on the kind of temperament that receives it, so that the return to Nature would come to mean simply the advance to a great personality. You would agree with that, I fancy. However, proceed with your article.

VIVIAN (*reading*): "Art begins with abstract decoration, with purely imaginative and pleasurable work dealing with what is unreal and non-existent. This is the first stage. Then Life becomes fascinated with this new wonder, and asks to be admitted into the charmed circle. Art takes life as part of her rough material, recreates it, and refashions it in fresh forms, is absolutely indifferent to fact, invents, imagines, dreams, and keeps between herself and reality the impenetrable barrier of beautiful style, of decorative or ideal treatment. The third stage is when Life gets the upper hand, and drives Art out into the wilderness. This is the true decadence, and it is from this that we are now suffering.

"Take the case of the English drama. At first in the hands of the monks Dramatic Art was abstract, decorative and mythological. Then she enlisted Life in her service, and using some of life's external forms, she created an entirely new race of beings, whose sorrows were more terrible than any sorrow man has ever felt, whose joys were keener than lover's joys, who had the rage of the Titans and the calm of the gods, who had monstrous and marvellous sins, monstrous and marvellous virtues. To them she gave a language different from that of actual use, a language full of resonant music and sweet rhythm, made stately by solemn cadence, or made delicate by fanciful rhyme, jewelled with wonderful words, and enriched with lofty diction. She clothed her children in strange raiment and gave them masks and at her bidding the antique world rose from its marble tomb. A new Caesar stalked through the streets of risen Rome, and with purple sail and flute-led oars another Cleopatra passed up the river to Antioch. Old myth and legend and dream took shape and substance. History was entirely re-written, and there was hardly one of the dramatists who did not recognise that the object of Art is not simple truth but complex beauty. In this they were perfectly right. Art itself is really a form of exaggeration; and selection, which is the very spirit of art, is nothing more than an intensified mode of over-emphasis.

"But Life soon shattered the perfection of the form. Even in Shakespeare we can see the beginning of the end. It shows itself by the gradual breaking-up of the blank-verse in the later plays, by the predominance given to prose, and by the over-importance assigned to characterisation. The passages in Shakespeare—and there are many—where the language is uncouth, vulgar, exaggerated, fantastic, obscene even, are entirely due to Life calling for an echo of her own voice and rejecting the intervention of beautiful style through which alone should life be suffered to find expression. Shakespeare is not by any means a flawless artist. He is too fond of going directly to life, and borrowing life's natural utterance. He forgets that when Art surrenders her imaginative medium she surrenders everything. Goethe says, somewhere:—

"It is in compression that the master first reveals himself."[7]

"It is in working within limits that the master reveals himself, and the limitation, the very condition of any art, is style. However, we need not linger any longer over Shakespeare's realism. The Tempest is the most perfect of palinodes. All that we desired to point out was that the magnificent work of the Elizabethan and Jacobean artists contained within itself the seeds of its own dissolution, and that, if it drew some of its strength from using life as rough material,

7. "In der Beschränkung zeigt sich erst der Meister."

it drew all its weakness from using life as an artistic method. As the inevitable result of this substitution of an imitative for a creative medium, this surrender of an imaginative form, we have the modern English melodrama. The characters in these plays talk on the stage exactly as they would off it; they have neither aspirations nor aspirates; they are taken directly from life and reproduce its vulgarity down to the smallest detail; they present the gait, manner, costume and accent of real people; they would pass unnoticed in a third-class railway carriage. And yet how wearisome the plays are! They do not succeed in producing even that impression of reality at which they aim, and which is their only reason for existing. As a method, realism is a complete failure.

"What is true about the drama and the novel is no less true about those arts that we call the decorative arts. The whole history of these arts in Europe is the record of the struggle between Orientalism, with its frank rejection of imitation, its love of artistic convention, its dislike to the actual representation of any object in Nature, and our own imitative spirit. Wherever the former has been paramount, as in Byzantium, Sicily and Spain, by actual contact or in the rest of Europe by the influence of the Crusades, we have had beautiful and imaginative work in which the visible things of life are transmuted into artistic conventions, and the things that Life has not are invented and fashioned for her delight. But wherever we have returned to Life and Nature, our work has always become vulgar, common and uninteresting. Modern tapestry, with its aerial effects, its elaborate perspective, its broad expanses of waste sky, its faithful and laborious realism, has no beauty whatsoever. The pictorial glass of Germany is absolutely detestable. We are beginning to weave possible carpets in England, but only because we have returned to the method and spirit of the East. Our rugs and carpets of twenty years ago, with their solemn depressing truths, their inane worship of Nature, their sordid reproductions of visible objects, have become, even to the Philistine, a source of laughter. A cultured Mahomedan once remarked to us, 'You Christians are so occupied in misinterpreting the fourth commandment that you have never thought of making an artistic application of the second.' He was perfectly right, and the whole truth of the matter is this: The proper school to learn art in is not Life but Art."

And now let me read you a passage which seems to me to settle the question very completely.

"It was not always thus. We need not say anything about the poets, for they, with the unfortunate exception of Mr. Wordsworth, have been really faithful to their high mission, and are universally recognised as being absolutely unreliable. But in the works of Herodotus, who, in spite of the shallow and ungenerous attempts of modern sciolists to verify his history, may justly be called the 'Father of Lies'; in the published speeches of Cicero and the biographies of Suetonius; in Tacitus at his best; in Pliny's *Natural History*; in Hanno's *Periplus*; in all the early chronicles; in the Lives of the Saints; in Froissart and Sir Thomas Malory; in the travels of Marco Polo; in Olaus Magnus, and Aldrovandus, and Conrad Lycosthenes, with his magnificent *Prodigiorum et Ostentorum Chronicon*; in the auto-biography of Benvenuto Cellini; in the memoirs of Casanova; in Defoe's *History of the Plague*; in Boswell's *Life of Johnson*; in Napoleon's despatches, and in the works of our own Carlyle, whose *French Revolution* is one of the most fascinating historical novels ever written, facts are either kept in their proper subordinate position, or else entirely excluded on the general ground of dullness. Now everything is changed. Facts are not merely finding a footing-place in history, but they are usurping the domain of Fancy, and have invaded the kingdom of Romance. Their chilling touch is over everything. They are vulgarising mankind. The crude commercialism of America, its materialising spirit, its indifference to the poetical side of things, and its lack of imagination and of high unattainable ideals, are entirely due to that country having adopted for its national hero a man who, according to his own confession, was incapable of telling a lie, and it is not too much to say that the story of George Washington and the cherry-tree has done more harm, and in a shorter space of time, than any other moral tale in the whole of literature."

CYRIL: My dear boy!

VIVIAN: I assure you it is the case, and the amusing part of the whole thing is that the story of the cherry-tree is an absolute myth.

However, you must not think that I am too despondent about the artistic future either of America or of our own country. Listen to this:—

"That some change will take place before this century has drawn to its close we have no doubt whatsoever. Bored by the tedious and improving conversation of those who have neither the wit to exaggerate nor the genius to romance, tired of the intelligent person whose reminiscences are always based upon memory, whose statements are invariably limited by probability, and who is at any time liable to be corroborated by the merest Philistine who happens to be present, Society sooner or later must return to its lost leader, the cultured and fascinating liar. Who he was who first, without ever having gone out to the rude chase, told the wondering cavemen at sunset how he had dragged the Megatherium from the purple darkness of its jasper cave, or slain the Mammoth in single combat and brought back its gilded tusks, we cannot tell, and not one of our modern anthropologists, for all their much-boasted science, has had the ordinary courage to tell us. Whatever was his name or race, he certainly was the true founder of social intercourse. For the aim of the liar is simply to charm, to delight, to give pleasure. He is the very basis of civilised society, and without him a dinner-party, even at the mansions of the great, is as dull as a lecture at the Royal Society, or a debate at the Incorporated Authors, or one of Mr. Burnand's farcical comedies.[8]

"Nor will he be welcomed by society alone. Art, breaking from the prison-house of realism, will run to greet him, and will kiss his false, beautiful lips, knowing that he alone is in possession of the great secret of all her manifestations, the secret that Truth is entirely and absolutely a matter of style; while Life—poor, probable, uninteresting human life—tired of repeating herself for the benefit of Mr. Herbert Spencer,[9] scientific historians, and the compilers of

8. Francis Cowley Burnand (1836–1917) manufactured several dozen plays, notably *Black-Eyed Susan* and *Cox and Box*, a musical version of John Maddison Morton's farce, between 1852 and the end of the century.

9. Herbert Spencer (1820–1903), English philosopher enormously influential in his time, particularly after his publication of a series of treatises on "evolutionary philosophy" from 1860 to 1887.

statistics in general, will follow meekly after him, and try to reproduce, in her own simple and untutored way, some of the marvels of
which he talks.

"No doubt there will always be critics who, like a certain writer
in the *Saturday Review*, will gravely censure the teller of fairy tales
for his defective knowledge of natural history, who will measure
imaginative work by their own lack of any imaginative faculty,
and will hold up their ink-stained hands in horror if some honest
gentleman, who has never been farther than the yew-trees of his
own garden, pens a fascinating book of travels like Sir John Mandeville, or, like great Raleigh, writes a whole history of the world,
without knowing anything whatsoever about the past. To excuse
themselves they will try and shelter under the shield of him who made
Prospero the magician, and gave him Caliban and Ariel as his
servants, who heard the Tritons blowing their horns round the
coral reefs of the Enchanted Isle, and the fairies singing to each
other in a wood near Athens, who led the phantom kings in dim
procession across the misty Scottish heath, and hid Hecate in a
cave with the weird sisters. They will call upon Shakespeare—they
always do—and will quote that hackneyed passage forgetting that
this unfortunate aphorism about Art holding the mirror up to
Nature, is deliberately said by Hamlet in order to convince the
bystanders of his absolute insanity in all art-matters."

CYRIL: Ahem! Another cigarette, please.

VIVIAN: My dear fellow, whatever you may say, it is merely a
dramatic utterance, and no more represents Shakespeare's real
views upon art than the speeches of Iago represent his real views
upon morals. But let me get to the end of the passage:—

"Art finds her own perfection within, and not outside of, herself.
She is not to be judged by any external standard of resemblance.
She is a veil, rather than a mirror. She has flowers that no forests
know of, birds that no woodland possesses. She makes and unmakes
many worlds, and can draw the moon from heaven with a scarlet
thread. Hers are the 'forms more real than living man,' and hers
the great archetypes of which things that have existence are but
unfinished copies. Nature has, in her eyes, no laws, no uniformity.
She can work miracles at her will, and when she calls monsters from

the deep they come. She can bid the almond tree blossom in winter, and send the snow upon the ripe cornfield. At her word the frost lays its silver finger on the burning mouth of June, and the winged lions creep out from the hollows of the Lydian hills. The dryads peer from the thicket as she passes by, and the brown fauns smile strangely at her when she comes near them. She has hawk-faced gods that worship her, and the centaurs gallop at her side."

CYRIL: I like that. I can see it. Is that the end?

VIVIAN: No. There is one more passage, but it is purely practical. It simply suggests some methods by which we could revive this lost art of Lying.

CYRIL: Well, before you read it to me, I should like to ask you a question. What do you mean by saying that life, "poor, probable, uninteresting human life," will try to reproduce the marvels of art? I can quite understand your objection to art being treated as a mirror. You think it would reduce genius to the position of a cracked looking-glass. But you don't mean to say that you seriously believe that Life imitates Art, that Life in fact is the mirror, and Art the reality?

VIVIAN: Certainly I do. Paradox though it may seem—and paradoxes are always dangerous things—it is none the less true that Life imitates art far more than Art imitates life. We have all seen in our own day in England how a certain curious and fascinating type of beauty, invented and emphasised by two imaginative painters, has so influenced Life that whenever one goes to a private view or to an artistic salon one sees, here the mystic eyes of Rossetti's dream, the long ivory throat, the strange square-cut jaw, the loosened shadowy hair that he so ardently loved, there the sweet maidenhood of "The Golden Stair," the blossom-like mouth and weary loveliness of the "Laus Amoris," the passion-pale face of Andromeda, the thin hands and lithe beauty of the Vivian in "Merlin's Dream." And it has always been so. A great artist invents a type, and Life tries to copy it, to reproduce it in a popular form, like an enterprising publisher. Neither Holbein nor Vandyck found in England what they have given us. They brought their types with them, and Life with her keen imitative faculty set herself to supply the master with models. The Greeks, with their quick

artistic instinct, understood this, and set in the bride's chamber the
statue of Hermes or of Apollo, that she might bear children as
lovely as the works of art that she looked at in her rapture or her
pain. They knew that Life gains from art not merely spirituality,
depth of thought and feeling, soul-turmoil or soul-peace, but that
she can form herself on the very lines and colours of art, and can
reproduce the dignity of Pheidias as well as the grace of Praxiteles.
Hence came their objection to realism. They disliked it on purely
social grounds. They felt that it inevitably makes people ugly, and
they were perfectly right. We try to improve the conditions of the
race by means of good air, free sunlight, wholesome water, and
hideous bare buildings for the better housing of the lower orders.
But these things merely produce health, they do not produce
beauty. For this, Art is required, and the true disciples of the great
artist are not his studio-imitators, but those who become like his
works of art, be they plastic as in Greek days, or pictorial as in
modern times; in a word, Life is Art's best, Art's only pupil.

As it is with the visible arts, so it is with literature. The most
obvious and the vulgarest form in which this is shown is in the case
of the silly boys who, after reading the adventures of Jack Sheppard
or Dick Turpin,[10] pillage the stalls of unfortunate apple-women,
break into sweet-shops at night, and alarm old gentlemen who are
returning home from the city by leaping out on them in suburban
lanes, with black masks and unloaded revolvers. This interesting
phenomenon, which always occurs after the appearance of a new
edition of either of the books I have alluded to, is usually attributed
to the influence of literature on the imagination. But this is a
mistake. The imagination is essentially creative, and always seeks
for a new form. The boy-burglar is simply the inevitable result of
life's imitative instinct. He is Fact, occupied as Fact usually is,
with trying to reproduce Fiction, and what we see in him is repeated
on an extended scale throughout the whole of life. Schopenhauer
has analysed the pessimism that characterises modern thought,
but Hamlet invented it. The world has become sad because a puppet

10. Jack Sheppard (1702–1724), an English highwayman executed at Tyburn,
was afterwards the subject of tracts by Defoe, plays, ballads, and novels. Richard
Turpin (1706–1739), also a highwayman, suffered the same fate as Sheppard.

was once melancholy. The Nihilist, that strange martyr who has no faith, who goes to the stake without enthusiasm, and dies for what he does not believe in, is a purely literary product. He was invented by Tourgenieff, and completed by Dostoevski. Robespierre came out of the pages of Rousseau as surely as the People's Palace rose out of the *débris* of a novel. Literature always anticipates life. It does not copy it, but moulds it to its purpose. The nineteenth century, as we know it, is largely an invention of Balzac. Our Luciens de Rubempré, our Rastignacs, and De Marsays made their first appearance on the stage of the *Comédie Humaine*. We are merely carrying out, with footnotes and unnecessary additions, the whim or fancy or creative vision of a great novelist. I once asked a lady, who knew Thackeray intimately, whether he had had any model for Becky Sharp. She told me that Becky was an invention, but that the idea of the character had been partly suggested by a governess who lived in the neighbourhood of Kensington Square, and was the companion of a very selfish and rich old woman. I inquired what became of the governess, and she replied that, oddly enough, some years after the appearance of *Vanity Fair*, she ran away with the nephew of the lady with whom she was living, and for a short time made a great splash in society, quite in Mrs. Rawdon Crawley's style, and entirely by Mrs. Rawdon Crawley's methods. Ultimately she came to grief, disappeared to the Continent, and used to be occasionally seen at Monte Carlo and other gambling places. The noble gentleman from whom the same great sentimentalist drew Colonel Newcome died, a few months after *The Newcomes* had reached a fourth edition, with the word "Adsum" on his lips. Shortly after Mr. Stevenson published his curious psychological story of transformation, a friend of mine, called Mr. Hyde, was in the north of London, and being anxious to get to a railway station, took what he thought would be a short cut, lost his way, and found himself in a network of mean, evil-looking streets. Feeling rather nervous he began to walk extremely fast, when suddenly out of an archway ran a child right between his legs. It fell on the pavement, he tripped over it, and trampled upon it. Being, of course, very much frightened and a little hurt, it began to scream, and in a few seconds the whole street was full of rough people who came pouring out of the houses like ants. They surrounded him, and asked him his name. He was just about to give it when he suddenly remembered the opening incident in Mr. Stevenson's story. He was so filled with horror at having realised in his own person that terrible and well-written scene, and at having done accidentally, though in fact, what the Mr. Hyde of fiction had done with deliberate intent, that he ran away as hard as he could go. He was, however, very closely followed, and finally he took refuge in a surgery, the door of which happened to be open, where he explained to a young assistant, who happened to be there, exactly what had occurred. The humanitarian crowd were induced to go away on his giving them a small sum of money, and as soon as the coast was clear he left. As he passed out, the name on the brass door-plate of the surgery caught his eye. It was "Jekyll." At least it should have been.

Here the imitation, as far as it went, was of course accidental. In the following case the imitation was self-conscious. In the year 1879, just after I had left Oxford, I met at a reception at the house of one of the Foreign Ministers a woman of very curious exotic beauty. We became great friends, and were constantly together. And yet what interested me most in her was not her beauty, but her character, her entire vagueness of character. She seemed to have no personality at all, but simply the possibility of many types. Sometimes she would give herself up entirely to art, turn her drawing-room into a studio, and spend two or three days a week at picture galleries or museums. Then she would take to attending race-meetings, wear the most horsey clothes, and talk about nothing but betting. She abandoned religion for mesmerism, mesmerism for politics, and politics for the melodramatic excitements of philanthropy. In fact, she was a kind of Proteus, and as much a failure in all her transformations as was that wondrous sea-god when Odysseus laid hold of him. One day a serial began in one of the French magazines. At that time I used to read serial stories, and I well remember the shock of surprise I felt when I came to the description of the heroine. She was so like my friend that I brought her the magazine, and she recognised herself in it immediately, and seemed fascinated by the resemblance. I should tell you, by the way, that the story was translated from some dead Russian writer, so that the author had not taken his type from my friend. Well, to put the matter briefly, some months afterwards I was in Venice, and finding the magazine in the reading-room of the hotel, I took it up casually to see what had become of the heroine. It was a most piteous tale, as the girl had ended by running away with a man absolutely inferior to her, not merely in social station, but in character and intellect also. I wrote to my friend that evening about my views on John Bellini, and the admirable ices at Florio's, and the artistic value of gondolas, but added a postscript to the effect that her double in the story had behaved in a very silly manner. I don't know why I added that, but I remember I had a sort of dread over me that she might do the same thing. Before my letter had reached her, she had run away with a man who deserted her in six months. I saw her in 1884 in Paris, where she was living with her mother, and I asked her whether the story had had anything to do with her action. She told me that she had felt an absolutely irresistible impulse to follow the heroine step by step in her strange and fatal progress, and that it was with a feeling of real terror that she had looked forward to the last few chapters of the story. When they appeared, it seemed to her that she was compelled to reproduce them in life, and she did so. It was a most clear example of this imitative instinct of which I was speaking, and an extremely tragic one.

However, I do not wish to dwell any further upon individual instances. Personal experience is a most vicious and limited circle. All that I desire to point out is the general principle that Life imitates Art far more than Art imitates Life, and I feel sure that if you think seriously about it you will find that it is true. Life holds the mirror up to Art, and either reproduces some strange type imagined by painter or sculptor, or realises in fact what has been dreamed in fiction. Scientifically speaking, the basis of life—the energy of life, as Aristotle would call it—is simply the desire for expression, and Art is always presenting various forms through which the expression can be attained. Life seizes on them and uses them, even if they be to her own hurt. Young men have committed suicide because Rolla did so, have died by their own hand because by his own hand Werther died. Think of what we owe to the imitation of Christ, of what we owe to the imitation of Caesar.

CYRIL: The theory is certainly a very curious one, but to make it complete you must show that Nature, no less than Life, is an imitation of Art. Are you prepared to prove that?

VIVIAN: My dear fellow, I am prepared to prove anything.

CYRIL: Nature follows the landscape painter, then, and takes her effects from him?

VIVIAN: Certainly. Where, if not from the Impressionists, do we get those wonderful brown fogs that come creeping down our streets, blurring the gas-lamps and changing the houses into monstrous shadows?[11] To whom, if not to them and their master, do we owe the lovely silver mists that brood over our river, and turn to faint forms of fading grace curved bridge and swaying barge? The extraordinary change that has taken place in the climate of London during the last ten years is entirely due to a particular school of Art. You smile. Consider the matter from a scientific or a metaphysical point of view, and you will find that I am right. For what is Nature? Nature is no great mother who has borne us. She is our creation. It is in our brain that she quickens to life. Things are because we see them, and what we see, and how we see it, depends on the Arts that have influenced us. To look at a thing is very different from seeing a thing. One does not see anything until one sees its beauty. Then, and then only, does it come into existence. At present, people see fogs, not because there are fogs, but because poets and painters have taught them the mysterious loveliness of such effects. There may have been fogs for centuries in London. I dare say there were. But no one saw them, and so we do not know anything about them. They did not exist till Art had invented them. Now, it must be admitted, fogs are carried to excess. They have become the mere mannersim of a clique, and the exaggerated realism of their method gives dull people bronchitis. Where the cultured catch an effect, the uncultured catch cold. And so, let us be humane, and invite Art to turn her wonderful eyes elsewhere.

11. Although Wilde is half-serious here, the reference is a parody (or plagiarism) of a famous description by Whistler, in his *Ten O'Clock Lecture* (given in 1885, published in 1888), of the "evening [mist] that clothes the riverside with poetry, as with a veil, and the poor buildings lose themselves in the dim sky, and the tall buildings become campanili, and the warehouses are palaces in the night...."

She has done so already, indeed. That white quivering sunlight that one sees now in France, with its strange blotches of mauve, and its restless violet shadows, is her latest fancy, and, on the whole, Nature reproduces it quite admirably. Where she used to give us Corots and Daubignys, she gives us now exquisite Monets and entrancing Pissaros. Indeed, there are moments, rare, it is true, but still to be observed from time to time, when Nature becomes absolutely modern. Of course she is not always to be relied upon. The fact is that she is in this unfortunate position. Art creates an incomparable and unique effect, and, having done so, passes on to other things. Nature, upon the other hand, forgetting that imitation can be made the sincerest form of insult, keeps on repeating this effect until we all become absolutely wearied of it. Nobody of any real culture, for instance, ever talks nowadays about the beauty of a sunset. Sunsets are quite old-fashioned. They belong to the time when Turner was the last note in art. To admire them is a distinct sign of provincialism of temperament. Upon the other hand they go on. Yesterday evening Mrs. Arundel insisted on my going to the window and looking at the glorious sky, as she called it. Of course I had to look at it. She is one of those absurdly pretty Philistines to whom one can deny nothing. And what was it? It was simply a very second-rate Turner, a Turner of a bad period, with all the painter's worst faults exaggerated and over-emphasized. Of course I am quite ready to admit that Life very often commits the same error. She produces her false Renés and her sham Vautrins, just as Nature gives us, on one day a doubtful Cuyp, and on another a more than questionable Rousseau. Still, Nature irritates one more when she does things of that kind. It seems so stupid, so obvious, so unnecessary. A false Vautrin might be delightful. A doubtful Cuyp is unbearable. However, I don't want to be too hard on Nature. I wish the channel, especially at Hastings, did not look quite so often like a Henry Moore, grey pearl with yellow lights, but then, when Art is more varied, Nature will, no doubt, be more varied also. That she imitates Art, I don't think even her worst enemy would deny now. It is the one thing that keeps her in touch with civilised man. But have I proved my theory to your satisfaction?

CYRIL: You have proved it to my dissatisfaction, which is better.

But even admitting this strange imitative instinct in Life and Nature, surely you would acknowledge that Art expresses the temper of its age, the spirit of its time, the moral and social conditions that surround it, and under whose influence it is produced.

VIVIAN: Certainly not! Art never expresses anything but itself. This is the principle of my new aesthetics; and it is this, more than that vital connection between form and substance, on which Mr. Pater dwells, that makes music the type of all the arts. Of course, nations and individuals, with that healthy natural vanity which is the secret of existence, are always under the impression that it is of them that the Muses are talking, always trying to find in the calm dignity of imaginative art some mirror of their own turbid passions, always forgetting that the singer of life is not Apollo but Marsyas.[12] Remote from reality and with her eyes turned away from the shadows of the cave, Art reveals her own perfection, and the wondering crowd that watches the opening of the marvellous many-petalled rose fancies that it is its own history that is being told to it, its own spirit that is finding expression in a new form. But it is not so. The highest art rejects the burden of the human spirit, and gains more from a new medium or a fresh material than she does from any enthusiasm for art, or from any lofty passion, or from any great awakening of the human consciousness. She develops purely on her own lines. She is not symbolic of any age. It is the ages that are her symbols.

Even those who hold that Art is representative of time and place and people cannot help admitting that the more imitative an art is the less it represents to us the spirit of its age. The evil faces of the Roman emperors look out at us from the foul porphyry and spotted jasper in which the realistic artists of the day delighted to work and we fancy that in those cruel lips and heavy sensual jaws we can find the secret of the ruin of the Empire. But it was not so. The vices of Tiberius could not destroy that supreme civilisation, any more

12. To the Romans, who erected statues to him, Marsyas symbolized man's rash urge for liberty. According to myth, the satyr Marsyas found an enchanted flute which played so well that music-god Apollo jealously challenged him to a contest of instruments. When Marsyas too quickly and willingly accepted, and inevitably lost to the wily god, Apollo took revenge by flaying him alive.

than the virtues of the Antonines could save it. It fell for other, for less interesting reasons. The sibyls and prophets of the Sistine may indeed serve to interpret for some that new birth of the emancipated spirit that we call the Renaissance; but what do the drunken boors and brawling peasants of Dutch art tell us about the great soul of Holland? The more abstract, the more ideal an art is the more it reveals to us the temper of its age. If we wish to understand a nation by means of its art, let us look at its architecture or its music.

CYRIL: I quite agree with you there. The spirit of an age may be best expressed in the abstract ideal arts, for the spirit itself is abstract and ideal. Upon the other hand, for the visible aspect of an age, for its look, as the phrase goes, we must of course go to the arts of imitation.

VIVIAN: I don't think so. After all, what the imitative arts really give us are merely the various styles of particular artists, or of certain schools of artists. Surely you don't imagine that the people of the Middle Ages bore any resemblance at all to the figures on mediaeval stained glass, or in mediaeval stone and wood carving, or on mediaeval metal-work, or tapestries, or illuminated MSS. They were probably very ordinary-looking people, with nothing grotesque, or remarkable, or fantastic in their appearance. The Middle Ages, as we know them in art, are simply a definite form of style, and there is no reason at all why an artist with this style should not be produced in the nineteenth century. No great artist ever sees things as they really are. If he did he would cease to be an artist. Take an example from our own day. I know that you are fond of Japanese things. Now, do you really imagine that the Japanese people, as they are presented to us in art, have any existence? If you do, you have never understood Japanese art at all. The Japanese people are the deliberate self-conscious creation of certain individual artists. If you set a picture by Hokusai, or Hokkei, or any of the great native painters, beside a real Japanese gentleman or lady, you will see that there is not the slightest resemblance between them. The actual people who live in Japan are not unlike the general run of English people; that is to say, they are extremely commonplace, and have nothing curious or extraordinary about them. In fact, the whole of Japan is a pure invention. There is no such country, there are no such people. One of our most

charming painters went recently to the Land of the Chrysanthemum
in the foolish hope of seeing the Japanese. All he saw, all he had the
chance of painting, were a few lanterns and some fans. He was quite
unable to discover the inhabitants, as his delightful exhibition at
Messrs. Dowdeswell's Gallery showed only too well. He did not know
that the Japanese people are, as I have said, simply a mode of style,
an exquisite fancy of art. And so, if you desire to see a Japanese effect,
you will not behave like a tourist and go to Tokio. On the contrary,
you will stay at home and steep yourself in the work of certain
Japanese artists, and then, when you have absorbed the spirit of
their style, and caught their imaginative manner of vision, you will
go some afternoon and sit in the Park or stroll down Piccadilly, and
if you cannot see an absolutely Japanese effect there, you will not
see it anywhere. Or, to return again to the past, take as another
instance the ancient Greeks. Do you think that Greek art ever
tells us what the Greek people were like? Do you believe that the
Athenian women were like the stately dignified figures of the
Parthenon frieze, or like those marvellous goddesses who sat in
the triangular pediments of the same building? If you judge from
the art, they certainly were so. But read an authority like Aristophanes, for instance. You will find that the Athenian ladies laced
tightly, wore high-heeled shoes, dyed their hair yellow, painted
and rouged their faces, and were exactly like any silly fashionable
or fallen creature of our own day. The fact is that we look back on
the ages entirely through the medium or art, and art, very fortunately, has never once told us the truth.

CYRIL: But modern portraits by English painters, what of them?
Surely they are like the people they pretend to represent?

VIVIAN: Quite so. They are so like them that a hundred years
from now no one will believe in them. The only portraits in which
one believes are portraits where there is very little of the sitter and
a very great deal of the artist. Holbein's drawings of the men and
women of his time impress us with a sense of their absolute reality.
But this is simply because Holbein compelled life to accept his
conditions, to restrain itself within his limitations, to reproduce his
type and to appear as he wished it to appear. It is style that makes
us believe in a thing—nothing but style. Most of our modern portrait

painters are doomed to absolute oblivion. They never paint what they see. They paint what the public sees, and the public never sees anything.

CYRIL: Well, after that I think I should like to hear the end of your article.

VIVIAN: With pleasure. Whether it will do any good I really cannot say. Ours is certainly the dullest and most prosaic century possible. Why, even Sleep has played us false, and has closed up the gates of ivory, and opened the gates of horn. The dreams of the great middle classes of this country, as recorded in Mr. Myers's two bulky volumes on the subject, and in the Transactions of the Psychical Society, are the most depressing things I have ever read.[13] There is not even a fine nightmare among them. They are commonplace, sordid and tedious. As for the Church, I cannot conceive anything better for the culture of a country than the presence in it of a body of men whose duty it is to believe in the supernatural, to perform daily miracles, and to keep alive that mythopoeic faculty which is so essential for the imagination. But in the English Church a man succeeds, not through his capacity for belief, but through his capacity for disbelief. Ours is the only Church where the sceptic stands at the altar, and where St. Thomas is regarded as the ideal apostle. Many a worthy clergyman, who passes his life in admirable works of kindly charity, lives and dies unnoticed and unknown; but it is sufficient for some shallow uneducated passman out of either University to get up in his pulpit and express his doubts about Noah's ark, or Balaam's ass, or Jonah and the whale, for half of London to flock to hear him, and to sit open-mouthed in rapt admiration at his superb intellect. The growth of common sense in the English Church is a thing very much to be regretted. It is really a degrading concession to a low form of realism. It is silly, too. It springs from an entire ignorance of psychology. Man can believe the impossible, but man can never believe the improbable. However, I must read the end of my article:—

"What we have to do, what at any rate it is our duty to do, is

13. F. W. H. Myers (1843–1901) was joint author of *Phantasms of the Living* (1886), which first embodied in print the results of the investigations of the Society for Psychical Research, which he had helped found.

to revive this old art of Lying. Much, of course, may be done in the way of educating the public, by amateurs in the domestic circle, at literary lunches, and at afternoon teas. But this is merely the light and graceful side of lying, such as was probably heard at Cretan dinner-parties. There are many other forms. Lying for the sake of gaining some immediate personal advantage, for instance—lying with a moral purpose, as it is usually called—though of late it has been rather looked down upon, was extremely popular with the antique world. Athena laughs when Odysseus tells her 'his words of sly devising,' as Mr. William Morris phrases it, and the glory of mendacity illumines the pale brow of the stainless hero of Euripidean tragedy, and sets among the noble women of the past the young bride of one of Horace's most exquisite odes. Later on, what at first had been merely a natural instinct was elevated into a self-conscious science. Elaborate rules were laid down for the guidance of mankind, and an important school of literature grew up round the subject. Indeed, when one remembers the excellent philosophical treatise of Sanchez [14] on the whole question, one cannot help regretting that no one has ever thought of publishing a cheap and condensed edition of the works of that great casuist. A short primer, 'When to Lie and How,' if brought out in an attractive and not too expensive a form, would no doubt command a large sale, and would prove of real practical service to many earnest and deep-thinking people. Lying for the sake of the improvement of the young, which is the basis of home education, still lingers amongst us, and its advantages are so admirably set forth in the early books of Plato's *Republic* that it is unnecessary to dwell upon them here. It is a mode of lying for which all good mothers have peculiar capabilities, but it is capable of still further development, and has been sadly overlooked by the School Board. Lying for the sake of a monthly salary is, of course, well known in Fleet Street, and the profession of a political leader-writer is not without its advantages. But it is said to be a somewhat dull occupation, and it certainly does not lead to much beyond a kind of ostentatious obscurity. The only form of lying that is absolutely beyond reproach is lying for its own sake,

14. Francisco Sanchez, who wrote "A Treatise on the Noble and High Science of Nescience" (1581).

and the highest development of this is, as we have already pointed out, Lying in Art. Just as those who do not love Plato more than Truth cannot pass beyond the threshold of the Academe, so those who do not love Beauty more than Truth never know the inmost shrine of Art. The solid, stolid British intellect lies in the desert sands like the Sphinx in Flaubert's marvellous tale, and fantasy, *La Chimère*, dances round it, and calls to it with her false, flute-toned voice. It may not hear her now, but surely some day, when we are all bored to death with the commonplace character of modern fiction, it will hearken to her and try to borrow her wings.

"And when that day dawns, or sunset reddens, how joyous we shall all be! Facts will be regarded as discreditable, Truth will be found mourning over her fetters, and Romance, with her temper of wonder, will return to the land. The very aspect of the world will change to our startled eyes. Out of the sea will rise Behemoth and Leviathan, and sail round the high-pooped galleys, as they do on the delightful maps of those ages when books on geography were actually readable. Dragons will wander about the waste places, and the phoenix will soar from her nest of fire into the air. We shall lay our hands upon the basilisk, and see the jewel in the toad's head. Champing his gilded oats, the Hippogriff will stand in our stalls, and over our heads will float the Blue Bird singing of beautiful and impossible things, of things that are lovely and that never happen, of things that are not and that should be. But before this comes to pass we must cultivate the lost art of Lying."

CYRIL: Then we must entirely cultivate it at once. But in order to avoid making any error I want you to tell me briefly the doctrines of the new aesthetics.

VIVIAN: Briefly, then, they are these. Art never expresses anything but itself. It has an independent life, just as Thought has, and develops purely on its own lines. It is not necessarily realistic in an age of realism, nor spiritual in an age of faith. So far from being the creation of its time, it is usually in direct opposition to it, and the only history that it preserves for us is the history of its own progress. Sometimes it returns upon its footsteps, and revives some antique form, as happened in the archaistic movement of late Greek Art, and in the pre-Raphaelite movement of our own day. At other times it entirely anticipates its age, and produces in one century work that it takes another century to understand, to appreciate, and to enjoy. In no case does it reproduce its age. To pass from the art of a time to the time itself is the great mistake that all historians commit.

The second doctrine is this. All bad art comes from returning to Life and Nature, and elevating them into ideals. Life and Nature may sometimes be used as part of Art's rough material, but before they are of any real service to Art they must be translated into artistic conventions. The moment Art surrenders its imaginative medium it surrenders everything. As a method Realism is a complete failure, and the two things that every artist should avoid are modernity of form and modernity of subject-matter. To us, who live in the nineteenth century, any century is a suitable subject for art except our own. The only beautiful things are the things that do not concern us. It is, to have the pleasure of quoting myself, exactly because Hecuba is nothing to us that her sorrows are so suitable a motive for a tragedy. Besides, it is only the modern that ever becomes old-fashioned. M. Zola sits down to give us a picture of the Second Empire. Who cares for the Second Empire now? It is out of date. Life goes faster than Realism, but Romanticism is always in front of Life.

The third doctrine is that Life imitates Art far more than Art imitates Life. This results not merely from Life's imitative instinct, but from the fact that the self-conscious aim of Life is to find expression, and that Art offers it certain beautiful forms through which it may realise that energy. It is a theory that has never been put forward before, but it is extremely fruitful, and throws an entirely new light upon the history of Art.

It follows, as a corollary from this, that external Nature also imitates Art. The only effects that she can show us are effects that we have already seen through poetry, or in paintings. This is the secret of Nature's charm, as well as the explanation of Nature's weakness.

The final revelation is that Lying, the telling of beautiful untrue things, is the proper aim of Art. But of this I think I have spoken at sufficient length. And now let us go out on the terrace, where "droops the milk-white peacock like a ghost," while the evening star "washes the dusk with silver." At twilight nature becomes a wonderfully suggestive effect, and is not without loveliness, though perhaps its chief use is to illustrate quotations from the poets. Come! We have talked long enough.

First published in *Nineteenth Century*, XXV (January, 1889), 35–56. Reprinted in revised form in *Intentions* (London, 1891), pp. 3–53.

# The Critic as Artist

With Some Remarks upon the
Importance of Doing Nothing

A Dialogue

Part I. PERSONS: *Gilbert and Ernest.*     SCENE: *the library
of a house in Piccadilly, overlooking the Green Park.*

GILBERT (*at the Piano*): My dear Ernest, what are you laughing
at?

ERNEST (*looking up*): At a capital story that I have just come across
in this volume of Reminiscences that I have found on your table.

GILBERT: What is the book? Ah! I see. I have not read it yet. Is
it good?

ERNEST: Well, while you have been playing, I have been turning
over the pages with some amusement, though, as a rule, I dislike
modern memoirs. They are generally written by people who have
either entirely lost their memories, or have never done anything
worth remembering; which, however, is, no doubt, the true explanation of their popularity, as the English public always feels perfectly
at ease when a mediocrity is talking to it.

GILBERT: Yes: the public is wonderfully tolerant. It forgives
everything except genius. But I must confess that I like all memoirs.
I like them for their form, just as much as for their matter. In literature mere egotism is delightful. It is what fascinates us in the
letters of personalities so different as Cicero and Balzac, Flaubert
and Berlioz, Byron and Madame de Sévigné.[1] Whenever we come
across it, and, strangely enough, it is rather rare, we cannot but
welcome it, and do not easily forget it. Humanity will always love
Rousseau for having confessed his sins, not to a priest, but to the
world, and the couchant nymphs that Cellini wrought in bronze

1. Madame de Sévigné (1626–1696), French writer and lady of fashion.

for the castle of King Francis, the green and gold Perseus, even, that in the open Loggia at Florence shows the moon the dead terror that once turned life to stone, have not given it more pleasure than has that autobiography in which the supreme scoundrel of the Renaissance relates the story of his splendour and his shame. The opinions, the character, the achievements of the man, matter very little. He may be a sceptic like the gentle Sieur de Montaigne, or a saint like the bitter son of Monica,[2] but when he tells us his own secrets he can always charm our ears to listening and our lips to silence. The mode of thought that Cardinal Newman[3] represented— if that can be called a mode of thought which seeks to solve intellectual problems by a denial of the supremacy of the intellect—may not, cannot, I think, survive. But the world will never weary of watching that troubled soul in its progress from darkness to darkness. The lonely church at Littlemore, where "the breath of the morning is damp, and worshippers are few," will always be dear to it, and whenever men see the yellow snapdragon blossoming on the wall of Trinity they will think of that gracious undergraduate who saw in the flower's sure recurrence a prophecy that he would abide for ever with the Benign Mother of his days—a prophecy that Faith, in her wisdom or her folly, suffered not to be fulfilled. Yes; autobiography is irresistible. Poor, silly, conceited Mr. Secretary Pepys has chattered his way into the circle of the Immortals, and, conscious that indiscretion is the better part of valour, bustles about among them in that "shaggy purple gown with gold buttons and looped lace" which he is so fond of describing to us, perfectly at his ease, and prattling, to his own and our infinite pleasure, of the Indian blue petticoat that he bought for his wife, of the "good hog's harslet," and the "pleasant French fricassee of veal" that he loved to eat, of his game of bowls with Will Joyce, and his "gadding after beauties," and his reciting of *Hamlet* on a Sunday, and his playing of the viol on week days, and other wicked or trivial things. Even in actual life egotism is not without its attractions. When

2. "The bitter son of Monica": St. Augustine (354–430).
3. John Henry Cardinal Newman (1801–1890), English prelate and writer. The references to Newman's early years paraphrase his famous spiritual autobiography, *Apologia pro Vita Sua* (1864).

people talk to us about others they are usually dull. When they talk to us about themselves they are nearly always interesting, and if one could shut them up, when they become wearisome, as easily as one can shut up a book of which one has grown wearied, they would be perfect absolutely.

ERNEST: There is much virtue in that If, as Touchstone would say. But do you seriously propose that every man should become his own Boswell? What would become of our industrious compilers of Lives and Recollections in that case?

GILBERT: What has become of them? They are the pest of the age, nothing more and nothing less. Every great man nowadays has his disciples, and it is always Judas who writes the biography.

ERNEST: My dear fellow!

GILBERT: I am afraid it is true. Formerly we used to canonise our heroes. The modern method is to vulgarise them. Cheap editions of great books may be delightful, but cheap editions of great men are absolutely detestable.

ERNEST: May I ask, Gilbert, to whom you allude?

GILBERT: Oh! to all our second-rate *littérateurs*. We are overrun by a set of people who, when poet or painter passes away, arrive at the house along with the undertaker, and forget that their one duty is to behave as mutes. But we won't talk about them. They are the mere body-snatchers of literature. The dust is given to one, and the ashes to another, and the soul is out of their reach. And now, let me play Chopin to you, or Dvorák? Shall I play you a fantasy by Dvorák? He writes passionate, curiously-coloured things.

ERNEST: No; I don't want music just at present. It is far too indefinite. Besides, I took the Baroness Bernstein down to dinner last night, and, though absolutely charming in every other respect, she insisted on discussing music as if it were actually written in the German language. Now, whatever music sounds like, I am glad to say that it does not sound in the smallest degree like German. There are forms of patriotism that are really quite degrading. No; Gilbert, don't play any more. Turn round and talk to me. Talk to me till the white-horned day comes into the room. There is something in your voice that is wonderful.

GILBERT (*rising from the piano*): I am not in a mood for talking to-night. I really am not. How horrid of you to smile! Where are the cigarettes? Thanks. How exquisite these single daffodils are! They seem to be made of amber and cool ivory. They are like Greek things of the best period. What was the story in the confessions of the remorseful Academician that made you laugh? Tell it to me. After playing Chopin, I feel as if I had been weeping over sins that I had never committed, and mourning over tragedies that were not my own. Music always seems to me to produce that effect. It creates for one a past of which one has been ignorant, and fills one with a sense of sorrows that have been hidden from one's tears. I can fancy a man who had led a perfectly commonplace life, hearing by chance some curious piece of music, and suddenly discovering that his soul, without his being conscious of it, had passed through terrible experiences, and known fearful joys, or wild romantic loves, or great renunciations. And so tell me this story, Ernest. I want to be amused.

ERNEST: Oh! I don't know that it is of any importance. But I thought it a really admirable illustration of the true value of ordinary art-criticism. It seems that a lady once gravely asked the remorseful Academician, as you call him, if his celebrated picture of "A Spring-Day at Whiteley's," or "Waiting for the Last Omnibus," or some subject of that kind, was all painted by hand?

GILBERT: And was it?

ERNEST: You are quite incorrigible. But, seriously speaking, what is the use of art-criticism? Why cannot the artist be left alone, to create a new world if he wishes it, or, if not, to shadow forth the world which we already know, and of which, I fancy, we would each one of us be wearied if Art, with her fine spirit of choice and delicate instinct of selection, did not, as it were, purify it for us, and give to it a momentary perfection. It seems to me that the imagination spreads, or should spread, a solitude around it, and works best in silence and in isolation. Why should the artist be troubled by the shrill clamour of criticism? Why should those who cannot create take upon themselves to estimate the value of creative work? What can they know about it? If a man's work is easy to understand, an explanation is unnecessary. . . .

GILBERT: And if his work is incomprehensible, an explanation is wicked.

ERNEST: I did not say that.

GILBERT: Ah! but you should have. Nowadays, we have so few mysteries left to us that we cannot afford to part with one of them. The members of the Browning Society, like the theologians of the Broad Church Party,[4] or the authors of Mr. Walter Scott's Great Writers Series, seem to me to spend their time in trying to explain their divinity away. Where one had hoped that Browning was a mystic they have sought to show that he was simply inarticulate. Where one had fancied that he had something to conceal, they have proved that he had but little to reveal. But I speak merely of his incoherent work. Taken as a whole the man was great. He did not belong to the Olympians, and had all the incompleteness of the Titan. He did not survey, and it was but rarely that he could sing. His work is marred by struggle, violence and effort, and he passed not from emotion to form, but from thought to chaos. Still, he was great. He has been called a thinker, and was certainly a man who was always thinking, and always thinking aloud; but it was not thought that fascinated him, but rather the processes by which thought moves. It was the machine he loved, not what the machine makes. The method by which the fool arrives at his folly was as dear to him as the ultimate wisdom of the wise. So much, indeed, did the subtle mechanism of mind fascinate him that he despised language, or looked upon it as an incomplete instrument of expression. Rhyme, that exquisite echo which in the Muse's hollow hill creates and answers its own voice; rhyme, which in the hands of the real artist becomes not merely a material element of metrical beauty, but a spiritual element of thought and passion also, waking a new mood, it may be, or stirring a fresh train of ideas, or opening by mere sweetness and suggestion of sound some golden door at which the Imagination itself had knocked in vain; rhyme, which can turn man's utterance to the speech of gods; rhyme, the one chord we have added to the Greek lyre, became in Robert Browning's hands a grotesque, misshapen thing, which at times made him masquerade in poetry as a low comedian, and ride Pegasus too often with his tongue in his cheek. There are moments when he wounds us by monstrous

4. The Broad Church Party was a liberal party in the Anglican communion during the second half of the nineteenth century.

music. Nay, if he can only get his music by breaking the strings of his lute, he breaks them, and they snap in discord, and no Athenian tettix, making melody from tremulous wings, lights on the ivory horn to make the movement perfect, or the interval less harsh. Yet, he was great: and though he turned language into ignoble clay, he made from it men and women that live. He is the most Shakespearian creature since Shakespeare. If Shakespeare could sing with myriad lips, Browning could stammer through a thousand mouths. Even now, as I am speaking, and speaking not against him but for him, there glides through the room the pageant of his persons. There, creeps Fra Lippo Lippi with his cheeks still burning from some girl's hot kiss. There, stands dread Saul with the lordly male-sapphires gleaming in his turban. Mildred Tresham is there, and the Spanish monk, yellow with hatred, and Blougram, and Ben Ezra, and the Bishop of St. Praxed's. The spawn of Setebos gibbers in the corner, and Sebald, hearing Pippa pass by, looks on Ottima's haggard face, and loathes her and his own sin, and himself. Pale as the white satin of his doublet, the melancholy king watches with dreamy treacherous eyes too loyal Strafford pass forth to his doom, and Andrea shudders as he hears the cousins whistle in the garden, and bids his perfect wife go down. Yes, Browning was great. And as what will he be remembered? As a poet? Ah, not as a poet! He will be remembered as a writer of fiction, as the most supreme writer of fiction, it may be, that we have ever had. His sense of dramatic situation was unrivalled, and, if he could not answer his own problems, he could at least put problems forth, and what more should an artist do? Considered from the point of view of a creator of character he ranks next to him who made Hamlet. Had he been articulate, he might have sat beside him. The only man who can touch the hem of his garment is George Meredith. Meredith is a prose Browning, and so is Browning. He used poetry as a medium for writing in prose.

ERNEST: There is something in what you say, but there is not everything in what you say. In many points you are unjust.

GILBERT: It is difficult not to be unjust to what one loves. But let us return to the particular point at issue. What was it that you said?

ERNEST: Simply this: that in the best days of art there were no art-critics.

GILBERT: I seem to have heard that observation before, Ernest. It has all the vitality of error and all the tediousness of an old friend.

ERNEST: It is true. Yes: there is no use your tossing your head in that petulant manner. It is quite true. In the best days of art there were no art-critics. The sculptor hewed from the marble block the great white-limbed Hermes that slept within it. The waxers and gilders of images gave tone and texture to the statue, and the world, when it saw it, worshipped and was dumb. He poured the glowing bronze into the mould of sand, and the river of red metal cooled into noble curves and took the impress of the body of a god. With enamel or polished jewels he gave sight to the sightless eyes. The hyacinth-like curls grew crisp beneath his graver. And when, in some dim frescoed fane, or pillared sunlit portico, the child of Leto stood upon his pedestal, those who passed by, διὰ λαμπροτάτου βαίνοντες ἀβρῶς αἰθέρος [treading delicately through the bright air], became conscious of a new influence that had come across their lives, and dreamily, or with a sense of strange and quickening joy, went to their homes or daily labour, or wandered, it may be, through the city gates to that nymph-haunted meadow where young Phaedrus bathed his feet, and, lying there on the soft grass, beneath the tall wind-whispering planes and flowering *agnus castus*, began to think of the wonder of beauty, and grew silent with unaccustomed awe. In those days the artist was free. From the river valley he took the fine clay in his fingers, and with a little tool of wood or bone, fashioned it into forms so exquisite that the people gave them to the dead as their playthings, and we find them still in the dusty tombs on the yellow hillside by Tanagra, with the faint gold and the fading crimson still lingering about hair and lips and raiment. On a wall of fresh plaster, stained with bright sandyx or mixed with milk and saffron, he pictured one who trod with tired feet the purple white-starred fields of asphodel, one "in whose eyelids lay the whole of the Trojan War," Polyxena, the daughter of Priam; or figured Odysseus, the wise and cunning, bound by tight cords to the mast-step, that he might listen without hurt to the singing of the Sirens, or wandering by the clear river of Acheron, where the ghosts of fishes flitted over the pebbly bed; or showed the Persian in trews and mitre flying before the Greek at Marathon, or the galleys clashing their beaks of brass in the little Salaminian bay. He drew with silver-point and charcoal upon parchment and prepared cedar. Upon ivory and rose-coloured terra-cotta he painted with wax, making the wax fluid with juice of olives, and with heated irons making it firm. Panel and marble and linen canvas became wonderful as his brush swept across them; and life seeing her own image, was still, and dared not speak. All life, indeed, was his, from the merchants seated in the market-place to the cloaked shepherd lying on the hill; from the nymph hidden in the laurels and the faun that pipes at noon, to the king whom, in long green-curtained litter, slaves bore upon oil-bright shoulders, and fanned with peacock fans. Men and women, with pleasure or sorrow in their faces, passed before him. He watched them, and their secret became his. Through form and colour he re-created a world.

All subtle arts belonged to him also. He held the gem against the revolving disk, and the amethyst became the purple couch for Adonis, and across the veined sardonyx sped Artemis with her hounds. He beat out the gold into roses, and strung them together for necklace or armlet. He beat out the gold into wreaths for the conqueror's helmet, or into palmates for the Tyrian robe, or into masks for the royal dead. On the back of the silver mirror he graved Thetis borne by her Nereids, or love-sick Phaedra with her nurse, or Persephone, weary of memory, putting poppies in her hair. The potter sat in his shed, and, flower-like from the silent wheel, the vase rose up beneath his hands. He decorated the base and stem and ears with pattern of dainty olive-leaf, or foliated acanthus, or curved and crested wave. Then in black or red he painted lads wrestling, or in the race: knights in full armour, with strange heraldic shields and curious visors, leaning from shell-shaped chariot over rearing steeds: the gods seated at the feast or working their miracles: the heroes in their victory or in their pain. Sometimes he would etch in thin vermilion lines upon a ground of white the languid bridegroom and his bride, with Eros hovering round them— an Eros like one of Donatello's angels, a little laughing thing with gilded or with azure wings. On the curved side he would write the name of his friend. ΚΑΛΟΣ ΑΛΚΙΒΙΑΔΗΣ [fair Alcibiades] or ΚΑΛΟΣ ΧΑΡΜΙΔΗΣ [fair Charmides] tells us the story of his days. Again, on the rim of the wide flat cup he would draw the stag browsing, or the lion at rest, as his fancy willed it. From the tiny perfume-bottle laughed Aphrodite at her toilet, and, with bare-limbed Maenads in his train, Dionysus danced round the wine-jar on naked must-stained feet, while, satyr-like, the old Silenus sprawled upon the bloated skins, or shook that magic spear which was tipped with a fretted fir-cone, and wreathed with dark ivy. And no one came to trouble the artist at his work. No irresponsible chatter disturbed him. He was not worried by opinions. By the Ilyssus, says Arnold somewhere, there was no Higginbotham. By the Ilyssus, my dear Gilbert, there were no silly art congresses bringing provincialism to the provinces and teaching the mediocrity how to mouth. By the Ilyssus there were no tedious magazines about art, in which the industrious prattle of what they do not understand. On the reed-grown banks of that little stream strutted no ridiculous journalism monopolising the seat of judgment when it should be apologising in the dock. The Greeks had no art-critics.

GILBERT: Ernest, you are quite delightful, but your views are terribly unsound. I am afraid that you have been listening to the conversation of some one older than yourself. That is always a dangerous thing to do, and if you will allow it to degenerate into a habit you will find it absolutely fatal to any intellectual development. As for modern journalism, it is not my business to defend it. It justifies its own existence by the great Darwinian principle of the survival of the vulgarest. I have merely to do with literature.

ERNEST: But what is the difference between literature and journalism?

GILBERT: Oh! journalism is unreadable, and literature is not read. That is all. But with regard to your statement that the Greeks had no art-critics, I assure you that is quite absurd. It would be more just to say that the Greeks were a nation of art-critics.

ERNEST: Really?

GILBERT: Yes, a nation of art-critics. But I don't wish to destroy the delightfully unreal picture that you have drawn of the relation of the Hellenic artist to the intellectual spirit of his age. To give an accurate description of what has never occurred is not merely the proper occupation of the historian, but the inalienable privilege of any man of parts and culture. Still less do I desire to talk learnedly. Learned conversation is either the affectation of the ignorant or the profession of the mentally unemployed. And, as for what is called improving conversation, that is merely the foolish method by which the still more foolish philanthropist feebly tries to disarm the just rancour of the criminal classes. No: let me play to you some mad scarlet thing by Dvorák. The pallid figures on the tapestry are smiling at us, and the heavy eyelids of my bronze Narcissus are folded in sleep. Don't let us discuss anything solemnly. I am but too conscious of the fact that we are born in an age when only the dull are treated seriously, and I live in terror of not being misunderstood. Don't degrade me into the position of giving you useful information. Education is an admirable thing, but it is well to remember from time to time that nothing that is worth knowing can be taught. Through the parted curtains of the window I see the moon like a clipped piece of silver. Like gilded bees the stars cluster round her. The sky is a hard hollow sapphire. Let us go out into the night. Thought is wonderful, but adventure is more wonderful still. Who knows but we may meet Prince Florizel of Bohemia, and hear the fair Cuban tell us that she is not what she seems?

ERNEST: You are horribly wilful. I insist on your discussing this matter with me. You have said that the Greeks were a nation of art-critics. What art-criticism have they left us?

GILBERT: My dear Ernest, even if not a single fragment of art-criticism had come down to us from Hellenic or Hellenistic days, it would be none the less true that the Greeks were a nation of art-critics, and that they invented the criticism of art just as they invented the criticism of everything else. For, after all, what is our primary debt to the Greeks? Simply the critical spirit. And, this spirit, which they exercised on questions of religion and science, of ethics and metaphysics, of politics and education, they exercised on questions of art also, and, indeed, of the two supreme and highest arts, they have left us the most flawless system of criticism that the world has ever seen.

ERNEST: But what are the two supreme and highest arts?

GILBERT: Life and Literature, life and the perfect expression of life. The principles of the former, as laid down by the Greeks, we may not realise in an age so marred by false ideals as our own. The principles of the latter, as they laid them down, are, in many cases, so subtle that we can hardly understand them. Recognising that the most perfect art is that which most fully mirrors man in all his infinite variety, they elaborated the criticism of language, considered in the light of the mere material of that art, to a point to which we, with our accentual system of reasonable or emotional emphasis, can barely if at all attain; studying, for instance, the metrical movements of a prose as scientifically as a modern musician studies harmony and counterpoint, and, I need hardly say, with much keener aesthetic instinct. In this they were right, as they were right in all things. Since the introduction of printing, and the fatal development of the habit of reading amongst the middle and lower classes of this country, there has been a tendency in literature to appeal more and more to the eye, and less and less to the ear which is really the sense which, from the standpoint of pure art, it should seek to please, and by whose canons of pleasure it should abide always. Even the work of Mr. Pater, who is, on the whole, the most perfect master of English prose now creating amongst us, is often far more like a piece of mosaic than a passage in music, and seems, here and there, to lack the true rhythmical life of words and the fine freedom and richness of effect that such rhythmical life produces. We, in fact, have made writing a definite mode of composition, and have treated it as a form of elaborate design. The Greeks, upon the other hand, regarded writing simply as a method of chronicling. Their test was always the spoken word in its musical and metrical relations. The voice was the medium, and the ear the critic. I have sometimes thought that the story of Homer's blindness might be really an artistic myth, created in critical days, and serving to remind us, not merely that the great poet is always a seer, seeing less with the eyes of the body than he does with the eyes of the soul, but that he is a true singer also, building his song out of music, repeating each line over and over again to himself till he has caught the secret of its melody, chaunting in darkness the words that are winged with light. Certainly, whether this be so or not, it was to his blindness, as an occasion, if not as a cause, that England's great poet owed much of the majestic movement and sonorous splendour of his later verse. When Milton could no longer write he began to sing. Who would match the measures of *Comus* with the measures of *Samson Agonistes*, or of *Paradise Lost* or *Regained*? When Milton became blind he composed, as every one should compose, with the voice purely, and so the pipe or reed of earlier days became that mighty many-stopped organ whose rich reverberant music has all the stateliness of Homeric verse, if it seeks not to have its swiftness, and is the one imperishable inheritance of English literature sweeping through all the ages, because above them, and abiding with us ever, being immortal in its form. Yes: writing has done much harm to writers. We must return to the voice. That must be our test, and perhaps then we shall be able to appreciate some of the subtleties of Greek art-criticism.

As it now is, we cannot do so. Sometimes, when I have written a piece of prose that I have been modest enough to consider absolutely free from fault, a dreadful thought comes over me that I may have been guilty of the immoral effeminacy of using trochaic and tribrachic movements, a crime for which a learned critic of the Augustan age censures with most just severity the brilliant if somewhat paradoxical Hegesias.[5] I grow cold when I think of it, and wonder to myself if the admirable ethical effect of the prose of that charming writer, who once in a spirit of reckless generosity towards the uncultivated portion of our community proclaimed the monstrous doctrine that conduct is three-fourths of life, will not some day be entirely annihilated by the discovery that the paeons have been wrongly placed.

ERNEST: Ah! now you are flippant.

GILBERT: Who would not be flippant when he is gravely told that the Greeks had no art-critics? I can understand it being said that the constructive genius of the Greeks lost itself in criticism, but not that the race to whom we owe the critical spirit did not criticise. You will not ask me to give you a survey of Greek art criticism from

5. Hegesias (ca. 300 or 250 B.C.), Greek orator and historian whose inflated oratory was deplored by ancient critics.

Plato to Plotinus. The night is too lovely for that, and the moon, if she heard us, would put more ashes on her face than are there already. But think merely of one perfect little work of aesthetic criticism, Aristotle's *Treatise on Poetry*. It is not perfect in form, for it is badly written, consisting perhaps of notes dotted down for an art lecture, or of isolated fragments destined for some larger book, but in temper and treatment it is perfect, absolutely. The ethical effect of art, its importance to culture, and its place in the formation of character, had been done once for all by Plato; but here we have art treated, not from the moral, but from the purely aesthetic point of view. Plato had, of course, dealt with many definitely artistic subjects, such as the importance of unity in a work of art, the necessity for tone and harmony, the aesthetic value of appearances, the relation of the visible arts to the external world, and the relation of fiction to fact. He first perhaps stirred in the soul of man that desire that we have not yet satisfied, the desire to know the connection between Beauty and Truth, and the place of Beauty in the moral and intellectual order of the Kosmos. The problems of idealism and realism, as he sets them forth, may seem to many to be somewhat barren of result in the metaphysical sphere of abstract being in which he places them, but transfer them to the sphere of art, and you will find that they are still vital and full of meaning. It may be that it is as a critic of Beauty that Plato is destined to live, and that by altering the name of the sphere of his speculation we shall find a new philosophy. But Aristotle, like Goethe, deals with art primarily in its concrete manifestations, taking Tragedy, for instance, and investigating the material it uses, which is language, its subject-matter, which is life, the method by which it works, which is action, the conditions under which it reveals itself, which are those of theatric presentation, its logical structure, which is plot, and its final aesthetic appeal, which is to the sense of beauty realised through the passions of pity and awe. That purification and spiritualising of the nature which he calls κάθαρσις [catharsis] is, as Goethe saw, essentially aesthetic, and is not moral, as Lessing fancied. Concerning himself primarily with the impression that the work of art produces, Aristotle sets himself to analyse that impression, to investigate its source, to see how it is engendered. As a physiologist and psychologist, he knows that the health of a function resides in energy. To have a capacity for a passion and not to realise it, is to make oneself incomplete and limited. The mimic spectacle of life that Tragedy affords cleanses the bosom of much "perilous stuff," and by presenting high and worthy objects for the exercise of the emotions purifies and spiritualises the man; nay, not merely does it spiritualise him, but it initiates him also into noble feelings of which he might else have known nothing, the word κάθαρσις having, it has sometimes seemed to me, a definite allusion to the rite of initiation, if indeed that be not, as I am occasionally tempted to fancy, its true and only meaning here. This is of course a mere outline of the book. But you see what a perfect piece of aesthetic criticism it is. Who indeed but a Greek could have analysed art so well? After reading it, one does not wonder any longer that Alexandria devoted itself so largely to art-criticism, and that we find the artistic temperaments of the day investigating every question of style and manner discussing the great Academic schools of painting, for instance, such as the school of Sicyon, that sought to preserve the dignified traditions of the antique mode, or the realistic and impressionist schools, that aimed at reproducing actual life, or the elements of ideality in portraiture, or the artistic value of the epic form in an age so modern as theirs, or the proper subject-matter for the artist. Indeed, I fear that the inartistic temperaments of the day busied themselves also in matters of literature and art, for the accusations of plagiarism were endless, and such accusations proceed either from the thin colourless lips of impotence, or from the grotesque mouths of those who, possessing nothing of their own, fancy that they can gain a reputation for wealth by crying out that they have been robbed. And I assure you, my dear Ernest, that the Greeks chattered about painters quite as much as people do nowadays, and had their private views, and shilling exhibitions, and Arts and Crafts guilds, and Pre-Raphaelite movements, and movements towards realism, and lectured about art, and wrote essays on art, and produced their art-historians, and their archaeologists, and all the rest of it. Why, even the theatrical managers of travelling companies brought their dramatic critics with them when they went on tour, and paid them very handsome salaries for writing laudatory notices. Whatever, in fact, is modern in our life we owe to the Greeks. Whatever is an anachronism is due to mediaevalism. It is the Greeks who have given us the whole system of art-criticism, and how fine their critical instinct was, may be seen from the fact that the material they criticised with most care was, as I have already said, language. For the material that painter or sculptor uses is meagre in comparison with that of words. Words have not merely music as sweet as that of viol and lute, colour as rich and vivid as any that makes lovely for us the canvas of the Venetian or the Spaniard, and plastic form no less sure and certain than that which reveals itself in marble or in bronze but thought and passion and spirituality are theirs also, are theirs indeed alone. If the Greeks had criticised nothing but language, they would still have been the great art-critics of the world. To know the principles of the highest art is to know the principles of all the arts.

But I see that the moon is hiding behind a sulphur-coloured cloud. Out of a tawny mane of drift she gleams like a lion's eye. She is afraid that I will talk to you of Lucian and Longinus, of Quintilian and Dionysius, of Pliny and Fronto and Pausanias, of all those who in the antique world wrote or lectured upon art matters. She need not be afraid. I am tired of my expedition into the dim, dull abyss of facts. There is nothing left for me now but the divine μονόχρονος ἡδονή [undivided pleasure] of another cigarette. Cigarettes have at least the charm of leaving one unsatisfied.

ERNEST: Try one of mine. They are rather good. I get them direct from Cairo. The only use of our *attachés* is that they supply their friends with excellent tobacco. And as the moon has hidden herself, let us talk a little longer. I am quite ready to admit that I was wrong in what I said about the Greeks. They were, as you have pointed out, a nation of art-critics. I acknowledge it, and I feel a little sorry for them. For the creative faculty is higher than the critical. There is really no comparison between them.

GILBERT: The antithesis between them is entirely arbitrary. Without the critical faculty, there is no artistic creation at all, worthy of the name. You spoke a little while ago of that fine spirit of choice and delicate instinct of selection by which the artist realises life for us, and gives to it a momentary perfection. Well, that spirit of choice, that subtle tact of omission, is really the critical faculty in one of its most characteristic moods, and no one who does not possess this critical faculty can create anything at all in art. Arnold's definition of literature as a criticism of life, was not very felicitous in form, but it showed how keenly he recognised the importance of the critical element in all creative work.

ERNEST: I should have said that great artists worked unconsciously, that they were "wiser than they knew," as, I think, Emerson remarks somewhere.

GILBERT: It is really not so, Ernest. All fine imaginative work is self-conscious and deliberate. No poet sings because he must sing. At least, no great poet does. A great poet sings because he chooses to sing. It is so now, and it has always been so. We are sometimes apt to think that the voices that sounded at the dawn of poetry were simpler, fresher and more natural than ours, and that the world which the early poets looked at, and through which they walked, had a kind of poetical quality of its own, and almost without changing could pass into song. The snow lies thick now upon Olympus, and its steep scarped sides are bleak and barren, but once, we fancy, the white feet of the Muses brushed the dew from the anemones in the morning, and at evening came Apollo to sing to the shepherds in the vale. But in this we are merely lending to other ages what we desire, or think we desire, for our own. Our historical sense is at fault. Every century that produces poetry is, so far, an artificial century, and the work that seems to us to be the most natural and simple product of its time is always the result of the most self-conscious effort. Believe me, Ernest, there is no fine art without self-consciousness, and self-consciousness and the critical spirit are one.

ERNEST: I see what you mean, and there is much in it. But surely you would admit that the great poems of the early world, the primitive, anonymous collective poems, were the result of the imagination of races, rather than of the imagination of individuals?

GILBERT: Not when they became poetry. Not when they received a beautiful form. For there is no art where there is no style, and no style where there is no unity, and unity is of the individual. No doubt Homer had old ballads and stories to deal with, as Shakespeare had chronicles and plays and novels from which to work, but they were merely his rough material. He took them, and shaped them into song. They became his, because he made them lovely. They were built out of music,

"And so not built at all,
And therefore built for ever."

The longer one studies life and literature, the more strongly one feels that behind everything that is wonderful stands the individual, and that it is not the moment that makes the man, but the man who creates the age. Indeed, I am inclined to think that each myth and legend that seems to us to spring out of the wonder, or terror, or fancy of tribe and nation, was in its origin the invention of one single mind. The curiously limited number of the myths seems to me to point to this conclusion. But we must not go off into questions of comparative mythology. We must keep to criticism. And what I want to point out is this. An age that has no criticism is either an age in which art is immobile, hieratic, and confined to the repro- duction of formal types, or an age that possesses no art at all. There have been critical ages that have not been creative, in the ordinary sense of the word, ages in which the spirit of man has sought to set in order the treasures of his treasure-house, to separate the gold from the silver, and the silver from the lead, to count over the jewels, and to give names to the pearls. But there has never been a creative age that has not been critical also. For it is the critical faculty that invents fresh forms. The tendency of creation is to repeat itself. It is to the critical instinct that we owe each new school that springs up, each new mould that art finds ready to its hand. There is really not a single form that art now uses that does not come to us from the critical spirit of Alexandria, where these forms were either stereotyped or invented or made perfect. I say Alexandria, not merely because it was there that the Greek spirit became most self-conscious, and indeed ultimately expired in scepticism and theol- ogy, but because it was to that city, and not to Athens, that Rome turned for her models, and it was through the survival, such as it was, of the Latin language that culture lived at all. When, at the Renaissance, Greek literature dawned upon Europe, the soil had been in some measure prepared for it. But, to get rid of the details of history, which are always wearisome and usually inaccurate, let us say generally, that the forms of art have been due to the Greek critical spirit. To it we owe the epic, the lyric, the entire drama in every one of its developments, including burlesque, the idyll, the romantic novel, the novel of adventure, the essay, the dialogue, the oration, the lecture, for which perhaps we should not forgive them, and the epigram, in all the wide meaning of that word. In fact, we owe it everything, except the sonnet, to which, however, some curious parallels of thought-movement may be traced in the Anthology, American journalism, to which no parallel can be found anywhere, and the ballad in sham Scotch dialect, which one of our most industrious writers has recently proposed should be made the basis for a final and unanimous effort on the part of our second-rate poets to make themselves really romantic. Each new school, as it appears, cries out against criticism, but it is to the critical faculty in man that it owes its origin. The mere creative instinct does not innovate, but reproduces.

ERNEST: You have been talking of criticism as an essential part of the creative spirit, and I now fully accept your theory. But what of criticism outside creation? I have a foolish habit of reading periodicals, and it seems to me that most modern criticism is perfectly valueless.

GILBERT: So is most modern creative work also. Mediocrity weighing mediocrity in the balance, and incompetence applauding its brother—that is the spectacle which the artistic activity of England affords us from time to time. And yet, I feel I am a little unfair in this matter. As a rule, the critics—I speak, of course, of the higher class, of those in fact who write for the sixpenny papers—are far more cultured than the people whose work they are called upon to review. This is, indeed, only what one would expect, for criticism demands infinitely more cultivation than creation does.

ERNEST: Really?

GILBERT: Certainly. Anybody can write a three-volumed novel. It merely requires a complete ignorance of both life and literature. The difficulty that I should fancy the reviewer feels is the difficulty of sustaining any standard. Where there is no style a standard must be impossible. The poor reviewers are apparently reduced to be the reporters of the police-court of literature, the chroniclers of the doings of the habitual criminals of art. It is sometimes said of them that they do not read all through the works they are called upon to criticise. They do not. Or at least they should not. If they did so, they would become confirmed misanthropes, or if I may borrow a phrase from one of the pretty Newnham graduates,[6] confirmed womanthropes for the rest of their lives. Nor is it necessary. To know the vintage and quality of a wine one need not drink the whole cask. It must be perfectly easy in half an hour to say whether a book is worth anything or worth nothing. Ten minutes are really sufficient, if one has the instinct for form. Who wants to wade through a dull volume? One tastes it, and that is quite enough—more than enough, I should imagine. I am aware that there are many honest workers in painting as well as in literature who object to criticism entirely. They are quite right. Their work stands in no intellectual relation to their age. It brings us no new element of pleasure. It suggests no fresh departure of thought, or passion, or beauty. It should not be spoken of. It should be left to the oblivion that it deserves.

ERNEST: But, my dear fellow—excuse me for interrupting you—you seem to me to be allowing your passion for criticism to lead you a great deal too far. For, after all, even you must admit that it is much more difficult to do a thing than to talk about it.

GILBERT: More difficult to do a thing than to talk about it? Not at all. That is a gross popular error. It is very much more difficult to talk about a thing than to do it. In the sphere of actual life that is of course obvious. Anybody can make history. Only a great man can write it. There is no mode of action, no form of emotion, that we do not share with the lower animals. It is only by language that we rise above them, or above each other—by language, which is the parent, and not the child, of thought. Action, indeed, is always easy, and when presented to us in its most aggravated, because most continuous form, which I take to be that of real industry, becomes simply the refuge of people who have nothing whatsoever to do. No, Ernest, don't talk about action. It is a blind thing dependent on external influences, and moved by an impulse of

6. Newnham College was the first women's college to be founded at Cambridge University.

whose nature it is unconscious. It is a thing incomplete in its essence, because limited by accident, and ignorant of its direction, being always at variance with its aim. Its basis is the lack of imagination. It is the last resource of those who know not how to dream.

ERNEST: Gilbert, you hold the world as if it were a crystal ball. You hold it in your hand, and reverse it to please a wilful fancy. You do nothing but re-write history.

GILBERT: The one duty we owe to history is to re-write it. That is not the least of the tasks in store for the critical spirit. When we have fully discovered the scientific laws that govern life, we shall realise that the one person who has more illusions than the dreamer is the man of action. He, indeed, knows neither the origin of his deeds nor their results. From the field in which he thought that he had sown thorns, we have gathered our vintage, and the fig-tree that he planted for our pleasure is as barren as the thistle, and more bitter. It is because Humanity has never known where it was going that it has been able to find its way.

ERNEST: You think, then, that in the sphere of action a conscious aim is a delusion?

GILBERT: It is worse than a delusion. If we lived long enough to see the results of our actions it may be that those who call themselves good would be sickened with a dull remorse, and those whom the world calls evil stirred by a noble joy. Each little thing that we do passes into the great machine of life which may grind our virtues to powder and make them worthless, or transform our sins into elements of a new civilisation, more marvellous and more splendid than any that has gone before. But men are the slaves of words. They rage against Materialism, as they call it, forgetting that there has been no material improvement that has not spiritualised the world, and that there have been few, if any, spiritual awakenings that have not wasted the world's faculties in barren hopes, and fruitless aspirations, and empty or trammelling creeds. What is termed Sin is an essential element of progress. Without it the world would stagnate, or grow old, or become colourless. By its curiosity Sin increases the experience of the race. Through its intensified assertion of individualism, it saves us from monotony of type. In its rejection of the current notions about morality, it is one with the higher ethics. And as for the virtues! What are the virtues? Nature, M. Renan[7] tells us, cares little about chastity, and it may be that it is to the shame of the Magdalen, and not to their own purity, that the Lucretias of modern life owe their freedom from stain. Charity, as even those of whose religion it makes a formal part have been compelled to acknowledge, creates a multitude of evils. The mere existence of conscience, that faculty of which people prate so much nowadays, and are so ignorantly proud, is a sign of our imperfect development. It must be merged in instinct before we become fine. Self-denial is simply a method by which man arrests his progress, and self-sacrifice a survival of the mutilation of the savage, part of that old worship of pain which is so terrible a factor in the history of the world, and which even now makes its victims day by day, and has its altars in the land. Virtues! Who knows what the virtues are? Not you. Not I. Not any one. It is well for our vanity that we slay the criminal, for if we suffered him to live he might show us what we had gained by his crime. It is well for his peace that the saint goes to his martyrdom. He is spared the sight of the horror of his harvest.

ERNEST: Gilbert, you sound too harsh a note. Let us go back to the more gracious fields of literature. What was it you said? That it was more difficult to talk about a thing than to do it?

GILBERT (*after a pause*): Yes: I believe I ventured upon that simple truth. Surely you see now that I am right? When man acts he is a puppet. When he describes he is a poet. The whole secret lies in that. It was easy enough on the sandy plains by windy Ilion to send the notched arrow from the painted bow, or to hurl against the shield of hide and flamelike brass the long ash-handled spear. It was easy for the adulterous queen to spread the Tyrian carpets for her lord, and then, as he lay couched in the marble bath, to throw over his head the purple net, and call to her smooth-faced lover to stab through the meshes at the heart that should have broken at Aulis. For Antigone even, with Death waiting for her as her bridegroom, it was easy to pass through the tainted air at noon, and climb the hill, and strew with kindly earth the wretched naked corse that had no tomb. But what of those who wrote about these

7. Ernest Renan (1823–1892), French philologist and historian, best known for his *Life of Jesus.*

things? What of those who gave them reality, and made them live for ever? Are they not greater than the men and women they sing of? "Hector that sweet knight is dead," and Lucian tells us how in the dim under-world Menippus saw the bleaching skull of Helen, and marvelled that it was for so grim a favour that all those horned ships were launched, those beautiful mailed men laid low, those towered cities brought to dust. Yet, every day the swanlike daughter of Leda comes out on the battlements, and looks down at the tide of war. The greybeards wonder at her loveliness, and she stands by the side of the king. In his chamber of stained ivory lies her leman. He is polishing his dainty armour, and combing the scarlet plume. With squire and page, her husband passes from tent to tent. She can see his bright hair, and hears, or fancies that she hears, that clear cold voice. In the courtyard below, the son of Priam is buckling on his brazen cuirass. The white arms of Andromache are around his neck. He sets his helmet on the ground, lest their babe should be frightened. Behind the embroidered curtains of his pavilion sits Achilles, in perfumed raiment, while in harness of gilt and silver the friend of his soul arrays himself to go forth to the fight. From a curiously carven chest that his mother Thetis had brought to his ship-side, the Lord of the Myrmidons takes out that mystic chalice that the lip of man had never touched, and cleanses it with brimstone, and with fresh water cools it, and, having washed his hands, fills with black wine its burnished hollow, and spills the thick grape-blood upon the ground in honour of Him whom at Dodona bare-footed prophets worshipped, and prays to Him, and knows not that he prays in vain, and that by the hands of two knights from Troy, Panthous' son, Euphorbus, whose love-locks were looped with gold, and the Priamid, the lion-hearted, Patroklus, the comrade of comrades, must meet his doom. Phantoms, are they? Heroes of mist and mountain? Shadows in a song? No: they are real. Action! What is action? It dies at the moment of its energy. It is a base concession to fact. The world is made by the singer for the dreamer.

ERNEST: While you talk it seems to me to be so.

GILBERT: It is so in truth. On the mouldering citadel of Troy lies the lizard like a thing of green bronze. The owl has built her nest in the palace of Priam. Over the empty plain wander shepherd and goatherd with their flocks, and where, on the surfaced, oily sea, οἶνοψ πόντος [wine-colored sea], as Homer calls it, copper-prowed and streaked with vermilion, the great galleys of the Danaoi came in their gleaming crescent, the lonely tunny-fisher sits in his little boat and watches the bobbing corks of his net. Yet, every morning the doors of the city are thrown open, and on foot, or in horse-drawn chariot, the warriors go forth to battle, and mock their enemies from behind their iron masks. All day long the fight rages, and when night comes the torches gleam by the tents, and the cresset burns in the hall. Those who live in marble or on painted panel, know of life but a single exquisite instant, eternal indeed in its beauty, but limited to one note of passion or one mood of calm. Those whom the poet makes live have their myriad emotions of joy and terror, of courage and despair, of pleasure and of suffering. The seasons come and go in glad or saddening pageant, and with winged or leaden feet the years pass by before them. They have their youth and their manhood, they are children, and they grow old. It is always dawn for St. Helena, as Veronese saw her at the window. Through the still morning air the angels bring her the symbol of God's pain. The cool breezes of the morning lift the gilt threads from her brow. On that little hill by the city of Florence, where the lovers of Giorgione are lying, it is always the solstice of noon, of noon made so languorous by summer suns that hardly can the slim naked girl dip into the marble tank the round bubble of clear glass, and the long fingers of the lute-player rest idly upon the chords. It is twilight always for the dancing nymphs whom Corot set free among the silver poplars of France. In eternal twilight they move, those frail diaphanous figures, whose tremulous white feet seem not to touch the dew-drenched grass they tread on. But those who walk in epos, drama, or romance, see through the labouring months the young moons wax and wane, and watch the night from evening unto morning star, and from sunrise unto sunsetting, can note the shifting day with all its gold and shadow. For them, as for us, the flowers bloom and wither, and the Earth, that Green-tressed Goddess as Coleridge calls her, alters her raiment for their pleasure. The statue is concentrated to one moment of perfection. The image stained upon the canvas possesses no spiritual element of growth or change. If they know nothing of death, it is because they know little of life, for the secrets of life and death belong to those, and those only, whom the sequence of time affects, and who possess not merely the present but the future, and can rise or fall from a past of glory or of shame. Movement, that problem of the visible arts, can be truly realised by Literature alone. It is Literature that shows us the body in its swiftness and the soul in its unrest.

ernest: Yes; I see now what you mean. But, surely, the higher you place the creative artist, the lower must the critic rank.

gilbert: Why so?

ernest: Because the best that he can give us will be but an echo of rich music, a dim shadow of clear-outlined form. It may, indeed, be that life is chaos, as you tell me that it is; that its martyrdoms are mean and its heroisms ignoble; and that it is the function of Literature to create, from the rough material of actual existence, a new world that will be more marvellous, more enduring, and more true than the world that common eyes look upon, and through which common natures seek to realise their perfection. But surely, if this new world has been made by the spirit and touch of a great artist, it will be a thing so complete and perfect that there will be nothing left for the critic to do. I quite understand now, and indeed admit most readily, that it is far more difficult to talk about a thing than to do it. But it seems to me that this sound and sensible maxim, which is really extremely soothing to one's feelings, and should be adopted as its motto by every Academy of Literature all over the world, applies only to the relations that exist between Art and Life, and not to any relations that there may be between Art and Criticism.

gilbert: But, surely, Criticism is itself an art. And just as artistic creation implies the working of the critical faculty, and, indeed, without it cannot be said to exist at all, so Criticism is really creative in the highest sense of the word. Criticism is, in fact, both creative and independent.

ernest: Independent?

gilbert: Yes; independent. Criticism is no more to be judged by any low standard of imitation or resemblance than is the work of poet or sculptor. The critic occupies the same relation to the work of art that he criticises as the artist does to the visible world of form and colour, or the unseen world of passion and of thought. He does not even require for the perfection of his art the finest materials. Anything will serve his purpose. And just as out of the sordid and sentimental amours of the silly wife of a small country doctor in the squalid village of Yonville-l'Abbaye, near Rouen, Gustave Flaubert was able to create a classic, and make a masterpiece of style, so, from subjects of little or of no importance, such as the pictures in this year's Royal Academy, or in any year's Royal Academy for that matter, Mr. Lewis Morris's poems, M. Ohnet's novels, or the plays of Mr. Henry Arthur Jones,[8] the true critic can, if it be his pleasure so to direct or waste his faculty of contemplation, produce work that will be flawless in beauty and instinct with intellectual subtlety. Why not? Dulness is always an irresistible temptation for brilliancy, and stupidity is the permanent *Bestia Trionfans* that calls wisdom from its cave. To an artist so creative as the critic, what does subject-matter signify? No more and no less than it does to the novelist and the painter. Like them, he can find his motives everywhere. Treatment is the test. There is nothing that has not in it suggestion or challenge.

ERNEST: But is Criticism really a creative art?

GILBERT: Why should it not be? It works with materials, and puts them into a form that is at once new and delightful. What more can one say of poetry? Indeed, I would call criticism a creation within a creation. For just as the great artists, from Homer and Aeschylus, down to Shakespeare and Keats, did not go directly to life for their subject-matter, but sought for it in myth, and legend, and ancient tale, so the critic deals with materials that others have, as it were, purified for him, and to which imaginative form and colour have been already added. Nay, more, I would say that the highest

---

8. Sir Lewis Morris (1833–1907) was a mediocre but popular English writer of religious and mythological poetry. Georges Ohnet (1848–1918) was a popular late-nineteenth-century French novelist. Henry Arthur Jones (1851–1929) was a popular English dramatist whose greatest successes were the melodramatic *The Silver King* (1882), *The Case of Rebellious Susan* (1894), and *Michael and His Lost Angel* (1896), which was praised by the critics, including Shaw, but was a box-office failure. His chief success in comedy came with *The Liars* in 1897.

Criticism, being the purest form of personal impression, is in its way more creative than creation, as it has least reference to any standard external to itself, and is, in fact, its own reason for existing, and, as the Greeks would put it, in itself, and to itself, an end. Certainly, it is never trammelled by any shackles of verisimilitude. No ignoble considerations of probability, that cowardly concession to the tedious repetitions of domestic or public life, affect it ever. One may appeal from fiction unto fact. But from the soul there is no appeal.

ERNEST: From the soul?

GILBERT: Yes, from the soul. That is what the highest criticism really is, the record of one's own soul. It is more fascinating than history, as it is concerned simply with oneself. It is more delightful than philosophy, as its subject is concrete and not abstract, real and not vague. It is the only civilised form of autobiography, as it deals not with the events, but with the thoughts of one's life; not with life's physical accidents of deed or circumstance, but with the spiritual moods and imaginative passions of the mind. I am always amused by the silly vanity of those writers and artists of our day who seem to imagine that the primary function of the critic is to chatter about their second-rate work. The best that one can say of most modern creative art is that it is just a little less vulgar than reality, and so the critic, with his fine sense of distinction and sure instinct of delicate refinement, will prefer to look into the silver mirror or through the woven veil, and will turn his eyes away from the chaos and clamour of actual existence, though the mirror be tarnished and the veil be torn. His sole aim is to chronicle his own impressions. It is for him that pictures are painted, books written, and marble hewn into form.

ERNEST: I seem to have heard another theory of Criticism.

GILBERT: Yes: it has been said by one whose gracious memory we all revere, and the music of whose pipe once lured Proserpina from her Sicilian fields, and made those white feet stir, and not in vain, the Cumnor cowslips, that the proper aim of Criticism is to see the object as in itself it really is. But this is a very serious error, and takes no cognisance of Criticism's most perfect form, which is in its essence purely subjective, and seeks to reveal its own secret and not the secret of another. For the highest Criticism deals with art not as expressive but as impressive purely.

ERNEST: But is that really so?

GILBERT: Of course it is. Who cares whether Mr. Ruskin's views on Turner are sound or not? What does it matter? That mighty and majestic prose of his, so fervid and so fiery-coloured in its noble eloquence, so rich in its elaborate symphonic music, so sure and certain, at its best, in subtle choice of word and epithet, is at least as great a work of art as any of those wonderful sunsets that bleach or rot on their corrupted canvases in England's [Tate] Gallery; greater indeed, one is apt to think at times, not merely because its equal beauty is more enduring, but on account of the fuller variety of its appeal, soul speaking to soul in those long-cadenced lines, not through form and colour alone, though through these, indeed, completely and without loss, but with intellectual and emotional utterance, with lofty passion and with loftier thought, with imaginative insight, and with poetic aim; greater, I always think, even as Literature is the greater art. Who, again, cares whether Mr. Pater has put into the portrait of Monna Lisa something that Lionardo never dreamed of? The painter may have been merely the slave of an archaic smile, as some have fancied, but whenever I pass into the cool galleries of the Palace of the Louvre, and stand before that strange figure "set in its marble chair in that cirque of fantastic rocks, as in some faint light under sea," I murmur to myself, "She is older than the rocks among which she sits; like the vampire, she has been dead many times, and learned the secrets of the grave; and has been a diver in deep seas, and keeps their fallen day about her; and trafficked for strange webs with Eastern merchants; and, as Leda, was the mother of Helen of Troy, and, as St. Anne, the mother of Mary; and all this has been to her but as the sound of lyres and flutes, and lives only in the delicacy with which it has moulded the changing lineaments, and tinged the eyelids and the hands." And I say to my friend, "The presence that thus so strangely rose beside the waters is expressive of what in the ways of a thousand years man had come to desire"; and he answers me, "Hers is the head upon which all 'the ends of the world are come,' and the eyelids are a little weary."

And so the picture becomes more wonderful to us than it really is, and reveals to us a secret of which, in truth, it knows nothing, and the music of the mystical prose is as sweet in our ears as was that flute-player's music that lent to the lips of La Gioconda those subtle and poisonous curves. Do you ask me what Lionardo would have said had any one told him of this picture that "all the thoughts and experience of the world had etched and moulded there in that which they had of power to refine and make expressive the outward form, the animalism of Greece, the lust of Rome, the reverie of the Middle Age with its spiritual ambition and imaginative loves, the return of the Pagan world, the sins of the Borgias?" He would probably have answered that he had contemplated none of these things, but had concerned himself simply with certain arrangements of lines and masses, and with new and curious colour-harmonies of blue and green. And it is for this very reason that the criticism which I have quoted is criticism of the highest kind. It treats the work of art simply as a starting-point for a new creation. It does not confine itself—let us at least suppose so for the moment—to discovering the real intention of the artist and accepting that as final. And in this it is right, for the meaning of any beautiful created thing is, at least, as much in the soul of him who looks at it, as it was in his soul who wrought it. Nay, it is rather the beholder who lends to the beautiful thing its myriad meanings, and makes it marvellous for us, and sets it in some new relation to the age, so that it becomes a vital portion of our lives, and a symbol of what we pray for, or perhaps of what, having prayed for, we fear that we may receive. The longer I study, Ernest, the more clearly I see that the beauty of the visible arts is, as the beauty of music, impressive primarily, and that it may be marred, and indeed often is so, by any excess of intellectual intention on the part of the artist. For when the work is finished it has, as it were, an independent life of its own, and may deliver a message far other than that which was put into its lips to say. Sometimes, when I listen to the overture to *Tannhäuser*, I seem indeed to see that comely knight treading delicately on the flower-strewn grass, and to hear the voice of Venus calling to him from the caverned hill. But at other times it speaks to me of a thousand different things, of myself, it may be, and my own life, or of the lives of others whom one has loved and grown weary of loving, or of the passions that man has known, or of the passions that man has not known, and so has sought for. To-night it may fill one with that ΕΡΩΣ ΤΩΝ ΑΔΥΝΑΤΩΝ, that *Amour de l'Impossible,* which falls like a madness on many who think they live securely and out of reach of harm, so that they sicken suddenly with the poison of unlimited desire, and, in the infinite pursuit of what they may not obtain, grow faint and swoon or stumble. To-morrow, like the music of which Aristotle and Plato tell us, the noble Dorian music of the Greek, it may perform the office of a physician, and give us an anodyne against pain, and heal the spirit that is wounded, and "bring the soul into harmony with all right things." And what is true about music is true about all the arts. Beauty has as many meanings as man has moods. Beauty is the symbol of symbols. Beauty reveals everything, because it expresses nothing. When it shows us itself, it shows us the whole fiery-coloured world.

ERNEST: But is such work as you have talked about really criticism?

GILBERT: It is the highest Criticism, for it criticises not merely the individual work of art, but Beauty itself, and fills with wonder a form which the artist may have left void, or not understood, or understood incompletely.

ERNEST: The highest Criticism, then, is more creative than creation, and the primary aim of the critic is to see the object as in itself it really is not; that is your theory, I believe?

GILBERT: Yes, that is my theory. To the critic the work of art is simply a suggestion for a new work of his own, that need not necessarily bear any obvious resemblance to the thing it criticises. The one characteristic of a beautiful form is that one can put into it whatever one wishes, and see in it whatever one chooses to see; and the Beauty, that gives to creation its universal and aesthetic element, makes the critic a creator in his turn, and whispers of a thousand different things which were not present in the mind of him who carved the statue or painted the panel or graved the gem.

It is sometimes said by those who understand neither the nature of the highest Criticism nor the charm of the highest Art, that the pictures that the critic loves most to write about are those that belong to the anecdotage of painting, and that deal with scenes taken out of literature or history. But this is not so. Indeed, pictures of this kind are far too intelligible. As a class, they rank with illustrations, and even considered from this point of view are failures, as they do not stir the imagination, but set definite bounds to it. For the domain of the painter is, as I suggested before, widely different from that of the poet. To the latter belongs life in its full and absolute entirety; not merely the beauty that men look at, but the beauty that men listen to also; not merely the momentary grace of form or the transient gladness of colour, but the whole sphere of feeling, the perfect cycle of thought. The painter is so far limited that it is only through the mask of the body that he can show us the mystery of the soul; only through conventional images that he can handle ideas; only through its physical equivalents that he can deal with psychology. And how inadequately does he do it then, asking us to accept the torn turban of the Moor for the noble rage of Othello, or a dotard in a storm for the wild madness of Lear! Yet it seems as if nothing could stop him. Most of our elderly English painters spend their wicked and wasted lives in poaching upon the domain of the poets, marring their motives by clumsy treatment, and striving to render, by visible form or colour, the marvel of what is invisible, the splendour of what is not seen. Their pictures are, as a natural consequence, insufferably tedious. They have degraded the invisible arts into the obvious arts, and the one thing not worth looking at is the obvious. I do not say that poet and painter may not treat of the same subject. They have always done so, and will always do so. But while the poet can be pictorial or not, as he chooses, the painter must be pictorial always. For a painter is limited, not to what he sees in nature, but to what upon canvas may be seen.

And so, my dear Ernest, pictures of this kind will not really fascinate the critic. He will turn from them to such works as make him brood and dream and fancy, to works that possess the subtle quality of suggestion, and seem to tell one that even from them there is an escape into a wider world. It is sometimes said that the tragedy of an artist's life is that he cannot realise his ideal. But the true tragedy that dogs the steps of most artists is that they realise their ideal too absolutely. For, when the ideal is realised, it is robbed of its wonder and its mystery, and becomes simply a new starting-point for an ideal that is other than itself. This is the reason why music is the perfect type of art. Music can never reveal its ultimate secret. This, also, is the explanation of the value of limitations in art. The sculptor gladly surrenders imitative colour, and the painter the actual dimensions of form, because by such renunciations they are able to avoid too definite a presentation of the Real, which would be mere imitation, and too definite a realisation of the Ideal, which would be too purely intellectual. It is through its very incompleteness that Art becomes complete in beauty, and so addresses itself, not to the faculty of recognition nor to the faculty of reason, but to the aesthetic sense alone, which, while accepting both reason and recognition as stages of apprehension, subordinates them both to a pure synthetic impression of the work of art as a whole, and, taking whatever alien emotional elements the work may possess, uses their very complexity as a means by which a richer unity may be added to the ultimate impression itself. You see, then, how it is that the aesthetic critic rejects those obvious modes of art that have but one message to deliver, and having delivered it become dumb and sterile, and seeks rather for such modes as suggest reverie and mood, and by their imaginative beauty make all interpretations true, and no interpretation final. Some resemblance, no doubt, the creative work of the critic will have to the work that has stirred him to creation, but it will be such resemblance as exists, not between Nature and the mirror that the painter of landscape or figure may be supposed to hold up to her, but between Nature and the work of the decorative artist. Just as on the flowerless carpets of Persia, tulip and rose blossom indeed and are lovely to look on, though they are not reproduced in visible shape or line; just as the pearl and purple of the sea-shell is echoed in the church of St. Mark at Venice; just as the vaulted ceiling of the wondrous chapel at Ravenna is made gorgeous by the gold and green and sapphire of the peacock's tail, though the birds of Juno fly not across it; so the critic reproduces the work that he criticises in a mode that is never imitative, and part of whose charm may really consist in the rejection of resemblance, and shows us in this way not merely the meaning but also the mystery of Beauty, and, by transforming each art into literature, solves once for all the problem of Art's unity.

But I see it is time for supper. After we have discussed some Chambertin and a few ortolans, we will pass on to the question of the critic considered in the light of the interpreter.

ERNEST: Ah! you admit, then, that the critic may occasionally be allowed to see the object as in itself it really is.

GILBERT: I am not quite sure. Perhaps I may admit it after supper. There is a subtle influence in supper.

First published in *Nineteenth Century*, XXVIII (July 1890), 123–147, as "The True Function and Value of Criticism." Reprinted, much revised, in *Intentions* (London, 1891), pp. 95–148. A second part, not reprinted here, was published in *Nineteenth Century*, September, 1890, 435–459, and reprinted in revised form in *Intentions*, pp. 151–213. It continues the discussion, but is more an elaboration of earlier material than a continuation. "It is to criticism that the future belongs," says Gilbert. "The duty of imposing form upon chaos does not grow less as the world advances. There was never a time when Criticism was more needed than it is now. It is only by its means that Humanity can become conscious of the point at which it has arrived." Concluding, he declares, "Creation is always behind the age. It is Criticism that leads us."

# Preface to *The Picture of Dorian Gray*

*The Picture of Dorian Gray was published in 1890. It is curious that Wilde signed his preface—a gratuitous and ostentatious gesture, since he was named as the author of the book anyway.*

*The novel introduced by the flippant preface, a composite of nineteenth-century ideas about dual personality, supernatural portraits, and Faustian compacts, seems almost a projection of Pater's phrase about "the dialogue of the soul with itself." Dorian Gray remains in life as young and attractive as in the painting of himself by Basil Hallward, whom he murders to protect his secret, for Gray, unchanging in outward appearance, lives the dissolute life reflected in the secreted, corrupting portrait. Wilde was symbolically separating his "Platonic" aesthetic theories from his half-hidden life; but in life as in his novel they inevitably come together to the subject's ruin.*

The artist is the creator of beautiful things.

To reveal art and conceal the artist is art's aim.

The critic is he who can translate into another manner or a new material his impression of beautiful things.

The highest, as the lowest, form of criticism is a mode of autobiography.

Those who find ugly meanings in beautiful things are corrupt without being charming. This is a fault.

Those who find beautiful meanings in beautiful things are the cultivated. For these there is hope.

They are the elect to whom beautiful things mean only Beauty.

There is no such thing as a moral or an immoral book. Books are well written, or badly written. That is all.

The nineteenth century dislike of Realism is the rage of Caliban seeing his own face in a glass.

The nineteenth century dislike of Romanticism is the rage of Caliban not seeing his own face in a glass.

The moral life of man forms part of the subject matter of the artist, but the morality of art consists in the perfect use of an imperfect medium. No artist desires to prove anything. Even things that are true can be proved.

No artist has ethical sympathies. An ethical sympathy in an artist is an unpardonable mannerism of style.

No artist is ever morbid. The artist can express everything.

Thought and language are to the artist instruments of an art.

Vice and virtue are to the artist materials for an art.

From the point of view of form, the type of all the arts is the art of the musician. From the point of view of feeling, the actor's craft is is the type.

All art is at once surface and symbol.

Those who go beneath the surface do so at their peril.

Those who read the symbol do so at their peril.

It is the spectator, and not life, that art really mirrors.

Diversity of opinion about a work of art shows that the work is new, complex, and vital.

When critics disagree, the artist is in accord with himself. We can forgive a man for making a useful thing as long as he does not admire it. The only excuse for making a useless thing is that one admires it intensely.

All art is quite useless.

OSCAR WILDE

*The Picture of Dorian Gray* (London, 1890).

# IV. ON HIMSELF

*In addition to the seven selections presented here, other Wildean letters-to-the-editor on his own work included one to the* St. James's Gazette *on* Dorian Gray (*June 30, 1890*), *one to the* Scots Observer *on the relation of art to morality* (*August 2, 1890*), *and one to the* Pall Mall Gazette *on* A House of Pomegranates (*December 11, 1891*).

# Letters on *Dorian Gray*

## MR. WILDE'S BAD CASE

To the Editor of the *St. James's Gazette.*

Sɪʀ,—I have read your criticism of my story, *The Picture of Dorian Gray*; and I need hardly say that I do not propose to discuss its merits or demerits, its personalities or its lack of personality. England is a free country, and ordinary English criticism is perfectly free and easy.

Besides, I must admit that, either from temperament or taste, or from both, I am quite incapable of understanding how any work of art can be criticised from a moral standpoint. The sphere of art and the sphere of ethics are absolutely distinct and separate; and it is to the confusion between the two that we owe the appearance of Mrs. Grundy, that amusing old lady who represents the only original form of humour that the middle classes of this country have been able to produce.

What I do object to most strongly is that you should have placarded the town with posters on which was printed in large letters:—

MR. OSCAR WILDE'S
LATEST ADVERTISEMENT:
A BAD CASE.

Whether the expression "A Bad Case" refers to my book or to the present position of the Government, I cannot tell. What was silly and unnecessary was the use of the term "advertisement."

I think I may say without vanity—though I do not wish to appear to run vanity down—that of all men in England I am the one who requires least advertisement. I am tired to death of being advertised —I feel no thrill when I see my name in a paper. The chronicle does not interest me any more. I wrote this book entirely for my own pleasure, and it gave me very great pleasure to write it. Whether it becomes popular or not is a matter of absolute indifference to me. I am afraid, Sir, that the real advertisement is your cleverly written article. The English public, as a mass, takes no interest in a work of art until it is told that the work in question is immoral, and your *réclame* will, I have no doubt, largely increase the sale of the magazine; in which sale I may mention with some regret, I have no pecuniary interest.—I remain, Sir, your obedient servant,

OSCAR WILDE.

*16 Tite Street, Chelsea, June 25.*

*St. James's Gazette,* June 26, 1890.


## MR. OSCAR WILDE AGAIN

SIR,—In your issue of to-day you state that my brief letter published in your columns is the "best reply" I can make to your article upon *Dorian Gray*. This is not so. I do not propose to discuss fully the matter here, but I feel bound to say that your article contains the most unjustifiable attack that has been made upon any man of letters for many years.

The writer of it, who is quite incapable of concealing his personal malice, and so in some measure destroys the effect he wishes to produce, seems not to have the slightest idea of the temper in which a work of art should be approached. To say that such a book as mine should be "chucked into the fire" is silly. That is what one does with newspapers.

Of the value of pseudo-ethical criticism in dealing with artistic work I have spoken already. But as your writer has ventured into the perilous grounds of literary criticism I ask you to allow me, in fairness not merely to myself but to all men to whom literature is a fine art, to say a few words about his critical method.

He begins by assailing me with much ridiculous virulence because the chief personages in my story are puppies. They *are* puppies. Does he think that literature went to the dogs when Thackeray wrote about puppydom? I think that puppies are extremely interesting from an artistic as well as from a psychological point of view.

They seem to me to be certainly far more interesting than prigs; and I am of the opinion that Lord Henry Wotton is an excellent corrective of the tedious ideal shadowed forth in the semi-theological novels of our age.

He then makes vague and fearful insinuations about my grammar and my erudition. Now, as regards grammar, I hold that, in prose at any rate, correctness should always be subordinate to artistic effect and musical cadence; and any peculiarities of syntax that may occur in *Dorian Gray* are deliberately intended, and are introduced to show the value of the artistic theory in question. Your writer gives no instance of any such peculiarity. This I regret, because I do not think that any such instances occur.

As regards erudition, it is always difficult, even for the most modest of us, to remember that other people do not know quite as much as one does one's self. I myself frankly admit I cannot imagine how a casual reference to Suetonius and Petronius Arbiter can be construed into evidence of a desire to impress an unoffending and ill-educated public by an assumption of superior knowledge. I should fancy that the most ordinary of scholars is perfectly well acquainted with the *Lives of the Caesars* and with the *Satyricon*.

The *Lives of the Caesars*, at any rate, forms part of the curriculum at Oxford for those who take the Honour School of *Literae Humaniores*; and as for the *Satyricon* it is popular even among pass-men, though I suppose they are obliged to read it in translations.

The writer of the article then suggests that I, in common with that great and noble artist Count Tolstoi, take pleasure in a subject because it is dangerous. About such a suggestion there is this to be said. Romantic art deals with the exception and with the individual. Good people, belonging as they do to the normal, and so, commonplace, type, are artistically uninteresting.

Bad people are, from the point of view of art, fascinating studies. They represent colour, variety and strangeness. Good people exasperate one's reason; bad people stir one's imagination. Your critic, if I must give him so honourable a title, states that the people in my story have no counterpart in life; that they are, to use his vigorous if somewhat vulgar phrase, "mere catchpenny revelations of the non-existent." Quite so.

If they existed they would not be worth writing about. The function of the artist is to invent, not to chronicle. There are no such people. If there were I would not write about them. Life by its realism is always spoiling the subject-matter of art.

The superior pleasure in literature is to realise the non-existent.

And finally, let me say this. You have reproduced, in a journalistic form, the comedy of *Much Ado About Nothing* and have, of course, spoilt it in your reproduction.

The poor public, hearing, from an authority so high as your own, that this is a wicked book that should be coerced and suppressed by a Tory Government, will, no doubt, rush to it and read it. But, alas! they will find that it is a story with a moral. And the moral is this: All excess, as well as all renunciation, brings its own punishment.

The painter, Basil Hallward, worshipping physical beauty far too much, as most painters do, dies by the hand of one in whose soul he has created a monstrous and absurd vanity. Dorian Gray, having led a life of mere sensation and pleasure, tries to kill conscience, and at that moment kills himself. Lord Henry Wotton seeks to be merely the spectator of life. He finds that those who reject the battle are more deeply wounded than those who take part in it.

Yes, there is a terrible moral in *Dorian Gray*—a moral which the prurient will not be able to find in it, but it will be revealed to all whose minds are healthy. Is this an artistic error? I fear it is. It is the only error in the book.—I remain, Sir, your obedient servant,

OSCAR WILDE.

*16 Tite Street, Chelsea, June 26.*

*St. James's Gazette,* June 27, 1890.


## MR. OSCAR WILDE'S DEFENCE

To the Editor of the *St. James's Gazette.*

SIR,—As you still keep up, though in a somewhat milder form than before, your attacks on me and my book, you not only confer on me the right, but you impose upon me the duty of reply.

You state, in your issue of to-day, that I misrepresented you when

I said that you suggested that a book so wicked as mine should be "suppressed and coerced by a Tory Government." Now, you did not propose this, but you did suggest it. When you declare that you do not know whether or not the Government will take action about my book, and remark that the authors of books much less wicked have been proceeded against in law, the suggestion is quite obvious.

In your complaint of misrepresentation you seem to me, Sir, to have been not quite candid.

However, as far as I am concerned, this suggestion is of no importance. What is of importance is that the editor of a paper like yours should appear to countenance the monstrous theory that the Government of a country should exercise a censorship over imaginative literature. This is a theory against which I, and all men of letters of my acquaintance, protest most strongly; and any critic who admits the reasonableness of such a theory shows at once that he is quite incapable of understanding what literature is, and what are the rights that literature possesses. A Government might just as well try to teach painters how to paint, or sculptors how to model, as attempt to interfere with the style, treatment and subject-matter of the literary artist, and no writer, however eminent or obscure, should ever give his sanction to a theory that would degrade literature far more than any didactic or so-called immoral book could possibly do.

You then express your surprise that "so experienced a literary gentleman" as myself should imagine that your critic was animated by any feeling of personal malice towards him. The phrase "literary gentleman" is a vile phrase, but let that pass.

I accept quite readily your assurance that your critic was simply criticising a work of art in the best way that he could, but I feel that I was fully justified in forming the opinion of him that I did. He opened his article by a gross personal attack on myself. This, I need hardly say, was an absolutely unpardonable error of critical taste.

There is no excuse for it except personal malice; and you, Sir, should not have sanctioned it. A critic should be taught to criticise a work of art without making any reference to the personality of the author. This, in fact, is the beginning of criticism. However, it was not merely his personal attack on me that made me imagine that he was actuated by malice. What really confirmed me in my first impression was his reiterated assertion that my book was tedious and dull.

Now, if I were criticising my book, which I have some thoughts of doing, I think I would consider it my duty to point out that it is far too crowded with sensational incident, and far too paradoxical in style, as far, at any rate, as the dialogue goes. I feel that from a standpoint of art these are true defects in the book. But tedious and dull the book is not.

Your critic has cleared himself of the charge of personal malice, his denial and yours being quite sufficient in the matter; but he has done so only by a tacit admission that he has really no critical instinct about literature and literary work, which, in one who writes about literature, is, I need hardly say, a much graver fault than malice of any kind.

Finally, Sir, allow me to say this. Such an article as you have published really makes me despair of the possibility of any general culture in England. Were I a French author, and my book brought out in Paris, there is not a single literary critic in France on any paper of high standing who would think for a moment of criticising it from an ethical standpoint. If he did so he would stultify himself, not merely in the eyes of all men of letters, but in the eyes of the majority of the public.

You have yourself often spoken against Puritanism. Believe me, Sir, Puritanism is never so offensive and destructive as when it deals with art matters. It is there that it is radically wrong. It is this Puritanism, to which your critic has given expression, that is always marring the artistic instinct of the English. So far from encouraging it, you should set yourself against it, and should try to teach your critics to recognise the essential difference between art and life.

The gentleman who criticised my book is in a perfectly hopeless confusion about it, and your attempt to help him out by proposing that the subject-matter of art should be limited does not mend matters. It is proper that limitation should be placed on action. It is not proper that limitation should be placed on art. To art belong all things that are and all things that are not, and even the editor of a London paper has no right to restrain the freedom of art in the selection of subject-matter.

I now trust, Sir, that these attacks on me and on my book will cease. There are forms of advertisement that are unwarranted and unwarrantable.—I am, Sir, your obedient servant,

OSCAR WILDE.

*16 Tite Street, S.W., June 27.*

*St. James's Gazette,* June 28, 1890.

## DORIAN GRAY

To the Editor of the *Daily Chronicle.*

SIR,—Will you allow me to correct some errors into which your critic has fallen in his review of my story, *The Picture of Dorian Gray*, published in to-day's issue of your paper?

I must admit, as one to whom contemporary literature is constantly submitted for criticism, that the only thing that ever prejudices me against a book is the lack of literary style; but I can quite understand how any ordinary critic would be strongly prejudiced against a work that was accompanied by a premature and unnecessary panegyric from the publisher. A publisher is simply a useful middleman. It is not for him to anticipate the verdict of criticism.

I may, however, while expressing my thanks to the "London Editor" for drawing my attention to this, I trust, purely American method of procedure, venture to differ from him in one of his criticisms. He states that he regards the expression "complete" as applied to a story, as a specimen of the "adjectival exuberance of the puffer." Here, it seems to me, he sadly exaggerates. What my story is is an interesting problem. What my story is not is a "novelette"—a term which you have more than once applied to it. There is no such word in the English language as novelette. It should not be used. It is merely part of the slang of Fleet Street.

In another part of your paper, Sir, you state that I received your assurance of the lack of malice in your critic "somewhat grudgingly." This is not so. I frankly said that I accepted that assurance "quite readily," and that your own denial and that of your own critic were sufficient.

Nothing more generous could have been said. What I did feel was that you saved your critic from the charge of malice by convicting him of the unpardonable crime of lack of literary instinct. I still feel that. To call my book an ineffective attempt at allegory, that in the hands of Mr. Anstey might have been made striking, is absurd.

Your critic states, to begin with, that I make desperate attempts to "vamp up" a moral in my story. Now, I must candidly confess that I do not know what "vamping" is. I see, from time to time, mysterious advertisements in the newspapers about "How to Vamp," but what vamping really means remains a mystery to me—a mystery that, like all other mysteries, I hope some day to explore.

However, I do not propose to discuss the absurd terms used by modern journalism. What I want to say is that, so far from wishing to emphasise any moral in my story, the real trouble I experienced in writing the story was that of keeping the extremely obvious moral subordinate to the artistic and dramatic effect.

When I first conceived the idea of a young man selling his soul in exchange for eternal youth—an idea that is old in the history of literature, but to which I have given new form—I felt that, from an aesthetic point of view, it would be difficult to keep the moral in its proper secondary place; and even now I do not feel quite sure that I have been able to do so. I think the moral too apparent. When the book is published in a volume I hope to correct this defect.

As for what the moral is, your critic states that it is this—that when a man feels himself becoming "too angelic" he should rush out and make a "beast of himself." I cannot say that I consider this a moral. The real moral of the story is that all excess, as well as all renunciation, brings its punishment, and this moral is so far artistically and deliberately suppressed that it does not enunciate its law as a general principle, but realises itself purely in the lives of individuals, and so becomes simply a dramatic element in a work of art, and not the object of the work of art itself.

Your critic also falls into error when he says that Dorian Gray, having a "cool, calculating, conscienceless character," was inconsistent when he destroyed the picture of his own soul, on the ground that the picture did not become less hideous after he had done what, in his vanity, he had considered his first good action. Dorian

Gray has not got a cool, calculating, conscienceless character at all. On the contrary, he is extremely impulsive, absurdly romantic, and is haunted all through his life by an exaggerated sense of conscience which mars his pleasures for him and warns him that youth and enjoyment are not everything in the world. It is finally to get rid of the conscience that had dogged his steps from year to year that he destroys the picture; and thus in his attempt to kill conscience Dorian Gray kills himself.

Your critic then talks about "obtrusively cheap scholarship." Now, whatever a scholar writes is sure to display scholarship in the distinction of style and the fine use of language; but my story contains no learned or pseudo-learned discussions, and the only literary books that it alludes to are books that any fairly educated reader may be supposed to be acquainted with, such as the *Satyricon* of Petronius Arbiter, or Gautier's *Emaux et Camées*. Such books as Le Conso's *Clericalis Disciplina* belong not to culture, but to curiosity. Anybody may be excused for not knowing them.

Finally, let me say this—the aesthetic movement produced certain curious colours, subtle in their loveliness and fascinating in their almost mystical tone. They were, and are, our reaction against the crude primaries of a doubtless more respectable but certainly less cultivated age. My story is an essay on decorative art. It reacts against the crude brutality of plain realism. It is poisonous if you like, but you cannot deny that it is also perfect, and perfection is what we artists aim at.—I remain, Sir, your obedient servant,

OSCAR WILDE.

*16 Tite Street, June 30.*

*Daily Chronicle,* July 2, 1890.


## MR. WILDE'S REJOINDER

To the Editor of the *Scots Observer*.

SIR,—You have published a review of my story, *The Picture of Dorian Gray*. As this review is grossly unjust to me as an artist, I ask you to allow me to exercise in your columns my right of reply.

Your reviewer, Sir, while admitting that the story in question is "plainly the work of a man of letters," the work of one who has "brains, and art, and style," yet suggests, and apparently in all seriousness, that I have written it in order that it should be read by the most depraved members of the criminal and illiterate classes. Now, Sir, I do not suppose that the criminal and illiterate classes ever read anything except newspapers. They are certainly not likely to be able to understand anything of mine. So let them pass, and on the broad question of why a man of letters writes at all let me say this.

The pleasure that one has in creating a work of art is a purely personal pleasure, it is for the sake of this pleasure that one creates. The artist works with his eye on the object. Nothing else interests him. What people are likely to say does not even occur to him.

He is fascinated by what he has in hand. He is indifferent to others. I write because it gives me the greatest possible artistic pleasure to write. If my work pleases the few I am gratified. If it does not, it causes me no pain. As for the mob, I have no desire to be a popular novelist. It is far too easy.

Your critic then, Sir, commits the absolutely unpardonable crime of trying to confuse the artist with his subject-matter. For this, Sir, there is no excuse at all.

Of one who is the greatest figure in the world's literature since Greek days, Keats remarked that he had as much pleasure in conceiving the evil as he had in conceiving the good. Let your reviewer, Sir, consider the bearings of Keats's fine criticism, for it is under these conditions that every artist works. One stands remote from one's subject-matter. One creates it and one contemplates it. The further away the subject-matter is, the more freely can the artist work.

Your reviewer suggests that I do not make it sufficiently clear whether I prefer virtue to wickedness or wickedness to virtue. An artist, Sir, has no ethical sympathies at all. Virtue and wickedness are to him simply what the colours on his palette are to the painter. They are no more and they are no less. He sees that by their means a certain artistic effect can be produced and he produces it. Iago may be morally horrible and Imogen stainlessly pure. Shakespeare, as Keats said, had as much delight in creating the one as he had in creating the other.

It was necessary, Sir, for the dramatic development of this story to surround Dorian Gray with an atmosphere of moral corruption. Otherwise the story would have had no meaning and the plot no issue. To keep this atmosphere vague and indeterminate and wonderful was the aim of the artist who wrote the story. I claim, Sir, that he has succeeded. Each man sees his own sin in Dorian Gray. What Dorian Gray's sins are no one knows. He who finds them has brought them.

In conclusion, Sir, let me say how really deeply I regret that you should have permitted such a notice as the one I feel constrained to write on to have appeared in your paper. That the editor of the *St. James's Gazette* should have employed Caliban as his art-critic was possibly natural. The editor of the *Scots Observer* should not have allowed Thersites to make mows in his review. It is unworthy of so distinguished a man of letters.—I am, etc.,

OSCAR WILDE.

*16 Tite Street, Chelsea, July 9.*

*Scots Observer*, July 12, 1890.

# Lady Windermere's Fan

## AN EXPLANATION

To the Editor of the *St. James's Gazette.*

Sɪʀ,—Allow me to correct a statement put forward in your issue of this evening to the effect that I have made a certain alteration in my play in consequence of the criticism of some journalists who write very recklessly and very foolishly in the papers about dramatic art. This statement is entirely untrue and grossly ridiculous.

The facts are as follows. On last Saturday night, after the play was over, and the author, cigarette in hand, had delivered a delightful and immortal speech, I had the pleasure of entertaining at supper a small number of personal friends; and as none of them was older than myself I, naturally, listened to their artistic views with attention and pleasure. The opinions of the old on matters of Art are, of course, of no value whatsoever. The artistic instincts of the young are invariably fascinating; and I am bound to state that all my friends, without exception, were of opinion that the psychological interest of the second act would be greatly increased by the disclosure of the actual relationship existing between Lady Windermere and Mrs. Erlynne—an opinion, I may add, that had previously been strongly held and urged by Mr. Alexander.

As to those of us who do not look on a play as a mere question of pantomime and clowning psychological interest is everything, I determined, consequently, to make a change in the precise moment of revelation. This determination, however, was entered into long before I had the opportunity of studying the culture, courtesy, and critical faculty displayed in such papers as the *Referee, Reynolds'*, and the *Sunday Sun.*

When criticism becomes in England a real art, as it should be, and when none but those of artistic instinct and artistic cultivation is allowed to write about works of art, artists will, no doubt, read criticisms with a certain amount of intellectual interest. As things are at present, the criticisms of ordinary newspapers are of no interest whatsoever, except in so far as they display, in its crudest form, the Boeotianism of a country that has produced some Athenians, and in which some Athenians have come to dwell.—I am, Sir, your obedient servant,

OSCAR WILDE.

*February 26.*

*St. James's Gazette*, February 27, 1892.

# *Salomé*

To the Editor of the *Times*.

SIR,—My attention has been drawn to a review of *Salomé* which
was published in your columns last week [February 23, 1893].
The opinions of English critics on a French work of mine have, of
course, little, if any, interest for me. I write simply to ask you to
allow me to correct a misstatement that appears in the review in
question.

The fact that the greatest tragic actress of any stage now living
saw in my play such beauty that she was anxious to produce it, to
take herself the part of the heroine, to lend to the entire poem the
glamour of her personality, and to my prose the music of her flute-
like voice—this was naturally, and always will be, a source of pride
and pleasure to me, and I look forward with delight to seeing Mme.
Bernhardt present my play in Paris, that vivid centre of art, where
religious dramas are often performed. But my play was in no sense
of the words written for this great actress. I have never written a
play for any actor or actress, nor shall I ever do so. Such work is
for the artisan in literature—not for the artist.—I remain, Sir,
your obedient servant,

OSCAR WILDE.

*Times*, March 2, 1893.

# Bibliography

The basic texts of Wilde's writing are the ten volumes of the 1908 London (Methuen and Co.) edition, edited by Robert Ross, and issued in the United States in 1921 (New York: Bigelow, Brown and Co.). Key volumes for a study of Wilde's criticism are IV (the essays in *Intentions*, together with the 1895 text of *The Soul of Man Under Socialism*), IX (*Reviews*) and X (*Miscellanies*, including art criticism, literary criticism and Wilde's many rejoinders to the press). For data on first publication of individual critical works, see the note on texts at the end of the present editor's Introduction. The most complete list of individual publications, including first appearances of each of Wilde's periodical contributions, signed and anonymous, appears in the *Bibliography of Oscar Wilde*, edited by Stuart Mason [Christopher Sclater Millard] and published in London (T. Werner Laurie, Ltd.) in 1914. It has not been superseded, although later scholarship has added some entries to the Wilde canon. As the Introduction to the present volume suggests, there are also numerous critical comments in Wilde's correspondence. The definitive edition, *The Letters of Oscar Wilde*, edited by Rupert Hart-Davis (London: Hart-Davis, 1962), includes not only the complete *De Profundis* letter-essay to Douglas but all of Wilde's numerous letters-to-the-editor.

There are few useful studies of Wilde's criticism, apart from sections devoted to this aspect of Wilde's work in the numerous biographies. Recommended are the following, some of which are only in part pertinent to Wilde as critic:

ABRAMS, M. H. *The Mirror and the Lamp*. New York: Oxford University Press, 1953, pp. 328 ff.

BEERBOHM, MAX. "A Lord of Language," *Vanity Fair*, March 2, 1905. Reprinted in H. Montgomery Hyde, *Oscar Wilde: The Aftermath*. (New York: Farrar, Straus, 1963), pp. 205–207.

ELLMANN, RICHARD. "The Critic as Artist as Wilde." In *Wilde and the Nineties: An Essay and an Exhibition,* ed. Charles Ryskamp. (Princeton, N.J.: Princeton University Library, 1966), pp. 1–21.

————. "Oscar and Oisin." In *Eminent Domain: Yeats Among Wilde, Joyce, Pound, Eliot, and Auden.* (New York: Oxford University Press, 1967), pp. 9–27.

HOUGH, GRAHAM. *The Last Romantics.* London: Duckworth, 1947, pp. 119 ff.

JACKSON, HOLBROOK. *The Eighteen Nineties.* New York: Knopf, 1927, pp. 72–90.

LUCAS, E. V., ED. *A Critic in Pall Mall.* London: Methuen, 1919.

SAN JUAN, EPIFANIO, JR. *The Art of Oscar Wilde.* Princeton, N.J.: Princeton University Press, 1967, pp. 74–104.

WELLEK, RENÉ. *A History of Modern Criticism.* New Haven and London: Yale University Press, 1965, IV, 407–416.

WOOD, ALICE. "Oscar Wilde as a Critic," *North American Review,* CCII (July–December 1915), 899–909.

# Index

Abrams, M. H., 247
Alexander, Sir George, 156, 244
Allingham, William, 95
Amman, Josse, 144 n.
Anderson, J. P., 44, 70–71
Aristotle, xvi–xvii, xix, 3, 209–210
Arnold, Matthew, 77, 103, 173, 205
Ashby-Sterry, Joseph, 42
Askew, Anne, 104
Austin, Alfred, xiii, 5–8

Baillie, Joanna, 106
Balfour, Arthur James, 13, 15
Balzac, Honoré de, xxx–xxxi, 9–12,
   140, 173–174, 184, 197
Barnard, Lady Anne, 105
Barrett, Wilson, 115, 153
Baudelaire, Charles, 4
Beerbohm, Max, xxxiv, 247
Behn, Mrs. Aphra, 104
Bennett, Arnold, xi n.
Berlioz, Hector, 197
Berners, Abbess Juliana, 104
Bernhardt, Sarah, 246
Binyon, Lawrence, xxiv
Black, William, 170
Blunt, Wilfrid Scawen, xxxii, 13–15
Boswell, James, 30, 179, 199
Bourchier, Arthur, 125
Bourget, Paul, 78, 172
Brawne, Fanny, 34
Brontë, Emily, 106
Brooke, Stopford, 107 n.
Browne, Sir Thomas, 63
Browning, Mrs. Elizabeth Barrett,
   xxv, 99–106

Browning, Robert, xxv, 77, 110–111,
   201–202
Buffon, Georges Louis, Comte de, 9
Bulwer Lytton, Edward, Lord, 53
Burnand, Francis Cowley, 180
Burns, Robert, 91
Byron, George Gordon, Lord, 197

Caine, Hall, xxvii, 40–44, 167, 170,
   172 n.
Campbell, Lady, 129, 154
Carew, Elizabeth, 104
Carlyle, Thomas, xiii, xxix, xxxi, 43, 61,
   103, 139, 179
Caro, Elmé Marie, 76–79
Carpenter, Edward, 107–109
Cellini, Benvenuto, 3, 179, 197–198
Centlivre, Mrs. Susannah, 105
Chapman, George, 46
Chatterton, Thomas, xxiv
Cicero, Marcus Tullius, 3, 179, 197
Colenso, Bishop, 173
Coleridge, Samuel Taylor, xxvii, 40–44,
   63, 219
Colvin, Sidney, 35–38
Colyns, Michael, 144
Cowley, Abraham, 105
Cowper, William, 46
Crane, Walter, 108
Crawford, Francis Marion, xxxi, 170,
   172 n.

Daudet, Alphonse, 171
Davenant, William, 32
Defoe, Daniel, 179, 183 n.
Dekker, Thomas, 31

249